G.V. COOPER DEL.

ON STONE BY J. CAMERON

LITH. OF G.W. LEWIS 111 NASSAU ST. N.Y.

PART OF SAN FRANCISCO,

from a sketch by G.W Casilear.

CALIFORNIA ILLUSTRATED:

INCLUDING

A DESCRIPTION

OF THE

PANAMA AND NICARAGUA ROUTES.

BY

A RETURNED CALIFORNIAN.

New York:
WILLIAM HOLDREDGE, PUBLISHER,
NO. 140 FULTON STREET.
1852.

E. O. JENKINS, PRINTER AND STEREOTYPER,
No. 114 Nassau Street, New York.

TO

Miss Hetta P. Letts,

OF

Wood Lawn, Staten Island,

THIS JOURNAL

IS

Most Respectfully Dedicated,

BY

THE AUTHOR.

Note to the Reader.

I HAVE, in these pages, endeavored to convey a correct impression, I have stated such facts *only* as I knew to be facts, and interspersed them with incidents that fell under my own observation. A season's residence in the mineral regions enabled me to obtain a correct *interior view* of life in California. The illustrations are truthful, and can be relied upon as faithfully portraying the scenes they are designed to represent. They were drawn upon the spot, and in order to preserve characteristics, *even the attitudes* of the individuals represented are truthfully given. The first part of this volume is written in a concise manner, with a view to brevity, as the reader is presumed to be anxious to make the shortest possible passage to the Eldorada.

THE AUTHOR.

Contents.

CALIFORNIA ILLUSTRATED,

INCLUDING A DESCRIPTION OF THE

PANAMA AND NICARAGUA ROUTES.

Chapter First.

SAIL FROM NEW YORK—OUR PILOT LEAVES US—LAND RECEDES FROM VIEW—SEA-SICKNESS—A WHALE—ENTER THE GULF STREAM—ENCOUNTER A GALE—ENTER THE TROPIC OF CANCER—"LAND, HO!"—CAYCOS AND TURK'S ISLANDS—ST. DOMINGO—CUBA—ENTER THE CARIBBEAN SEA—SPORTING—SUNDAY—STANDING IN FOR THE PORT OF CHAGRES—BEAUTIFUL SCENE—DROP ANCHOR.

DEAR READER:—If you have visited California, you will find nothing in these pages to interest you; if you have not, they may serve to kill an idle hour. On the 27th of January, 1849, having previously engaged passage, I had my baggage taken on board the bark "Marietta," lying at Pier No. 4, East River, preparatory to sailing for Chagres, *en route* to California. It was 9, A.M. A large concourse of friends and spectators had collected on the pier to witness our departure, and after two hours of confusion and excitement, we let go our hawser—and, as we swung around into the stream, recèived the last adieus of our friends on shore. We were taken in tow by a steam-tug, and were soon under way, our bowsprit pointing seaward. We occupied our time, while running down the bay, in writing notes to our friends, our pilot having kindly volunteered to deliver them. We passed Forts Hamilton and Diamond at 1, P.M., and at three had made Sandy Hook. Our pilot's boat, which had been laying off, came along side to receive him; we gave our last thoughts into his charge, and bade him adieu.

We had now passed Sandy Hook, and putting our helm down, we stood away to the South. The wind being light, we bent on studding sails, and were soon making our course at the rate of five knots. The excitement had now subsided; and, as the hills were fast receding, we were most painfully admonished that we were leaving home and friends. We soon sunk the highest points of land below the horizon, and felt that we were fairly launched upon the ocean, and that we were traveling to a scene of adventure, the result of which no one could divine. We felt that sinking of spirit one only feels on such occasions; and, at this particular time, clouds as dark as night hung in the horizon of the future. Night came on, and with it a stiff breeze, creating a heavy sea. This caused most of the passengers to forget their friends, and bestow their undivided care upon themselves.

For some cause, at this particular juncture, the passengers were affected with peculiar sensations, mostly in the region of the stomach. They did not think it was sea-sickness. Whatever the cause may have been, the effect was most distressing. It assumed an epidemic form. The symptoms were a sickening sensation and nausea at the stomach; the effect, distressing groans and copious discharges at the mouth. The captain felt no alarm; said he had had similar cases before on board his ship. The night was spent in the most uncomfortable manner imaginable. Many of the passengers, too sick to reach their berths, were lying about on deck, and at every surge would change sides of the vessel. All being actuated by the same impulse, performed the same evolutions.

With the dawn of the 28th, the wind lulled, and our canvas was again spread to a three knot breeze. At noon we took our first observation, and at evening passed a ship, although not within speaking distance. The dawn of the 29th is accompanied by a seven-knot breeze, and we stand away on our course with all sail set. At 3 P.M., we were saluted by a whale, and at 4 entered the Gulf Stream. We here first observe luminous substances in the water, which at night appear like an ocean of fire. During the night it blew a gale, and we ran under double-reefed topsails, with mainsail furled. 30th. Leave the Gulf Stream, the wind blowing a terrific gale. We are tossed about on mountainous waves, and all sick. 31st. All sail set, and running six knots; dolphins and porpoises playing about the ship. We are again saluted by a whale.

1st Feb. Pleasant; all appear at table; enter the trade winds; hoist studding-sails; lovely day; 4, P.M., mate catches a dolphin, and brings him on deck. 2d. Calm summer day. 3d. All on deck; extremely pleasant. 4th. Sunday; pleasant; pass a ship; fine breeze; throw the log; are running eight knots. 5th. Pass through schools of flying-fish, one of which flies on board. We enter the tropic of Cancer. A flock of black heron are flying through the air; we take an observation; are eighty miles from Caycos and Turk's Island; making for the Caycos passage. 7th. 5, P.M. The captain discovers land from the mast-head, and we are cheered with the cry of "Land, Ho!" We pass around Caycos Island, and through the passage; and on the morning of the 8th, are in sight of St. Domingo, sixty miles distant. It looms up from the horizon like a heavy black cloud. 9th. Pass the island of Cuba, and on the 10th enter the Caribbean Sea. We passed near the island of Nevassa, a small rocky island, inhabited only by sea-fowl. They mistaking our vessel for a fowl of a larger species, came off in flocks, until our rigging was filled, and the sun almost obscured. They met with a *foul* reception. There were eighty passengers on board, all armed. They could not resist the temptation, but wantonly mutilated the unsuspecting birds, many of which expiated with their lives the crime of confiding in strangers. One would receive a charge of shot, with which it would fly back to the island, uttering the most unharmonious screeches, when a new deputation would set off for us, many of them destined to return to the island in the same musical mood. Fortunately, we were driven along by the breeze, and they returned to their homes, and have, no doubt, spent many an evening around the family hearth, speculating upon the peculiar sensations experienced on that occasion. The enthusiasm of the passengers did not immediately subside, but they spent the afternoon in shooting at targets.

11th. Thermometer standing at 80°. We are carried along with a three-knot breeze; our ship bowing gracefully to the undulations of the sea. It being Sunday, home presents itself vividly to our imagination. 13th. Standing in for the coast of

New Grenada; at 6 P. M., the captain cries out from the mast-head, "Land Ho!" We shorten sail, and on the morning of the 14th are standing in for the port of Chagres.

A most beautiful scene is spread out before us; we are making directly for the mouth of the river, the left point of the entrance being a bold, rocky promontory, surmounted by fortifications. (See Plate). The coast to the left is bold and rocky, extending a distance of five miles, and terminating in a rocky promontory, one of the points to the entrance of Navy Bay, the anticipated terminus of the Panama railroad. The coast to the right is low, stretching away as far as the eye can reach. In the background is a succession of elevations, terminating in mountains of considerable height, the valleys, as well as the crests of the hills, being covered with a most luxuriant growth of vegetation, together with the palm, cocoa-nut, and other tropical trees of the most gigantic size. As we neared the port, we passed around the steamer Falcon, which had just come to anchor, and passing on to within half a mile of the mouth of the river, we rounded to, and let go our anchor.

G. V. COOPER DEL.

LITH. OF G. W. LEWIS, 111 NASSAU ST. N. Y.

CHAGRES FROM THE ANCHORAGE.

Chapter Second.

NATIVES AND "BUNGOES"—CRESCENT CITY ARRIVES—WE SAIL INTO THE MOUTH OF THE RIVER—PREPARE FOR A FIGHT—FASHIONS AND FORTIFICATIONS—AN HONEST ALCALDE—NON-FULFILLMENT OF CONTRACTS.

OUR attention was first attracted to the natives who were rowing off to us in "bungoes," or canoes of immense size, each manned by eight, ten, or twelve natives, apparently in a state of nudity. Their manner of propelling their craft was as novel as their appearance was ludicrous. They rise simultaneously, stepping up on a high seat, and, uttering a peculiar cry, throw themselves back on their oars, and resume their former seats. This is done with as much uniformity as if they were an entire piece of machinery. In the afternoon the Crescent City came to anchor, together with several sailing vessels, bringing, in all, about one thousand passengers.

We remained outside until the 17th, when we weighed anchor and passed into the mouth, making fast to the right bank, now called the American side of the river. We found an abundance of water in the channel, but at the entrance several dangerous rocks. As this coast is subject to severe northers, it is an extremely difficult port to make. The steamers still anchor some two miles out. We found several vessels near the mouth, beached and filled.

It was amusing to see the passengers preparing to make their advent on land. It is well understood that no one started for California without being thoroughly fortified, and as we had arrived at a place, where, as we thought, there must be, at least, *some* fighting to do, our first attention was directed to our *armor.* The revolvers, each man having at least two, were first overhauled, and the six barrels charged. These were put in our belt, which also contained a bowie knife. A brace of smaller pistols are snugly pocketed inside our vest; our rifles are liberally charged; and with a cane in hand, (which of course contains a dirk), and a *slung shot* in our pockets, we step off and look around for the enemy.

We crossed the river to Chagres, which consists of about thirty huts constructed of reeds, and thatched with palm-leaves, the inhabitants, the most squalid set of beings imaginable. They are all good Catholics, but do not go to the Bible for the fashions. There are fig-leaves in abundance, yet they are considered by the inhabitants quite superfluous, they preferring the garments that nature gave them, sometimes, however, adding a Panama hat.

We visited the fortifications, which were in a dilapidated state, the walls fast falling to decay. The only sentinels at the time of our visit, were three goats and two children. (See Plate.) It has a commanding position, and has been a work of much strength, but the guns are now dismounted, and the inhabitants ignorant of their use. In returning from the fort, we crossed a stream where a party of *ladies* were undressing for a bath, i. e., they were taking off their hats. We passed on, and after viewing the "lions," returned to our vessel, not very favorably impressed with the manners or customs of the town.

We had contracted with the Alcalde for canoes to carry us up the river. The steamboat Orus, then plying on the river, having contracted to take up the Falcon's passengers, had offered an advanced price, and secured all the canoes, including ours. Our Alcalde had been struck down to the highest bidder, and I will here say that, although many charges have been brought against the New Grenadians, they have never been accused of fulfilling a contract, especially if they could make a "*real*" by breaking it. We did not relish the idea of remaining until the canoes returned, as Chagres had the name, (and it undoubtedly deserved it,) of being the most unhealthy place in Christendom. Many of our passengers had their lives insured before starting, and there was a clause in each policy, that remaining at Chagres over night would be a forfeiture.

The trunks of the steamers' passengers, particularly those of the Crescent City, were landed on the bank of the river, while their owners were endeavoring to secure passage up. The

B. V. COOPER DEL.

LITH. OF G. W. LEWIS, 111 NASSAU ST N.Y.

INTERIOR OF THE CASTLE,

AT CHAGRES

"bungoes" had all gone up with the Orus. There were left two or three small canoes, and the scenes of competition around these were exciting, and often ludicrous in the extreme. Now a man would contract for passage for himself and friend, and while absent to arrange some little matter preparatory to a start, some one would offer the worthy *Padrone* (captain) a higher price, when he would immediately put the trunks of the first two on shore, and take on board those of the latter, together with their owners, and shove out into the stream. Now the first two would appear, with hands filled with refreshments for the voyage, and begin to look around for their boat. In a moment their eyes fall upon their trunks, and the truth flashes across their imagination. Now the scene of excitement begins. The boat is ordered to the shore, it don't come, and they attempt to wade out to it. The first step convinces them of the impracticability of this expedient, as they sink into the mud to their necks. Revolvers are flourished, but they can be used by both parties, consequently are not used at all.

Chapter Third.

FIRST ATTEMPT AT BOAT BUILDING—EXCITEMENT "ON 'CHANGE"—A LAUNCH AND CLEARANCE—THE CREW—A MUTINY—QUELLED—POOR ACCOMMODATIONS—A NIGHT IN ANGER—AN ANTHEM TO THE SUN—NATURE IN FULL DRESS.

WE saw but one alternative, which was, to construct a boat ourselves, and work it up the river. Upon this we decided, and purchasing the temporary berths of our vessel, soon had a boat on the stocks, 6 feet by 19, and in three days it was afloat at the side of the "Marietta," receiving its freight. We called it the "*Minerva*," and she was probably the first American-bottom ever launched at this port. A misfortune here befel me which I will relate somewhat minutely, as it was undoubtedly the cause of the death of a party concerned. In going out one morning to assist in the construction of the boat, I left my vest, which had a sum of money sewed up in the upper side pocket, in my berth, covered in such a manner I thought no one could discover it. I did not give it a thought during the day, but on going to my berth in the evening, I noticed the covering had been disturbed, and as my room-mates were in the habit of helping themselves to prunes, from a box in my berth, I imagined they had discovered and taken care of it. I was the more strongly impressed that this was the case from the fact that they had frequently spoken of my carelessness. I immediately saw them; they had seen nothing of it. Watches were stationed and the ship searched, but no trace of the money. A person who had had access to the cabin on that day for the first time was strongly suspected, but no trace of the money found. Our suspicions, however, were well founded, as the sequel will show. The passengers very kindly offered to make up a part of the loss, but as I had a little left I most respectfully declined its acceptance. We had about 3000 lbs. of freight and nine persons,

G.V. COOPER DEL.

LITH OF G. W. LEWIS 111 NASSAU ST. N.Y.

ENTRANCE TO THE RIVER CHAGRES

and at 2 P. M., 22d Feb., gave the word, "let go," run up our sail, and as it was blowing a stiff breeze from the ocean, glided rapidly along up the river, our worthy captain, Dennison, and his accomplished mate, Wm. Bliss, of the "Marietta," calling all hands on deck, and giving us three times three as we parted, to which *adios* we responded with feeling hearts. Now, as there is a straight run of three miles, a fair wind, and nothing to do but attend to our sail and tiller, we will take a survey of craft and crew. We are freighted with trunks, shovels, pick-axes, India-rubber bags, smoked ham, rifles, camp-kettles, hard-bread, swords and cheese. Our crew, commencing at the tallest, (we had no first officer,) consisted of two brothers, Dodge, young men of intelligence and enterprise; the eldest a man of the most indomitable perseverance, the younger of the most unbounded good humor, both calculated to make friends wherever they go, and to ride over difficulties without a murmur. They had associated with them three Germans, Shultz, Eiswald, and Hush. Shultz was a young man of energy, fond of music, a good singer, gentlemanly and companionable; Eiswald, full of humor and mirth, extracting pleasure from every incident, always at his post, a fine companion and good navigator; Hush, was a small man, with exceedingly large feet; he appeared to be entirely out of his element; he was disposed to do all he could, but his limbs would not obey him; his arms appeared to be mismated; his legs, when set in motion, would each take an opposite direction, and his feet were everywhere, except where he wanted to have them. We were quite safe when he was still, but when set in motion we found him a dangerous companion. Mr. Russ, a young lawyer of New York, Mr. Cooper, an artist, also of New York, a man of energy, perseverance and genius, and one of the most efficient men of the party. Mr. Beaty, an elderly man, extremely tall and slender, and very moral and exemplary in his habits; being in feeble health, he was to act as cook for the voyage. Ninthly and lastly, myself, an extremely choleric young man, of whom delicacy forbids me to say more.

We have now arrived at the bend of the river, and as here is a spring of excellent water, we make fast and fill our water-keg. Water is obtained here for the vessels in port, by sending up small boats. It can be obtained in any quantity, and a more lovely place cannot well be conceived of. After adjusting our baggage preparatory to manning our oars, we again shoved out into the stream. We manned four oars, consequently kept a reserve. We were all fresh and vigorous, and, being much elated with the novelty of our voyage, resolved to work the boat all night. It was already quite dark, but with the aid of a lamp we kept on our course. The river here was walled up on either side by gigantic trees, their branches interchanging over our heads, almost shutting out the stars. Sometimes the branches stretching out but little above the surface of the river, were filled with water fowls, the white heron presenting a strange and most striking appearance. They would start with fright at our approach, striking wildly in the dark with their wings; some would find secure resting-places on the more elevated branches, while others would settle down through the dense foliage to the margin of the river. Innumerable bats, attracted by our light, were flitting along the surface of the river, but aside from these all nature appeared to be hushed in sleep.

We moved along with much spirit until about eleven o'clock, when there were symptoms of disaffection. Some were weary, others sleepy; some declared they would work no longer, others that the boat should not stop. We had all the premonitory symptoms of a mutiny. It was suggested that we should uncork a bottle of brandy, which was accordingly done, and it was soon *unanimously* declared that our prospects had never appeared so flattering. I am *sure* our boat was never propelled with such energy. I am not prepared to say that the brandy *didn't* have an influence. We moved along rapidly for an hour when we had a relapse of the same disaffection. We resolved to stop; but we were in a dilemma. We had left home under the impression that the Chagres river was *governed* by alligators and anacondas, assisted by all the venomous reptiles in the "whole dire catalogue," consequently, to run to the shore was to run right into the jaws of death, which we did not care to do at this particular time. We pulled along until we came in contact with a limb, which stretched out over the surface of the river, to which we made fast. After detailing two of the party as a watch, we stowed ourselves away as best we could. I was in a half-sitting posture—my feet hanging outside the boat, my back coming in contact with the chime of our water-keg. I tried for some time to sleep, but in vain. I tried to persuade myself that I was at home in a comfortable bed, just falling into a doze, but my back was not to be deceived in that way; and after spending two hours in my uncomfortable position, I got up. I found that my companions had been as badly lodged as myself, and all as anxious to man the oars. We were soon under way, and soon the approaching day was proclaimed by the incessant howl of the animal creation, including the tiger, leopard, cougar, monkeys, &c., &c., accompanied by innumerable parrots and other tropical birds. All nature seemed to be in motion. The scene is indelibly impressed upon my memory. The trees on the margin of the river were of immense size, clothed to their tops with morning-glories and other flowers of every conceivable hue, their tendrils stooping down, kissing the placid bosom of the river. Birds of the most brilliant plumage were flying through the air, in transports of joy. All nature seemed to hail the sun with bursts of rapture. Everything appeared to me so new and strange. My transition from a northern winter to this delightful climate, seemed like magic, and appeared like a scene of enchantment, like the dawning of a new creation.

Chapter Fourth.

BREAKFAST—PRIMITIVE MODE OF LIFE—MEET THE "ORUS"—MUTINY AND RAIN—A STEP BACKWARDS—ENCAMPMENT—A "FORTIFIED" AND FRIGHTENED INDIVIDUAL—SPORTING—MOSQUITOS.

We moved along until the sun had ascended the horizon, when we made fast to the shore and took breakfast. Being somewhat fatigued, we remained until after dinner. We were visited here by two native men and a little boy, all dressed in black, the suits that nature gave them. They were cutting poles with big knives or machets; they had brought their dinner with them, which consisted of a piece of sugar-cane, a foot in length.

We again manned our oars and worked our boat until about sunset, when we drew along shore at a pleasant point designing to encamp. Some of the party were anxious to gain a higher point on the river, and we again pushed out. As we were gaining the middle of the stream, a canoe turned the point containing two boys; they immediately cried out, "vapor! vapor!" (steamboat, steamboat,) and before we could reach the shore, the "Orus" came dashing around the point, throwing her swell over the sides of our boat, and we were near being swamped. This caused great consternation and excitement, which soon subsided, and we were again under way. We were, however, destined not to end our day's journey, without additional difficulties. We worked an hour without finding a suitable place to spend the night. Those having proposed stopping below, now strongly demurred to going on, and after an *eloquent* and *spirited* discussion, it was decided by a majority vote, that we should run back. It commenced to rain about this time, and we returned in not the most amiable mood.

We erected an india rubber tent on shore and, laying our

masts fore and aft, threw our sail over it as a protection to the boat; and, after supper, detailed our watch, when another attempt was made to sleep. Mr. Hush and myself, were on the first watch. I took my station in the boat, but there being a strange commotion in the water, and the sides of the boat not being very high, Mr. H. preferred the shore. He armed himself with a brace of revolvers, and one of horse pistols, a bowie-knife, a large German rifle and broad sword, and stepped on shore. The night was extremely quiet, and at ten o'clock it ceased to rain. Nothing was heard except the peculiar whistle of a bird, which much resembled that of a school boy. The river, however, was in a constant agitation, which we presumed to be caused by alligators rushing into schools of fish.

At 12, Mr. H. thought he heard a strange noise in the forest, approaching the encampment, and in a few minutes uttering a most unearthly yell, he jumped for the boat. His feet hanging a little "too low on the edge," caught under a root, and he brought up in the river. This being full of alligators, only added to his fright, and the precise time it took him to get out, I am unable to say.

The morning was again hailed by universal acclamation, and after an early breakfast we resumed our voyage. We had a pleasant run during the day, stopping frequently to secure pheasants, pigeons, toucans, parrots, &c. The latter are not very palatable, but we were not disposed to be fastidious, and every thing we shot, except alligators, went into the camp-kettle. Late in the afternoon we met a bungo, the natives pointing to a tree, the top of which was filled with wild turkeys. We pulled along under the tree, discharged a volley, and succeeded in frightening them to another. Having a carbine charged with shot, I brought one to the ground. I climbed up the bank, but found the forest impenetrable. The under growth was a dense chaparal, interlaced with vines, every shrub and tree armed with thorns. I, however, with my *machet*, reached the turkey. There being a sandy beach near, we resolved to encamp for the night; and while we were pitching our tent, Mr. B. dressed and cooked our turkey.

We were here attacked by the most ravenous swarm of musquitos it was ever my lot to encounter. We had promised ourselves a comfortable night's rest, but it was like most of the promises one makes himself. We entered the campaign with the greatest zeal; but before morning, would have been glad to capitulate on any terms. The morning dawned as it only dawns within the tropics. Being Sunday we resolved to rest, and called our place of encampment, Point Domingo.

Chapter Fifth.

FIRST RAPID—AN UNFORTUNATE INDIVIDUAL—A STEP BACKWARDS—SEVERAL INDIVIDUALS IN A STATE OF EXCITEMENT—TIN PANS NOT EXACTLY THE THING—A BREAKFAST EXTINGUISHED—SPORTING—MONKEY AMUSEMENTS—A "FLASH IN THE PAN"—TWO FEET IN OUR PROVISION BASKET—POVERTY OF THE INHABITANTS AND THEIR DOGS—ARRIVAL AT GORGONA.

MONDAY morning, having an early breakfast, we were again under way. We shot several alligators, and at 10, A.M., arrived at the first rapid. We uncorked a bottle of brandy and prepared for hard work. As Mr. Hush did not help work the boat, (*it was not safe to give him a pole*) it was suggested that he should walk. We commenced the ascent, and after an hour of hard labor, gained the summit. We drew up along shore, and Mr. H. attempted to jump on board. His feet, as usual, taking the wrong direction, he stumbled and caught hold of an India rubber bag for support, which not being securely fastened, went overboard. The current being strong it passed rapidly down, and there was no alternative but to follow it with the boat. We soon found ourselves going with the greatest velocity, down the rapid we had just toiled so hard to ascend. We overtook the bag at the foot, and making fast to the shore, we held a *very animated* colloquy, which was embellished with an occasional oath by way of emphasis. Mr. H. suspected that he was the subject of our animadversions, but there was *nothing said.*

We again ascended the rapid, and worked on until rain and night overtook us. We were obliged to encamp on an unpleasant rocky shore, and cook supper in the rain. We passed an uncomfortable night; and in the morning it was still raining in torrents. We were furnished with India rubber *ponchos* and were making preparations to start while Mr. Cooper and Mr. Beaty were preparing breakfast. It was difficult to get fuel, and still more difficult to make it burn. They however succeeded in kindling the fire. We usually boiled our coffee-water in the camp-kettle, but this being full of game, we filled a large tin pan with water, and placed it over the fire, supported by three stones. The ham was frying briskly by the fire, our chocolate dissolving, and every thing going on *swimmingly*, when one of the stones turned, capsizing the tin pan, putting out every particle of fire, and filling the chocolate and ham with ashes. (See plate.) Mr. Cooper was frantic with rage, doffing his hat, throwing the ham into the river, kicking over the chocolate cup, cursing every thing in general, and tin pans in particular, while Mr. Beaty, with a most rueful countenance, clasped his hands, exclaiming, "Oh! my!!!"

Mr. Dodge came to the rescue, and we had a warm breakfast, and were soon under way. At ten, the sun came out, and we had a pleasant run, using our sail. We encamped in a delightful place on the left bank of the river, and had a comfortable night's rest. When we awoke in the morning, the air was filled with parrots, toucans, tropical pheasants, etc. Our guns were immediately brought into requisition, and we soon procured a full supply, including seven pheasants. One of the party and myself finding a path that had been beaten by wild beasts resolved to follow it, and penetrate more deeply into the forest. After going some distance we heard a strange noise, which induced my companion to return. Being well armed I proceeded on, and soon came upon a party of monkeys taking their morning exercise. There were about twenty of them, in the top of a large tree. The larger ones would take the smaller and pretend they were about to throw them off; the little ones, in the mean time, struggling for life. There was one very large one, with a white face, who appeared to be doing the honors of the occasion, viz., laughing when the little ones were frightened. If I had been within speaking distance of *his honor*, I would have informed him that his uncouth laugh had diminished the audience on the present occasion by at least one half. I did not break in upon their sports, but, following the path, soon found myself at a bend of the river.

A native was passing, who informed me that there were turkeys on the other side. I stepped into his canoe, and in a

G. W. COOPER DEL. ON STONE BY J. CAMERON LITH. OF G. W. LEWIS 111. NASSAU ST. N.Y.

PREPARING BREAKFAST

on the Chagres River.

moment we were climbing the opposite bank. When within shooting distance I raised my gun; it missed fire, and the turkeys flew away, the native exclaiming "*mucho malo.*" We recrossed, and I soon reached the encampment. Our game was cooked, and the party ready to embark. We shoved out, but, unfortunately, Hush had forgotten his bowie knife. We floated back, he ascended the bank, and succeeded in finding it. In returning, he found it difficult to reach the boat; the bank being quite abrupt, he, however, determined to jump, and, after making a few peculiar gyrations with his arms, he *did* jump, and landed both feet in our provision basket, breaking several bottles, and in his effort to extricate himself kicked the basket overboard. He would have followed it, had it not been for timely assistance.

The day was excessively hot, the river rapid, and our progress slow. In the after part of the day, we passed a rancho where there were a few hills of corn, the first sign of industry we had seen along the river. One can hardly conceive of a country susceptible of a higher cultivation. They have a perpetual summer; tropical fruits grow spontaneously; they have the finest bottom lands for rice, tobacco, cotton, corn, or sugar plantations perhaps on this continent; yet, with the exception of a very little corn and sugar, nothing is cultivated. The enterprise of the States would make the country a paradise.

We encamped at night where the river had a peculiar bend, forming a horse-shoe, and one of the most delightful spots I ever saw. I selected it for my own use—as a rice and sugar plantation—but have not *yet* had the title examined. In the middle of the night a canoe passed down in which was the man suspected of having borrowed my vest. He spoke to one of our party, said he was on his way to Chagres, on business, but would return to Gorgona immediately. We took an early start in the morning, and at nine stopped at a rancho to purchase cigars. Such a squalid family I never saw. There were three women, two or three young ladies, and half a dozen children—none of them were dressed, excepting a little boy who had on a checked palm leaf hat. We asked for cigars, they had none, but would make some for us, "poco tiempo," (little time). We couldn't wait. We were much struck with the appearance of the dog, which was so poor that, in attempting to bark at us, it turned a summerset. We were now not far from Gorgona, and exerted every nerve to reach our destination. At noon, while at dinner, a young native approached us from the forest, and proposed to help work the boat up to Gorgona. As he was a tall, athletic young fellow, and *didn't charge anything*, we accepted his proposition, and gave him his dinner. We were now six miles from Gorgona, and with the aid of our native there was a prospect of arriving in good time. The river was shallow, with frequent rapids, and, although our boat drew only nine inches water, we were frequently obliged to get out and tow it up. (See Plate). Your humble servant is standing on the bow of the boat with a long pole. Cooper is "*boosting*" at the side. Hush is doing duty—the first on the rope. Dodge is in a passion and in the act of addressing some emphatic remark to *gentlemen* on board. Natives are seen in their canoes, and just above, seated on the limb of a tree, is a monkey who appears to be looking on enjoying the scene. As we passed under the tree he came down upon one of the lower branches, and seemed disposed to take passage. An alligator is seen on the bank below, and in the air innumerable parrots. The noise of these is one of the annoyances of this country, their screeching incessant and intolerable. Late in the afternoon we arrived within half a mile of Gorgona, which was behind a bend of the river, where our native wished to land. We soon passed the bend, when the town was in full view, and in a few moments our labors were at an end. Our friends had felt some solicitation for us. Seven days was an unusual passage *at this season of the year*, and if they had wished to effect an insurance on us it is doubtful whether it could have been done in Gorgona at the usual rates.

CO...ER DEL.

ON STONE BY J. CAMERON

LITH. OF G. W. LEWIS, 111. NASSAU ST. N. Y.

PASSING A RAPPID,

on Chagres river.

Chapter Sixth.

CUSTOMS AND DRESS OF THE NOBILITY—A SUSPICIOUS INDIVIDUAL—JOURNEY TO PANAMA—A NIGHT PROCESSION—A WEALTHY LADY IN "BLOOMER"—AN AGREEABLE NIGHT SURPRISE—"HUSH" ON HORSE BACK—CAPTAIN TYLER SHOT—A MOUNTAIN PASS AT NIGHT—THUNDER STORM IN THE TROPICS.

THE town is pleasantly situated about fifty feet above the level of the river, and contains some eight hundred inhabitants. At the time of our arrival, there were about five hundred Americans encamped in the town. The buildings are mostly constructed of reed, thatched with palm-leaf. (See Plate). A hammock is slung under the eave of one of these houses, occupied by the mother, in the act of administering to the wants of a little one; an open countenanced dog is near, as if waiting to relieve the child, a señora is shelling corn, and a hog is looking on, one foot raised, in readiness to obey the *first* summons.

The people dress, as in Chagres, with the addition, in some cases, of half a yard of linen and a string of beads. The Alcalde and his lady were generally well dressed; but, as strange as it may appear, they were always accompanied in their morning walks by their son, a lad of fourteen, his *entire* costume consisting of a Panama hat. In the evening of the day of our arrival, we observed our worthy boatman making himself familiar around the American tents. Soon the police were on the alert, and we were informed that he was one of the most notorious thieves in the country. He had landed back, thinking it safer to come into town at night. We had our baggage carried up, and were soon residents of the American part of the town. I was here put in possession of facts which strengthened my suspicions of the individual who passed down the river on the previous night; and, in the sequel, instead of returning to Gorgona, he, on his arrival at Chagres, hired a native to carry him to a vessel that was about to sail for New Orleans, and in attempting to climb on board he missed his footing, fell into the water and was drowned. His hat came to the surface, but his body was never recovered.

There was, at this time, no means of conveyance from Panama to San Francisco, and people preferred remaining, and consuming their provisions in Gorgona, to paying exorbitant prices to have it transported to Panama. After remaining some days I purchased a horse, and started for Panama, twenty-five miles distant.

It is a pleasant ride across, being a succession of mountains and valleys, each valley containing a spring-brook of the purest water. Two miles out of Gorgona you enter a mule path running through a dense forest, the branches interchanging overhead, forming an arbor sufficiently dense to exclude the sun. You sometimes pass through gullies in the side of the mountain, sufficiently wide at the bottom to admit the mule and his rider, and looking up, you find yourself in a chasm with perpendicular sides, twenty feet in depth, into which the sun has never shone. Here, as in all Spanish countries, are numerous crosses, marking the resting-place of the assassin's victim. When within three miles, the country opens, disclosing to the view the towers of the cathedral, indicating the location of Panama. The balance of the road is paved with cobble stones, the work of convicts, who are brought out in chain-gangs. One mile out, you cross the national bridge, a stone structure of one arch; here is also an extensive missionary establishment, now in ruins. When within half a mile of the wall of the city, you pass a stone tower, surmounted by a cross. You are now in the suburbs of the city. The street is paved, and on either side are ruins, some of considerable extent, having been costly residences, with highly cultivated gardens attached. You pass a plaza, on one side of which is an extensive church. You now enter between two walls, which gradually increase in height, as you approach the gate, until, crossing a deep moat which surrounds the city, they are joined to the main wall.

On entering the gate the first thing that presents itself is a chapel, where you are expected to return thanks for your safe arrival. I rode through, put my horse in the court-yard of the

"Washington House," took supper, surveyed the town, and retired. At about three in the morning, I was aroused by a strange noise. On going to the window I saw a procession of nuns and priests passing through the street, escorted by a band of music. They presented a strange appearance. The priests were dressed in black robes and tights, wearing black hats with broad brims, rolled up and fastened to the crown; the nuns, with white scarfs passing over the head and sweeping the ground, each carried a lighted taper, presenting the appearance of a procession of ghosts. They would all join in chanting some wild air, when the band would play the chorus. Nothing could be more impressive than such a scene as this. Aroused from sleep at the dead of night, by such wild strains, uttered in such impassioned tones, as if pleading for mercy at the very gates of despair. They seemed like doomed spirits, wandering about without a guiding star, under the ban of excommunication.

I rose early in the morning, bathed in the Pacific, and after breakfast mounted for Gorgona, where I arrived in the evening. I went to a *rancho*, half a mile distant, for sugar-cane for my horse. I was waited upon by the proprietress who accompanied me to the cane-field, and used the machet with her own hands. After cutting a supply for the horse, she presented me with a piece for my own use, which I found extremely palatable. This *lady* is one of the most extensive landholders in New Grenada, and one of the most wealthy. She lived in a thatched hovel, the sides entirely open, with the earth for a floor. Her husband was entirely naked, and seemed to devote his attention to the care of the children, of whom there were not less than a dozen, all dressed like "Pa." She dressed in "Bloomer," i. e., she wore a half-yard of linen, and a palm-leaf hat. My horse was stolen during the night. I went to the Alcalde next morning, offered him $5 reward, and before night I was obliged to invest another *real* in sugar-cane for my worthy animal. Money here is a much more effectual searcher than eyes, particularly for stolen horses.

After remaining a few days I again started for Panama. It was after noon, and after riding some distance my horse was taken sick. I stopped until evening, when I again mounted, but was soon obliged to dismount and prepare for spending the night in the woods. It was quite dark, and as I was taking the saddle off my horse five very suspicious-looking natives came up, and were disposed to be inquisitive. To rid myself of them, I told them I expected a "companiero." They left with apparent reluctance. After kindling the fire, fearing they might renew their visit, I put caps on my revolver, preparatory to loading it. As I was in the act of so doing my horse startled, looked wildly about, and, in a moment, I heard footsteps approaching. As they drew near, I thought they were in boots, and consequently Americans. I cried out, "Americano?" They immediately called my name. My surprise and pleasure can well be imagined as I recognized the voices of the Dodges, Shultz, Eiswald, and Hush.

After mutual congratulations we prepared supper, and were soon seated around the fire, recalling the incidents of our voyage up the river. The elder Dodge was lying on a trunk near the fire, and late in the evening, as the muleteer was attempting to drive the horses back, one of them took fright, wheeled about, and in attempting to jump over the trunk, his forefeet came in contact with Dodge, knocking him off, and planting his hind feet into his back. We were struck with horror, supposing him dead, but after straightening him up, and washing his face and head, he was able to speak. He was still in a critical condition, and we were obliged to attend him during the night. The next morning, after a long hunt for our horses, we rode a short distance to an American tent, and leaving the Dodges and company, I rode on to Panama. The next day Mr. Dodge arrived, in a very feeble state of health, but eventually recovered.

In a few days I returned to Gorgona, and sold the "Minerva." She was drawn up into town, inverted, making the roof of the "United States Hotel," the first framed building erected in Gorgona. On my way back to Panama, as I had got about half way through, I was surprised at meeting Mr. Hush. He informed me that he did not think Panama a healthy place, and that he was on his return to the States. He sat on his horse with a good deal of ease, his feet appearing to have on their best behavior. He could not get them into the stirrups, still they appeared to go quietly along by the sides of the horse. Why he thought Panama unhealthy, was a mystery to some. I am not prepared to say that his party ever *insinuated* anything of the kind. In the after part of the day, I was overtaken by Maj. Sewall, lady, and suite. They descended the mountain, and as they were about to cross the brook at its base, Capt. Tyler, one of the party, dismounted, and as he was crossing over, a double-barrelled gun accidentally discharged within four feet of him, he receiving the entire charge in his hip. This caused the greatest consternation. The Capt. having Mrs. Sewall's child in his arms, it was feared it had received a part of the charge. This fortunately did not prove to be the case. The Capt. was immediately stripped, the wound dressed, and through the kind assistance of the Engineering corps of the Panama Railroad, who were encamped near, a litter was constructed, and he was taken through to Panama on the shoulders of the natives.

I was detained until the sun had disappeared behind the mountain, and it was with some difficulty my horse found his way. I ascended the next mountain, and in attempting to descend, lost my way. I dismounted, and after a long search, found the gully through which it was necessary to pass. There was not a ray of light—it was the very blackness of darkness—and on arriving at the end of the gully, I was again obliged to dismount, and after groping about for half an hour, found what I presumed to be the path. My horse was of a different opinion. The matter was discussed—I carried the "point." After riding a short distance, he stopped, and on examining the path, I found that it dropped abruptly into a chasm twenty feet in depth. My horse now refused to move in any direction, which left no alternative but to encamp. I succeeded in finding canebrake, which I cut for him, and spreading out my India rubber blanket, using my saddle as a pillow, I stretched myself out for the night. A most profound stillness reigned through the forest. All nature seemed to be hushed in sleep. Occasionally a limb would crack, struggling with the weight of its own foliage, and once, not far distant, a gigantic tree, a patriarch of the forest, came thundering to the ground. A slight breeze passed mournfully by, as if sighing its requiem, and again all was still.

This solemnity was painfully ominous. There appeared to be something foreboding in the very solemnity that reigned. If

I ever realized the companionship of a horse, it was on this occasion; and I believe it was reciprocal, for when I would speak to him, he would neigh, and seem to say, "I love you, too."

In the middle of the night I was attracted by the barking of a monkey, which very much resembled that of a dog. This called to mind home, and caused many a bright fancy to flit through my imagination. I was soon, however, drawn from my reverie by the low muttering of distant thunder, portending an approaching deluge, which, in this climate, invariably follows. It grew near, and was accompanied by the most vivid flashes of lightning. This revealed to me my situation. I was on the side of the mountain, at the base of an almost perpendicular elevation, which was furrowed by deep gullies, giving fearful token of approaching devastation. Very near was a gigantic palm-tree, the earth on the lower side of which appeared to have been protected by it. I removed my saddle and blanket, and my horse, asking to accompany me, was tied near. The lightning grew more vivid, and the thunder, as peal succeeded peal, caused the very mountains to quake. The clouds, coming in contact with the peaks, instantaneously discharged the deluge, which, rushing down, carried devastation in its track. The sight was most terrific. By the incessant flashes I could see the torrents rushing down, chafing, foaming, and lashing the sides of the mountains, as if the *furies* were trying to vie with each other in madness. In an hour the rage of the elements had ceased, the thunder muttering a last adieu, fell back to his hiding place, and again all was still. My blanket had protected me from the rain; and if I am ever on a committee to award premiums for valuable inventions, Mr. Goodyear will be at the head of my list. I slept until morning, when I had an opportunity of viewing the devastation of the night. I mounted, and at 10 o'clock arrived at Panama.

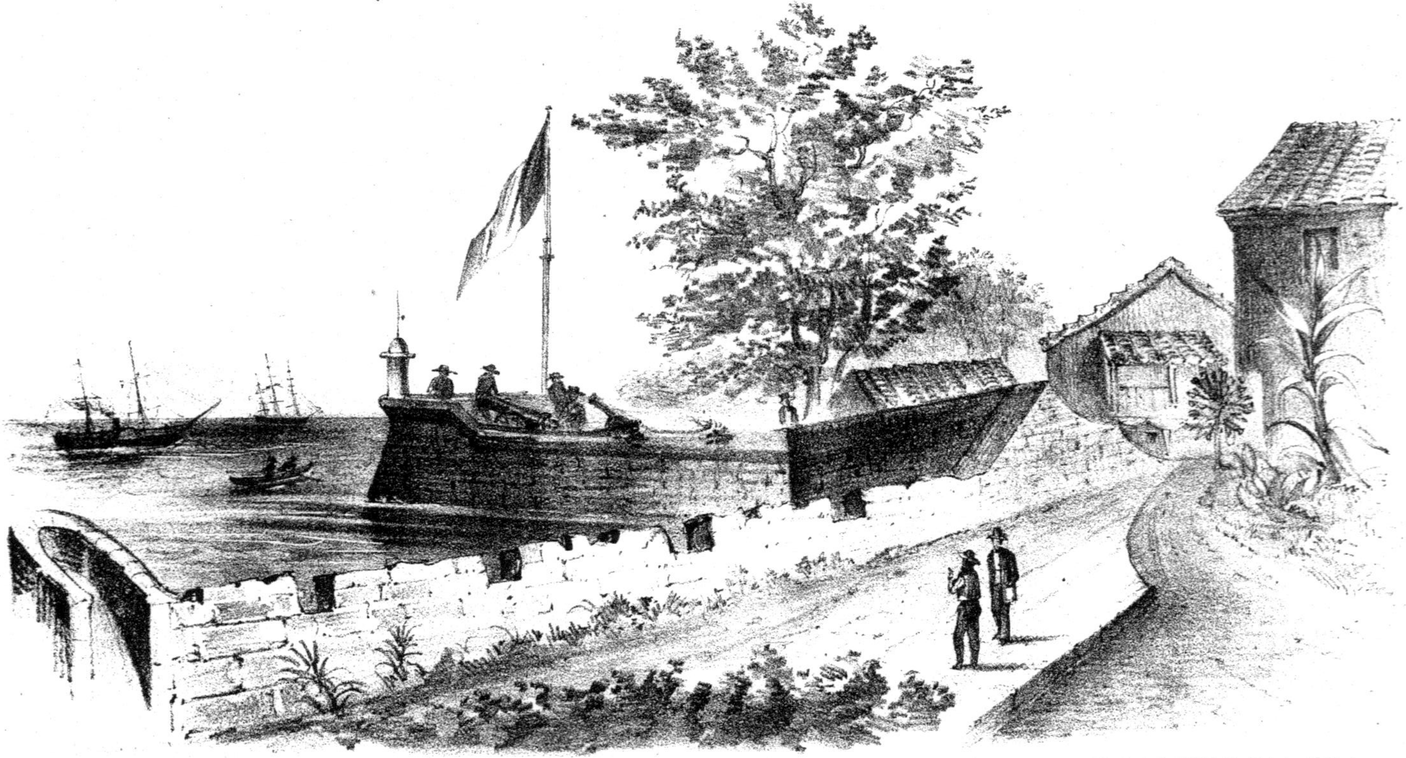

COOPER DEL. ON STONE BY J. CAMERON LITH. OF G. W. LEWIS 111 NASSAU ST. N.Y.

BATTERY, PANAMA.

Chapter Seventh.

PANAMA—CATHEDRAL AND CONVENTS—RELIGIOUS CEREMONIES—AMALGAMATION—FANDANGO.

PANAMA, under the Spanish dominion, was a city of twelve thousand inhabitants, and was the commercial mart of the Pacific. The old city having been destroyed by buccaneers, the present site was selected. The military strength of the city is a true index to the state of the country at the time of its construction; and its present condition a lamentable commentary on the ruthless spirit that has pervaded the countries of South America. The number and extent of the churches and monasteries are a monument to the indomitable zeal and perseverance for which the Catholic Church has been justly celebrated. Old Panama is seven miles distant. An ivy-grown tower is all that remains to mark the spot. The city is inclosed by a wall of much strength, outside of which is a deep moat. It has one main and one side entrance by land, and several on the water-side. The base of the wall on the water-side is washed by the ocean at flood tide, but at the ebb the water recedes a mile, leaving the rocks quite bare. Thére was formerly a long line of fortifications, but at present the guns are dismounted, excepting on an elbow of the wall, called the "battery." (See Plate.) In the centre of the town is the main plaza, fronting which is the cathedral, the government house, and the prison. (See Plate.) Here is seen a "Padre," walking with a señorita; an "hombre," mounted on a donkey, with a large stone jar on each side, from which he serves his customers with water; a "chain-gang" of prisoners, carrying bales of *carna*, guarded by a barefooted soldier. And still further to the left is a sentinel watching the prison. I will here state, that most of the Panama hats that are made here, are manufactured in this prison.

3

The principal avenues, running parallel, are "Calle San Juan de Dio," "Calle de Merced," and "Calle de Obispo." There are numerous extensive churches, the principal one being the cathedral. This is a magnificent structure, and of colossal dimensions. In the end fronting the plaza are niches, in which are life-size statues of the twelve Apostles, of marble. It has two towers, the upper sections of which are finished with pearl. The interior was furnished without regard to expense. It is now somewhat dilapidated, but still has a fine organ. The convent, "La Mugher," is an extensive edifice, being 300 feet in length. The roof of most parts has fallen in, and the walls are fast falling to decay. The only tenant is a colored woman who has a hammock slung in the main entrance. She has converted the convent into a stable, charging a *real* a night for a horse or mule —they board themselves; they, however, have the privilege of selecting their own apartments. It encloses a large court, in which there are two immense wells, and numerous fig, and other fruit trees. There is a tower still standing on one end of the building, without roof or window; it has, however, several bells still hanging. The convent of "San Francisco," is also an extensive structure, in a dilapidated state; one part of it is still tenanted by nuns. It has a tower with bells still hanging. These buildings, as well as all the buildings of Panama, are infested by innumerable lizards, a peculiarity of the city that first strikes the stranger. They are harmless, but to one unaccustomed to seeing them, are an unpleasant sight.

The people here, as in all catholic countries, are very attentive to religious rites and ceremonies, and almost every day of the week is ushered in by the ringing of church and convent bells. The ringing is constant during the day; and people are seen passing to and from church, the more wealthy classes accompanied by their servants, bearing mats, upon which they kneel on their arrival. Almost every day is a saint's day, when all business is suspended to attend its celebration.

Good Friday is the most important on the calendar. All business is suspended, all attend church during the day, and at night they congregate *en masse* in the plaza in front of one of the churches outside the walls. Inside the church, held by a native in Turkish costume, is an ass, mounted on which is a

G.V. COOPER DEL. ON STONE BY J. CAMERON LITH. OF G.W. LEWIS, 111 NASSAU

GRAND CATHEDERAL, PANAMA.

life-size wax figure of the Saviour. There are also life-size figures of Mary, St. Peter, St. Paul, and St. John, each mounted on a car, and each car illuminated by one hundred tapers, which are set in candelabras of silver, and borne by sixteen men. Incense is burned, a chant is sung accompanied by the organ, and at the ringing of a small bell, all rise from their knees; the bell rings again, and the procession moves. The ass is first led out, followed by the figures of Mary and the Apostles in order; next, the band of music and the procession follows, which is illuminated by innumerable tapers. They move toward the main gate, all joining in the chant. The passage of the first of the procession through the gate, is announced by the simultaneous discharge of rockets which illumine the very heavens. The discharging of rockets is continued, and, after passing through the principal streets, they return to the church and deposit the images. They again return to the city, seize an effigy of Judas Iscariot and after hanging it up by the neck, cut it down and burn it. The celebration closes with the usual night procession of nuns and priests. These celebrations and processions are conducted with the greatest solemnity, the people all engaging in them as if they thought them indispensable to salvation.

The priests are quite ultra in their dress, wearing a black silk gown, falling below the knee, black silk tights, patent-leather shoes, fastened with immense silver buckles, a black hat, the brim of the most ungovernable dimensions, rolled up at the sides and fastened on the top of the crown. Their zeal in religion is equalled only by their passion for gaming and cock-fighting. It appears strange to see men of their holy calling enter the ring with a cock under each arm, gafted for the sanguinary conflict, and, when the result is doubtful, enter into a most unharmonious wrangle, with the *faithful* under their charge.

The citizens of Panama are composed of all grades of color, from the pure Sambo, (former slaves or their descendants,) to the pure Castilian. The distinctive lines of society are not very tightly drawn. At the fandangoes all colors are represented, and a descendant of Spain will select, as a partner, one of the deepest dye. In this hot climate the waltz or quadrille soon throws all parties into a most profuse perspiration, which causes *that other* characteristic of the African race to manifest itself. I would recommend my American friends to select partners of the lighter color, as I am not prepared to say the *odor* is altogether pleasant. The order of the evening is to fill the floor; the music and dance commence; when a gentleman gives out, another takes his partner, and so on, until it is time for refreshments. The ladies never tire.

G. V. COOPER DEL. ON STONE BY J. CAMERON LITH. OF C. W. LEWIS, 111 NASSAU ST. N. Y.

THE ISLANDS, FROM PANAMA

Chapter Eighth.

BAY OF PANAMA—ISLANDS—SOLDIERS—ARRIVAL OF $1,000,000 IN GOLD AND SILVER—A CONDUCTA—"BUNGOES" "UP" FOR CALIFORNIA—WALL STREET REPRESENTED—SAIL FOR SAN FRANCISCO—CHIMBORAZO—CROSS THE EQUATOR—A CALM—A DEATH AT SEA.

IN the bay of Panama (called the "Pearl Archipelago," from the numerous pearls obtained in its waters,) there are innumerable islands, all of great fertility, supplying the city with vegetables, tropical fruits, eggs, fowls, &c. (See Plate.) It is from these islands vessels are supplied with provisions and water, the latter being obtained at Toboga, one of the largest of the group. A more enchanting scene than is presented from the higher points of these islands, cannot be imagined. The bay as placid as a mirror, Panama in full view, with mountains rising in the background. Looking along down the coast of South America, you see a succession of lofty mountains, some by their conical peaks proclaiming their volcanic origin, some still clouded in smoke, giving token of the fierce struggle that is going on within. Still farther to the right the bay opens into the broad Pacific; that little ripple that is now running out, will go on gathering strength, until it breaks upon the shores of the "Celestial Empire." Still farther to the right, a tower, shrouded in ivy, seems weeping over the tomb of a city.

In the background mountain succeeds mountain, until the last is buried in clouds. Ships and steamers are lying quietly at anchor; numerous islands are blooming at your feet, clothed with tropical fruits, growing and ripening spontaneously. Nature reigns supreme, the hand of man has not marred her perfection; if his rude habitation is sometimes seen, it is nestling quietly in the bosom of some grove planted by the hand of Nature, interlaced by vines, their tendrils entwining, forming an arbor over his head, and presenting fruit and wine at his door. It seems a paradise. It would seem that man might be happy here. He has not to care for to-morrow, but to partake of the bounties of nature as they are presented. But, alas! man spends his life struggling for the thousand phantasies his own diseased imagination has engendered, while nature has placed happiness within his reach, and only asks contentment on the part of the recipient of her bounties.

The markets of Panama, as well as the retail trade in other departments, are under the supervision of females. They are generally well supplied with every variety of fruit from the islands, together with eggs, fowls, &c. The beef and pork are sold by the *yard*. Beef is cut in thin strips and dried in the sun; this is packed or sewed up in skins, and is an article of export from many of the South American Republics. The inhabitants have a great passion for "fighting-cocks." There is not a house that is not furnished with from one to a dozen. They generally occupy the best aparments, and, on entering a house, your first salutation is from "chanticleer," he having a strange propensity to do the loud talking. They also venerate the turkey-buzzard, with which the city is sometimes clouded. They are the carrion bird of the south, and no doubt good in their place, but the most loathsome of all the feathered tribe.

The citizens of Panama, as well as of other tropical countries, have the happy faculty of devoting most of their time to the pursuit of pleasure, i.e., they divide time between business and pleasure, giving to the latter a great predominance. Before the innovations made by "los Americanos," stores were open from 9 to 10 A. M., and 4 to 5 P. M., the balance of the day was spent in smoking, drinking coffee, chocolate, or cocoa, gambling, cock-fighting, attending church, or wooing sleep in hammocks. The city is generally healthy, yet at some seasons of the year, is subject to fevers of a malignant type. It has been visited several times by that scourge the cholera, which swept off many of its inhabitants, and, at one time, seemed destined to depopulate the country. The priests clad themselves in sackcloth, and devoted every moment to the rites of the church, burning incense and invoking the patron saint of the city to stay the ravages of the disease. The vaults in which the dead are deposited, are a succession of arches in mason-work, resembling large ovens. When one of these is full it is closed up, and the adjoining one filled.

The city has a small garrison of soldiers, their only duty being to guard the prison, and conduct prisoners out in chain-gangs to labor, paving the streets, repairing the walls, carrying goods, &c. A gang will be seen in front of the cathedral, in the accompanying plate. The appearance of the under-officers, is ludicrous in the extreme. They are seen parading the streets with an air of authority, in full uniform, and barefooted.

Soon after my arrival at Panama, one of the British steamers came in from Valparaiso with $1,000,000 in gold and silver. This was deposited in front of the custom-house, and guarded during the night by soldiers; and, in the morning, packed on mules, preparatory to crossing the Isthmus. It required thirty-nine mules to effect the transportation. A detachment of nine first started, driven by a single soldier, armed with a musket, and barefooted. The second, third, and fourth detachments started at intervals of half an hour, each guarded like the first. The mules were driven in droves, without bridle or halter. The route being through an unbroken forest of twenty-five miles, it would seem a very easy matter to rob the "conducta." But, strange to say, although $1,000,000 per month, for several years, has passed over the route, no such attempt has ever been made. In the immediate vicinity, and overlooking the city, is a mountain called "Cerro Lancon," which was once fortified by an invading foe, from which the city was bombarded and taken. On the summit a staff is now seen, from which the stars and stripes float proudly in the breeze. This was erected by the Panama Railroad Company, to point out, during the survey, the location of the city.

Great anxiety was felt by the Americans at Panama to proceed on to California. The sun had passed overhead, and was settling in the north, indicating the approach of the rainy season. Many were sick of the fever, many had died, which added to the general anxiety. Many had procured steamer tickets before leaving home. The steamers had passed down to San Francisco, been deserted by their crews, and were unable to return, and there were no seaworthy vessels in port. The indomitable go-a-head-ativeness of the Yankee nation could not remain dormant, and soon several "bungoes" were "up" for California. Schooners of from thirteen to twenty-five tons, that had been abandoned as worthless, were soon galvanized, by pen and type, into "*the new and fast sailing schooner.*" These were immediately filled up at from $200 to $300 per ticket, passengers finding themselves. In the anxiety to get off, a party purchased an iron boat on the Chagres River, carried it across to Panama on their shoulders, fitted it out, and sailed for California. The first "bungo" that sailed, after getting out into the bay some three or four miles, was struck by a slight flaw of wind, dismasted, and obliged to put back for repairs. This caused a very perceptible decline in "bungo" stocks. Many took passage in the British steamer for Valparaiso, in hopes to find conveyance from that port. The passengers of one of "*the fast sailing schooners*" when going on board, preparatory to sailing, found that the owners, in their *zeal to accommodate their countrymen*, had sold about three times as many tickets as said vessel would carry. Instead of allowing fourteen square feet to the man, as the law requires, they appear to have taken the *exact-dimensions* of the passengers, and filled the vessel accordingly. The passengers refused to let the captain weigh anchor, and sent a deputation on shore to demand the return of their money; but lo! the disinterested gentlemen were "non est inventus." After a long search, they succeeded in finding one of the worthies, and notwithstanding his disinterested efforts in behalf of the *public*, he was locked up. The captain fearing personal violence, left the vessel privately, and for several days was nowhere to be found. The passengers, however, entered into a compromise with themselves, the first on the list going on board. The mate informed the captain and they were soon under way. The owner, who had been so persecutingly locked up, having formerly been an operator in Wall street, resolved to slight the hospitalities of the city, and took his leave when the barefooted sentinel wasn't looking.

One circumstance that added much to the annoyance of our detention was, that the letters from our friends were all directed to San Francisco, and were then lying in the letter-bags at Panama, but not accessible to us. I felt this annoyance most sensibly. I would have given almost any price for one word of intelligence from home. On returning one evening from Gorgona I was informed by Mr. Pratt, my room-mate, that a gentleman had called during my absence with a letter. I left the supper table to go in search of him; some one knocked at the door; and imagine my surprise and pleasure as Mr. D. Trembley, an old acquaintance from New York was ushered into the room. He had letters for me dated two months subsequent to my departure. He was accompanied by his brother, and I had the pleasure of making the passage up the Pacific in their company.

The prospect, at this time, of getting passage to California was extremely doubtful, and many returned to the States. During the latter part of April, however, several vessels arrived in port, and were "put up" for San Francisco. I had sent to New York for a steamer ticket—which was due, but there being no steamer in port, and being attacked with the fever, I was advised to leave at the earliest possible moment. I secured passage in the ship "Niantic," which was to sail on the 1st of May. On the morning of that day bungoes commenced plying between the shore and ship, which was at anchor some five miles out, and at 4 P. M., all the passengers were on board. The captain was still on shore, and there was an intense anxiety manifested. Many had come on board in feeble health; some who had purchased tickets had died on shore; many on board were so feeble that they were not expected to live. I was one of the number; we all felt that getting to sea was our only hope, and all eyes were turned toward shore, fearing the captain might be detained. At half-past five his boat shoved off, when all on board were electrified. As he neared the ship all who were able prepared to greet him, and some, whose lungs had been considered in a feeble and even precarious state, burst out into the most vociferous acclamations. The captain mounted the quarter-deck and sung out, "Heave ahead," when the clanking of the chain and windlass denoted that our anchor was being drawn from its bed. At half-past six the "Niantic" swung from her moorings, and was headed for the mouth of the "Gulf of Panama." Again the shouts were deafening. No reasonable politician could have wished a greater display of enthusiasm, and a nominee would consider his election quite certain, whose pretensions were backed up by two hundred and forty pairs of *such* lungs. We had a light breeze and moored slowly out—the lights of the city gradually settling below the horizon. As we passed the islands an occasional light would appear and immediately vanish. Soon all nature was shrouded in darkness, and with the exception of an occasional creaking of the wheel, and a slight ripple at the prow, everything was still.

In the morning we were running down along the coast of South America, the captain wishing to cross the equator, in order to fall in with the trade winds. We passed along very near the coast, having the Andes constantly in view, some of the peaks towering up, their heads buried in the blue ether of Heaven.

We were often saluted by whales, sometimes coming up near the ship, throwing up a column of water, and passing under our keel, displaying to us their gigantic dimensions. We would sometimes run into schools of porpoises, extending almost to the horizon in every direction. We were constantly followed by sharks, accompanied by their pilots—the latter a most beautiful fish, from eight to twelve inches in length, striped in white and grey. It seemed strange that they should have been created to act as pilots to the "terror of the deep." The shark is always accompanid by one, and sometimes two or three. They generally swim a little in advance, but sometimes nestle along on the back of their huge master—as if to rest, and in case of emergency, are said to take refuge in his mouth.

On the 6th we came in sight of "Chimborazo," the highest peak of the Andes, and the highest mountain on the western continent. It appears to penetrate the very heavens. It was surmounted by belts or layers of clouds, with sufficient space between to disclose the mountain. Below and above the first belt there was vegetation, above the second sterility, above the third, and towering on up, a covering of eternal snow.

On the 12th we reached the Gallipagos islands, a group of volcanic formation, directly under the equator. They are not inhabited by man, but are the home of the terrapin. We passed very near, but as it was almost sunset, we did not lower our boat. We crossed the equator, and made one degree south latitude. Then standing west, in order to fall in with the trade winds, we reached 110° west longitude. We then headed north on our course to San Francisco, but there was no wind. We had a calm for several days, accompanied with rain and mist. The weather was excessively hot, causing everything on board to mildew. Our clothes, boots, trunks, &c., were covered with mould. Those who were sick became worse, and others were attacked. Our ship rolled about like a log, without sufficient air to cause a ripple. There was a general uneasiness manifested, and something foreboding in every face; all were indisposed; we felt that there was a destitution of vitality in the atmosphere. On the 6th of June one of the passengers was attacked with the ship-fever, which immediately proved fatal. He died at three o'clock in the morning, and at ten was brought out, sewed up in canvas, and laid upon the gang plank. A bag of sand was tied to his feet, a prayer read, and, at the signal, the end of the plank was raised, and he slid gently into his grave. It being calm, we watched the spot until the last bubble had risen to the surface. This was to us an afflicting scene; a gloom seemed to rest upon every countenance. That one of our number should have been taken away by a disease thought to be contagious, and one so malignant in its character, gave rise to emotions of the most painful dejection. The ship was immediately cleansed, disinfecting fluid was distributed profusely, and we escaped the farther appearance of the disease.

Chapter Ninth.

STAND IN FOR SAN FRANCISCO—INDICATIONS OF LAND—THE COAST—ENTER THE "GOLDEN GATE"—INNER BAY—SAN FRANCISCO—LUMPS OF GOLD—NOTES OF ENTERPRISE—SURROUNDING SCENE—GAMBLING.

WE soon fell in with the north-east trade winds, which carried us along rapidly, causing us to make so much lee-way however, that on arriving at 38° north latitude, (the latitude of San Francisco), we were at 140° west longitude. We then tacked ship and stood in for the coast of California. We had baffling winds and calms for several days, but falling in with the north-west trades, we were carried rapidly along, the wind increasing until it blew a gale. This lasted for two days. The ship laid over so that her main studding-sail boom touched the water, and on the 1st July the gale carried away our gib. On the 3d, we discovered weeds and logs floating in the water, indicating our proximity to land. We take an observation, and ascertain that we are sixty miles from San Francisco. This we ought to make by 8 o'clock the next morning. The passengers are all engaged in packing up. The retorts, crucibles, gold tests, pick-axes, shovels, and tin-pans, are put into a separate bag, and laid on the *top*; each determined to be the first off for the mines. Each one having conceived a different mode of keeping his gold, one would exhibit an ingenious box with a secret lock, another, a false bottom to his trunk, a fourth a huge belt, while a fifth was at work on the fifteenth buckskin bag, each of 20 lbs. capacity. All were looking to the glorious future with a faith that would have removed mountains, particularly if they were suspected of having gold concealed underneath. On the morning of the 4th, the sun rose in a cloud of mist. We were all expectation and excitement. Some were at mast-head, others in the shrouds, and all on the "*qui vive*" for land. The fog was so dense we could not take an observation, but still stood in toward land. At 12 o'clock we felt a slight breeze, and the mist rose like a curtain, displaying to our astonished vision the coast of California. A simultaneous shout burst forth, and our very ship seemed to bound with enthusiasm. We find by taking an observation that we are twenty miles north of the entrance to the bay. We had a fair wind, and passed along very near the coast, which is bold and rocky, rising and terminating in the coast range of mountains, and in the back ground the famed "Sierra Nevada," (mountains of snow).

At 3 o'clock, P. M., we arrived off a bold rocky promontory, which is the north point to the entrance of the outer bay of San Francisco, called "De los Reys," or King's Point. We soon changed our course, standing in for the entrance to the inner bay, some twenty miles distant. The air was filled with geese, brant, loons, ducks, &c. We here saw the hair-seal, somewhat resembling a tiger. They would come to the surface, display themselves, and disappear. We saw, also, a very large whale coming directly toward the ship, alternately diving and reappearing, and the third time he came to the surface, he was quite near us. He threw up a column of water, and diving headlong toward the bottom, threw his huge tail into the air. Not wishing to come to anchor before morning, we shortened sail, and all "*turned in.*"

In the morning we were a short distance from the "*Golden Gate*," the entrance to the inner bay, making for it with a fair breeze. A large ship was abreast of us, making for the same point. A schooner spoke us, and wished to pilot us in, but our captain not relishing California price ($200), declined. The strait through which we were about to pass, is an opening through the coast-range of mountains, about a mile in width, and has the appearance of having been cut through by the action of the inland waters. The capes at either side are bold, and that on the right is fortified. We could not have made a more auspicious entrance. It was a delightful morning, with a fresh breeze, and the tide rushing in at eight knots. When we had made the entrance, we could see through into the inner bay, directly in the centre of which is an island of considerable elevation, which serves as a beacon to inward-bound vessels. The passage in was entirely without interruption, and the scene most enchanting. It seemed to us that the gates had been thrown open, and we ushered in to view some fairy scene. At our left was the little bay of "Saucelito" (Little Willow), where several vessels were lying cosily under the bank, taking in water. Here is a small island, inhabited only by sea-fowl—there a strait which is the mouth of the Sacramento and San Joaquin rivers, beyond which the shore of the bay is bold with mountains in the background. We still head toward the island in the centre. At our right, the shore is bold, and still further on, a point of considerable elevation juts out into the bay. The tide is still bearing us along with headlong speed, and we are obliged to take in all sail with the exception of the flying-jib. As we neared the point we changed our course, making as near it as practicable, and, as we round it, San Francisco is spread out before us, where rides a fleet of two hundred sail. We feel that we have attained the acme of our ambition, that we have really entered the "Golden Gates." We pass along, and passing several vessels, come to the United States man-of-war, "Gen. Warren." Our patriotism, at this particular time, was not of a nature to be smothered into silence. We took off our hats, opened our mouths, and it was soon evident that our lungs had lost none of their vigor by exposure to the sea air. We passed most of the shipping, and finding a convenient place our captain cried out "haul down the flying jib," "let go the anchor," and our ship rounded to, as if willing to rest after a run of sixty-five days.

We were immediately boarded by boatmen, and I was soon in a row-boat on my way to the shore. On landing, my first move was for the post-office. I had gone but a few paces in this city of strangers, before some one called my name. I turned around; he did not recognize my six months' beard, and apologized. I recognized him as a New York friend, and assured him there was no offence, that I was the identical individual he was looking for. I accompanied him to his store, where he exhibited several specimens of gold, weighing twenty-seven ounces, twenty-five ounces, and down to a single ounce. These were no unwelcome sight to me, and served to stimulate the fever. My greatest anxiety, however, was to hear from home, and with the least possible delay, I hurried to the post office. I had heard from home but once in six months, and my anxiety and pleasure can well be imagined, when, in answer to my inquiry, I was handed a half-dozen letters. I went to a restaurant, read my letters, ate a $3.50 beefsteak, and felt as rich as men are generally supposed *to feel* after a six months' residence. I could neither get room nor lodgings in town. Many of the business men, and all the transient people, lived in tents. My tent was still on board the ship, and my friend above spoken of, offered me the hospitalities of his own for the night.

In the morning I took my writing-desk, and climbed to an eminence in the vicinity of the city, to write to my friends at home. Seating myself under a cluster of small trees which protected me from the sun, I commenced, and, with the exception of an interval for dinner, spent the day in writing. The scene around me was animated. Everything appeared to be propelled by the most indomitable perseverance. The frame of a house would be taken from the ship in the morning, and at night it was fully tenanted. The clatter of the innumerable hammers, each answered by a thousand echoes, seemed the music by which the city was being marshalled into existence. Ships were constantly arriving; coming to anchor a mile out, they would immediately disgorge their cargoes, which, taken by lighters, were conveyed to the shore, and thrown into heaps, their owners running about to contract for their immediate transportation into the interior. Others were seen rowing off to vessels, which, after receiving their complement of passengers, would weigh anchor and stand for the strait, which is the joint mouth of the Sacramento and San Joaquin Rivers.

Towards evening the scene became less animated, and the noise more subdued. I could but look with admiration upon the heightened beauty of the scene, as Nature was about to repose. A smile of approbation seemed to play upon her countenance as she was taking the last view of this, the perfection of her works.

The sun is almost down, tinging only some of the highest peaks of the surrounding mountains. The city, extending from the bay up the left base and side of the mountain, is about to cease her notes of enterprise, and light her lamps. At the base, directly under my feet, is an encampment of one hundred tents, occupied by Americans and Chilians. Two hundred ships are lying at anchor, displaying their various ensigns, comprising almost all the commercial nations of the world; and looming up conspicuously in the offing, is the man-of-war, "Gen. Warren," her majestic appearance proclaiming the superiority of American naval architecture. But the most striking feature in the scene is this beautiful bay; surrounded by mountains which protect it from the winds, it sleeps in perfect calm, the flood and ebb tide carrying vessels in and out, at from seven to eight knots an hour. At this moment, although the wind is blowing in the mountains, the bay is as placid as a mirror. In the centre of the bay is a beautiful island, as if nature had set in pearl one of her choicest emeralds. But "night has let her curtain down, and pinned it with a star." In the evening I strolled about with my friends, and was surprised to see that all of the best houses on the main streets were gambling houses. The rooms were brilliantly lighted, and each contained several *monte* tables, loaded with gold and silver coin, together with many rich specimens from the mines. To allure their victims, they were usually furnished with music, a bar, and an interesting señorita to deal the cards. Gamblers understand that the only *sure* way of making a man courageous is to get him drunk, consequently, at about every second dealing of the cards, all the betters are "treated." A man bets on a card and loses. His last drink is beginning to effervesce, and, of course, he is too *shrewd* to let the gambler have his money. He doubles the bet, putting the money on the same card, thinking that a card must, at least, win every other time. I have noticed that gamblers are very considerate, always *managing* to throw out just the card the victim wishes to bet upon. Again he loses, and again is "treated." His courage is up: the third time *his* card must certainly win. The "deal" takes place, and, strange to say, *his* card is turned up, and seems to say, in its very face that it is to win. In order to win back his former losses, he stakes, this time, half his purse. The other betters and bystanders now begin to manifest an interest in the affair. The gambler now begins to draw the cards, and, lo! the victim's card don't win. He is excited; he sees that others are looking at him, and displays the greatest amount of courage by taking another drink, and calling for another deal. Again *his* card is turned up. It cannot possibly lose four times in succession. He throws on his entire purse. It is lost. He goes out penniless. Another *shrewd* man was standing by, betting small sums on the opposite card, and consequently had won four times in succession. He had discovered the remarkable *fact*, that the card opposite the above described unlucky one, would *invariably* win. He determined to make a fortune by his discovery. The deal takes place, the unlucky card comes out, and he puts a large sum on the *other* one. The cards are drawn, and, strange as it may seem, the *unlucky* card wins. This appeared doubly strange to the *shrewd* man. He took another drink, and felt positive it could not happen so again. Another deal, and the indefatigable *unlucky* card is again in the field. Again the shrewd man bets, and again the *unlucky* card wins. The shrewd man displays as much courage as his predecessor, and is soon prepared to leave in the same financial condition.

The bystanders grow a little suspicious. The cards are again dealt, small bets are made and won by the bystanders. The gambler "treats," bystanders again bet, win, are "treated," and grow courageous. A better state of feeling exists; the gambler grows more complacent, and treats oftener. All are anxious to bet, the gambler is considered one of the best of fellows—one of that kind of men who would a little prefer *losing* money to *winning* it. Again bets are made and won, and all appear anxious to share the gambler's money, as it is, doubtless, about to be distributed among the *fortunate* bystanders. All drink and bet liberally; but this time they lose. This is, however, the first loss, and they bet again, but it so happens that they lose this time also. They drink and bet again, and again lose. They now find that they have only half as much money as they commenced with. They now resolve to recover what they have lost, and quit. But, alas! when the victim arrives at this point in the drama, he is lost. He loses every bet, until, seized by a feeling of reckless desperation, he risks *all*, and is immolated upon the altar of avarice.

Hundreds who have never risked, and who think it impossible they ever could risk, a dollar in a game of chance, are daily drawn into the vortex. They come to town with well-filled purses, the proceeds, perhaps, of six months' hard labor, to buy the necessary provisions and clothing, get their letters, &c. They meet old friends, drink, go to the gambling house, drink again, and finally bet a small amount, and perhaps win. They bet again, and again win. A feeling of avarice is now excited, and they risk a large sum. But after repeated bets, with varied success, they discover that they are losers. They now make the *fatal resolve* that they will win back what they have lost and quit; the next moment they are ruined.

Chapter Ten.

THE "HOUNDS"—VILLAINY—INDIGNATION MEETING—VIGILANCE COMMITTEE.

SAN FRANCISCO was, at this time, infested by a gang of desperados disposed to repudiate all laws, and be governed only by their own fiendish propensities. They styled themselves "hounds," and neither life nor property were secure against their depredations. They felt so secure in their strength and numbers, that they did not seek the protection of night, but frequently committed the most revolting crimes at noon-day, and under the eye of the public authorities. They would enter public houses, demand whatever they wished, always forgetting to pay for the same, and, perhaps, before leaving, demolish every article of furniture on the premises. This would be a mere prelude or introductory to a night of fiendish revelry. They would plunder houses, commit the most diabolical acts upon the inmates, murder in case of resistance, then commit the building to the flames to hide their infamy.

On the first Sunday after my arrival, several of the leaders of the gang returned to town, after a few days' absence. They crossed over from the opposite side of the bay, having with them a fife and drum, the music of which was accompanied by yells, groans and hisses, such as one would only expect to hear from demons. After landing they marched into the main plaza, and executing a few peculiar evolutions, dispensed with their music, at least the instrumental part of it, and commenced their foray. I was seated in a restaurant as the captain and five of his followers entered. He drew up to a table upon which were several glasses, decanters, &c., together with sundry plates of refreshments. He raised his foot, kicked over the table, smashing the crockery into atoms, then taking his cigar from his mouth said, with the utmost *nonchalance*, "waiter, bring me a gin-cocktail, G—d d—n you." After having satisfied their thirst and hunger, they sallied forth without taking the trouble to learn the precise amount of damage done.

During the night, after committing several robberies, they entered a Chilian tent, and, after committing the most brutal outrages upon the mother and daughter, murdered the former, and in their struggle with the latter, she, after receiving several severe wounds, caught a bowie-knife from the hand of one of them and, after dealing him a deadly blow, made her escape. She immediately gave the alarm, and although robberies had been committed with impunity, this outrage upon defenceless females, awakened an impulse that was irresistible. The excitement was most intense; citizens flocked together, armed with a determination to meet out summary punishment to the perpetrators of this inhuman outrage.

Several arrests were made, and, although many were in favor of summary vengeance, better counsel prevailed, and they were put into the hands of the authorities and locked up. They refused to give any information as to the stolen property, but upon searching the tent of an accomplice, various articles were found, and snugly stowed away in a mattress was a large amount in gold dust, the wages of their infamy. A few hours after the above arrests, a demonstration was made by accomplices, in order to force open the jail, and release their comrades. This caused the strongest feelings of indignation, and the citizens assembled *en masse* in the plaza, all armed to the teeth, determined to avenge this additional aggravation to the atrocious crimes already perpetrated. They immediately organized themselves into a police, and determined to act with decision upon any proposition that might be sanctioned by the meeting. Had a resolution passed to hang the prisoners it would have been carried into immediate effect. Notwithstanding the excitement of the moment, many of the "hounds" had the effrontery to show themselves, and during a speech by one of the citizens, made some menacing jestures, upon which the speaker drew a revolver from his bosom, and with a determined emphasis requested all those who sympathized with the prisoners to separate from the crowd. Had they complied, the determination manifested in every countenance gave fearful token of the doom that awaited them. It was resolved, in consideration of the insecurity of the jail, to transfer the prisoners to the man-of-war, "General Warren." This was carried into immediate effect, the citizens forming a double file from the jail to the shore.

This demonstration secured but five of the numerous horde that infested the city, and it was not to be expected that the arrests of these would prove a salutary check, nor did it. The desperados stood in greater fear of this self-constituted police than of the regular authorities. This organization was undoubtedly the germ from which the "Vigilance Committee" eventually grew. It is well known that, upon the breaking out of the gold excitement, the cities of the world sent forth their vilest scum, consisting of gamblers, pickpockets, murderers, and thieves, and California was the receptacle. They immediately fraternized, and were at once the most adroit, wily and experienced embodiment of villainy with which the prospects of a city were ever blighted. They were not men broken down in their *profession* at home, but the very *aristocracy* of crime. Too well-skilled to be detected, they had escaped the meshes of the law in their own country, and resorted to California for its superior *business* prospects. As if to have the organization complete, the convict islands of Great Britain vomited forth a herd that seemed almost *festering* with crime. This sealed the doom of San Francisco. She was infested by an organization, the very incarnation of infamy. They would fire the city for plunder, and commit murder to screen themselves from detection.

The city had grown to the stature of a giant; all were reaping the reward of their enterprise, when on the 5th December following, the torch of the incendiary was applied, and within a few short hours San Francisco was in ashes. Citizens who had assumed their pillows in wealth awoke in penury. Many, after a year of toil and anxiety, were preparing to return to their families in affluence, but in one brief moment their dreams of happiness were blighted, and their riches a heap of smouldering ruins. The city was immediately rebuilt, but citizens had barely entered their new habitations, when it was again devastated by fire. Again it rose, Phenix-like, from its own ashes, and again business was resumed, but for the third time it was in ruins.

The citizens were appalled. That it was the work of incendiaries no one doubted, yet to detect them seemed impossible, so skillfully were their plans laid, and so adroitly executed. Added to this, the sequel proved that some of their number had got into "high places," were conniving at their acts, and sharing their ill-gotten booty. This, in part, accounts for the tardy proceedings against those who were arrested, and the numerous reprieves of those who were clearly proved guilty. Property to the value of some twenty millions of dollars had already been destroyed, hundreds of citizens had been reduced from affluence to bankruptcy, others were in momentary fear of sharing the same fate. They had lost confidence in the city authorities, and there seemed no alternative but to take the matter into their own hands. They consequently organized themselves into what was termed a "Vigilance Committee," with the determination of bringing every suspicious person to a strict account. Many of the most influential and wealthy citizens were the first to enrol themselves, and they called upon all to join them in their effort at self-protection. Their head-quarters was at the engine-house of a fire company, the tolling of the bell being the signal for all to assemble. This well-known signal was always heard when an arrest was made, and became the death-knell to many a wretch, who for his villainies was hastily summoned into another world. The meetings of the Committee were strictly private, none but members being admitted. The proceedings were summary, and if the prisoner was proved guilty his sentence was carried into immediate effect. None were executed, however, without the unanimous consent of members present, this being one of the provisions of their constitution. Those who were executed were not only proved guilty, but confessed their guilt before their execution. Most of those who fell under the ban of the Committee were "Sidney convicts," and subsequently they were all ordered to leave the country within a specified time, upon the pain of death. The Mayor issued a proclamation against the proceedings of the Committee, and the coroner's juries summoned over the bodies of those who were executed, found against them; yet it is a question of doubt, whether *any one* was secretly opposed to their proceedings.

Persons living in well-regulated communities, and looking at the matter in the distance, may feel disposed to censure the Committee and its proceedings as hasty and precipitate; but, when we take into consideration that not only property to an immense amount, but life itself, was in jeopardy—the want of facilities for securing and retaining criminals during the tardy process of law, the numerous rescues by accomplices, and the frequent pardons by the authorities when the accused were notoriously guilty,—I say, when we take these things into consideration, together with the fact that not an individual was executed who was not clearly proved guilty, and even confessed his guilt; we can look upon the acts of the Committee not only as just—but imperative. In the confessions of some of those who were executed they implicated men in authority, in such a manner that not a doubt was left upon the public mind. The result of these summary measures is apparent to all. Crime, since the organization of the Committee, has decreased one half, and they have now ceased to make arrests, leaving all to the jurisdiction of the proper authorities. They, however, maintain their organization, and would, no doubt, act in case of emergency.

Chapter Eleventh.

START FOR THE MINERAL REGIONS—BANKS OF THE SACRAMENTO RIVER—SHOT AT—GOLD VS. MICA—SUTTERVILLE—PRIMITIVE MODE OF LIFE—SACRAMENTO CITY—AN INDIVIDUAL WHO HAD "SEEN THE ELEPHANT."

I SPENT the interval between the 5th of July and the 19th in preparing for the mines. I found many of the miners in town on account of the high state of water in the rivers. My friends who had visited the interior, spoke discouragingly of the mines, preferring the mercantile business. But goods were at the time selling at less than New York prices, and rents were enormously high. Many of the merchants were anxious to sell out and go into the mines, and I came to the conclusion that mining was the only sure way of making a fortune.

On the 19th July I went on board the brig "North Bend," with three men who had been hired in New York and sent out by a company in which I had an interest, and sailed for the Sacramento river. We crossed the bay, and in an hour were in the strait, running up with a stiff breeze, passing numerous small islands inhabited by water fowl and covered with "guano." There were innumerable ducks, brant, loons, and geese flying through the air; the scenery delightful, the first fifty miles being a succession of small bays, all studded with islands. At the right the bank rises gradually to the height of from twenty to fifty feet, covered with wild oats, with an occasional "live oak" tree, and relieved by frequent ravines through which small streams find their way to the strait. This plain, during the rainy season, furnishes pasture for heads of wild cattle—elk, deer, and antelope, but at this season they had retired to the marshes and lower lands; and the whole of the right bank, as far back as the eye could reach, appeared one immense field of ripened grain. The left bank, on the immediate margin, presents the same appearance, but relieved in the background by the coast range of mountains with which we were running parallel. This range appears a continuous ledge of granite, destitute of vegetation, and at one point towers up into a peak of considerable height, called Monte Diablo, (Devil's Mount).

At 12 M., we arrived at Benicia, now a port of entry and United States naval station. The man of man-of-war, "Southampton," was anchored in the stream—guarding the passage—to prevent smuggling. As soon as we came in sight they lowered their boat, and pulled out toward the middle of the stream to intercept us, and examine our papers—at the same time hoisting a signal for us to come to. Our captain was an "old salt," and, in his estimation, the greatest blessing conferred upon man is a fair wind. He had every inch of canvas set, and manifested a determination not to shorten sail; we were running before a ten-knot breeze, and flew by them like a shadow. They hailed us, but not being obeyed they fired a gun from the ship, when our captain ordered the helm put down, and in an instant our sails were fluttering in the breeze; we had distanced the jolly-boat—they being obliged to row half a mile against the current to reach us. The officer boarded us in not the most amiable mood; it was quite apparent that we were enjoying a joke he thought somewhat expensive to himself. He informed us that a foreign vessel had passed them a few days previous; but they were now on their guard and would have given us the next shot in our rigging. He pronounced our papers satisfactory, and pulled off for the ship, being most heartily cheered by us.

We were soon under way dashing along at lightning speed; soon arriving at the confluence of the Sacramento and San Joaquin rivers, fifty miles above San Francisco, the latter river coming in from the east, the former from the north. The strait up which we had sailed, running in the same direction, is called, by many, the Sacramento river. At the junction of the two rivers there is a marsh, of some extent, in the midst of which is located the "New York of the Pacific," of newspaper notoriety. I am informed that it now contains *one house.* There were not so many when we passed up. It is said there has never been a death in the city. We soon entered "Sui Sun" bay, which is an extensive, but very shallow body of water, requiring careful pilotage to take vessels through in safety. We again enter the Sacramento, which now presents a different appearance—the immediate margin being walled up by heavy timber, beyond which the marsh extends as far as the eye can reach. The depth of water on these marshes frequently covers the grass, presenting the appearance of a succession of lakes—all swarming with water fowls. Soon after reëntering the river our pilot brought us to a dead stand by running us on a sand bar. It was ebb tide, and there was no alternative but to await the flood. We loaded our rifles, lowered a boat, and pulled for the shore, preparatory to a hunt.

On landing, we were greeted by the most ravenous swarm of mosquitos it was ever my fortune to fall in with. They seemed to constitute the very atmosphere, and for size and spirit, I think they are without rivals, even in the "Montezuma swamp." We did not at first retreat, but soon came to the conclusion that game must be poor, where there are so many *bills* presented. We carried a few of them on board, and they were so well pleased, they remained till morning. At 10, A.M., the tide flooded us off, and we were again under way. We soon left the river, and entered what is called the "slough," which is a part of the river running out twenty miles above, and by passing through it, half the distance is saved. On both sides the "slough," it is densely timbered; the branches hanging over the stream, and many of the trees inclining over, it required the greatest care to avoid their coming in contact with our spars. We had a fine breeze, and each of the passengers took his turn at the wheel. None of them attracted the attention of the captain, until it became my turn. Whether it was that I understood navigation better than my fellow-passengers, I am not prepared to say, but, certain it is, that I had stood at the wheel but a moment, when, without consulting the compass, I found myself at a dead stand in a tree-top. I did not claim much credit for it, *and did not receive any.*

After cutting away branches, grapevines, etc., we were again under way, with the captain at the wheel. He proved as skillful as myself, and made fast to the first tree-top. We soon reëntered the main channel, and were passing through a more

G. V. COOPER DEL.

ON STONE BY J. CAMERON

LITH. OF G. W. LEWIS, 111 NASSAU ST. N. Y.

SUTTER

3 miles below Sac City

pleasant country, being a succession of forest and plain. At 4, P.M., in passing the mouth of a small stream, we again found ourselves aground, with a prospect of waiting twelve hours for the next tide. A boat was lowered, and some of the passengers went off to hunt. There were fish here in abundance. We offered them refreshments, but they seemed to "loathe the sight." The passengers who had gone on shore, had disappeared in the forest, but soon two of the number were seen hurrying toward the shore. They pushed off the small boat, and were soon coming over the side of the brig. They appeared much agitated, and, after consulting a friend in whispers, the three started for the shore.

After an hour's absence, they returned with their handkerchiefs filled with something, which was evidently not for the public eye. It was immediately put under lock and key. From the self-satisfied air and knowing winks of the three fortunate individuals, it was apparent that their fortune was full of hope. After mature reflection, they, no doubt, came to the conclusion, that as there was enough for all, as it was in their power, with a word, to place wealth within the grasp of all, it was their duty to make all happy, without delay, and, with great magnanimity, informed us that they had ascended the stream some distance, and, as they approached the ripple, to their astonishment, they found the water gurgling through pebbles of gold. They had each secured a competence, assuring us that we could go and do likewise. Some evil-disposed person stood by, who informed us that he noticed the same thing, and did not think it was gold. The three above-mentioned individuals, to reassure us, unlocked their trunks, but, lo! their fortunes, like fancy-stocks at the present day, had a downward tendency. It proved to be mica. It had somewhat the appearance of gold, but on separating it from the sand, it was found to be very light, having the appearance of small pieces of gilt paper. It was a most *blighting* illustration of the adage, that "all is not gold that glitters," particularly to the three above-mentioned individuals. The bed of the river at this place had the appearance of being constituted of golden sands. The same has been noticed in almost all the streams in California, and has, undoubtedly, given rise to many of the golden reports. At 10, A.M., (Sunday,) we were again under way, the day excessively hot, and at 12, M., arrived at "Sutterville;" and, when opposite the *town*, found ourselves out of the channel, and aground. We all went on shore, and had the pleasure of making the acquaintance of one of the proprietors, with whom we walked a mile back from the *town*, to view "*Capitol Hill*," the *anticipated* site of the State House. Although we did not break ground for the corner-stone, we were among the first to know the *precise spot*. The *town* is situated four miles below Sacramento City, and three from the fort. It contained three houses, visible to the *natural* eye, but, to the eye of the worthy proprietor's imagination, it numbered many thousands. This had caused a very perceptible rise in the value of city lots.

It afterwards became a town of some twenty houses. The owners offered to a company owning the bark "Josephine," thirty lots provided they would land their effects and make improvements. The proposition was accepted, and the improvements commenced. (See Plate.) A cannon is seen in the foreground which was taken from the Josephine, and used to salute vessels in passing up and down the river, as occasion might require. At the left, are two Oregonians riding at full speed, and in the centre is seen the Indian chief, Olympia, his squaw, and several natives of lesser note. The Josephine is seen at the river bank. She was subsequently sold and sailed for Oregon.

I here visited a family that had been wandering about since 1845, without having entered a house. There were two men, a woman, and three children, from three months to five years of age. They started from one of the Eastern States, with a wagon, two yoke of oxen, and two cows, passed through Missouri, crossed the Rocky Mountains into Oregon, and finally drove down to California. The children were all natives of the forest except the eldest. They were encamped under a large oak-tree a short distance from the river. The bed was made up on the ground, the sheets of snowy whiteness, the kitchen furniture was well arranged against the root of the tree, the children were building a playhouse of sticks, while the mother was sitting in a "Boston rocker" reading the Bible, with a Methodist hymn-book in her lap. The infant lay croaking on a white flannel-blanket, looking like a blown up life-preserver. While I

G. V. COOPER DEL.

ON STONE BY J. CAMERON

LITH OF G. W. LEWIS 111 NASSAU ST. N. Y.

ENCAMPMENT AT SAC CITY, NOV. 1849.

My own tent.

was conversing with the woman, one of the men went into the back room to change his linen, *i. e.*, he stepped behind the tree. They were all enjoying good health and appeared happy. I am disposed to think their house will be a poor protection during the rainy season; but for a summer-house, one could not well conceive of one better ventilated.

The next morning the flood-tide swept us into the channel, and at ten, we made fast to the bank at Sacramento city. This is at the junction of the American river with the Sacramento, 150 miles from San Francisco. Here, all was confusion and dust, each generating the other. This is the point from which the first move is made, by land, for the mines, and every man was on the run; mule-teams were moving in every direction, some loading, others preparing to load, each surrounded by a halo of dust which rendered mules and driver invisible. We were just in time to find one tree unoccupied, consequently settled down and commenced "keeping house." We designed to remain in town until the next morning. (See Plate.) This is my own tent. At this time, there were about one hundred houses and tents in town; but it seemed that every man landed with a house, and put it up the same day. Our brig had no less than thirteen on board, finished even to the glazing. Goods of every description were piled up on the river-bank, awaiting the carman. The owners were, in many instances, obliged to erect temporary shelters and sell them on the ground.

I met several persons who had been in the mines and seen the "Elephant." Among others, a fellow passenger on the "Niantic." He had been in the country two weeks, and in the mines half an hour. He had just returned, and was traveling through town trying to sell his utensils, preparatory to returning to the States. He was completely decorated with his wares, and looked like a country kitchen in disorder. He had a pair of grained boots and a smoked ham in one hand, a piece of perforated sheet-iron, a coffee-pot and frying-pan in the other, a pair of long India Rubber boots, with pants attached, thrown over one shoulder, and a pair of blankets under the arm. Over the other shoulder, was a long-handled shovel, from which was suspended a camp-kettle, containing a pepper-box, a pair of mining shoes, a piece of smoked beef, a Spanish grammar, several sea-biscuit, a pick-axe without a handle, and one pound each of sugar, coffee and bar-soap. All the above were offered at cost "*to close the concern.*" Every thing here was on the highest key. The town was only two months old, and lots were commanding New York prices. I was advised to embark in trade; but my heart was in the high-land, and the next morning at nine o'clock, we were moving for the interior, a party of a dozen having hired a six mule-team.

Chapter Twelve.

SUTTER'S FORT—A HERD OF CATTLE—"LASSOING"—RIO DE LOS AMERICANOS—A DISAPPOINTED HUNTER—A CAIFORNIAN SERENADE—A MULE AND HIS RIDER—PARTING COMPANY—THIRST—SERENADES SUPPORTED BY DIRECT TAXATION—SIERRA NEVADAS.

WE drove out a mile, to the margin of an extensive plain, where we stopped at a well, filled our flasks, and moved on, a gentleman who had a friend in the hospital at the fort, and myself, going in advance of the team. The fort at the time of its construction, was an extensive work, but now it is all in ruins excepting the inner inclosure, in which are situated the dwelling, hospital and out-houses. (See Plate). It is constructed of adobes, or unburned brick, prepared and laid up by Indian labor; and I will here remark, that the Indians on the ranchos in California, are considered as stock, and are sold with it as cattle, and the purchaser has the right to work them on the rancho, or take them into the mines. They are extremely squalid in appearance, and in the most abject servitude. I have never found the natives, anywhere, in a condition so degraded. We found the sick man in a very feeble state, having been in the hospital six weeks with dysentery, which he had contracted in the mines; and at this time there was but little hope of his recovery.

The fort is situated in the midst of an extensive plain, three miles from Sacramento city, and the same distance from the ferry and ford of the American river, (Rio Del Americano). It is said the proprietor, in one season, harvested nearly two thousand acres of wheat. At some distance back of the fort we saw grazing one of those immense herds of cattle for which California has been celebrated, (see Plate,) estimated at from two to three thousand head. Before the gold was discovered hides and tallow were the only articles of export, and cattle were raised and slaughtered for these articles alone. They run in large herds, feeding on the marshes in summer, and on the plains during the rainy season, kept from the grain by ditches and embankments, with which the fields are surrounded. They receive no care from the proprietors, and consequently are shy, and taken only with the "lasso." These are made of raw hide, cut and platted like a whip-lash about fifty feet in length, and the size of the finger. It has a small loop or pully in one end, through which the other is passed and drawn up to a coil about five feet in diameter. The other end is then fastened to the pommel of the saddle; the rider taking the coil in his right hand coils the balance to the same size, and mounts.

There are probably no better horsemen in the world, not excepting the Cossacks, than the whites, half-breeds, and some of the Indians of California. It has been said, that their only homes are upon the backs of their horses, and nothing could possibly exceed the spirit and reckless daring displayed on an occasion like this. Their dresses are extremely picturesque. A high crowned hat with a black glazed covering, trimmed with a gold-lace band and bell-buttons; a hunting shirt fastened at the waist by a blue or red sash, and a belt containing a brace of pistols, black velvet breeches, open at the side of the leg, the edges trimmed with bell-buttons, showing the white drawers underneath. Below the knee the leg is dressed in tanned skins, which are wound around and fastened with strings; a pair of boots with a pair of massive iron spurs, trimmed with heavy chains; the hind tree, as well as the pommel of the saddle, rises quite abruptly, enabling one to retain his seat either at a rear or plunge of his horse; the pommel terminating in an eagle's head, which prevents the lasso from slipping from the neck. The trimming of the saddle covers the entire back of the horse, the stirrups are of wood, made very large, with a leather covering in front, protecting the foot and leg from mud, brush, &c.; the bridle has a heavy iron bit and generally but one rein.

Thus mounted, a party of fifteen or twenty will approach a herd of cattle, horses, or elk, as the case may be. As they approach the herd takes fright, one snorts and starts, which is a signal for all, and they dash away. The horsemen, each selecting his victim, now bear down upon them with the speed of lightning. The herd, now aware of their pursuit, redouble

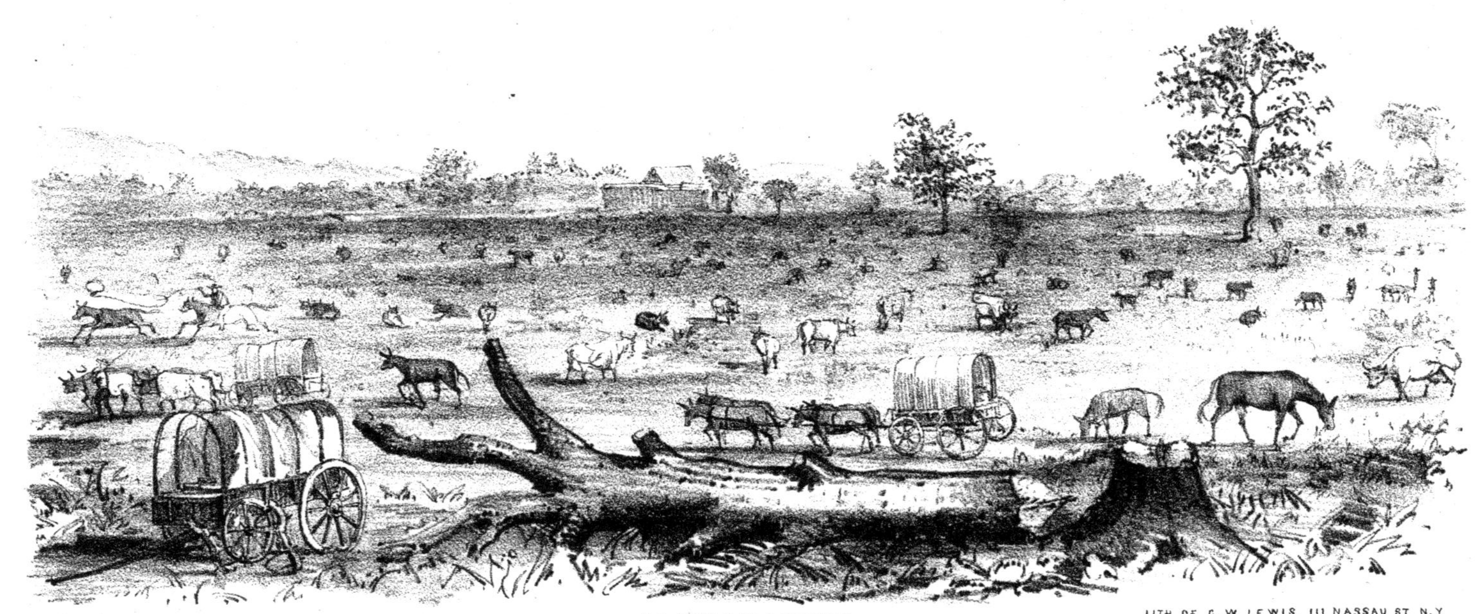

G. V. COOPER DEL. ON STONE BY J. CAMERON LITH OF G. W. LEWIS, 111 NASSAU ST N.Y.

Rear of Sutters Fort

their energies, straining every nerve, the earth fairly quaking beneath their hoofs. The horses, as they near, display as much enthusiasm as their riders, and seem to scorn the very earth. They are now upon them. The herd, frantic and dismayed, begin to scatter. The horse now sees his victim and bounds with the most reckless impetuosity. The horseman, now rising in his saddle, throws his weight into the left stirrup, and with his right hand swings the lasso until the coil is sufficiently open, when it flies with the velocity and precision of an arrow, taking effect around the horns or neck of the victim. The horse, understanding the business, now slackens his speed, and prepares for the first shock, by taking a bracing position. The victim straitens the lasso, bounds into the air, and falls to the ground. The horseman dismounts, keeping his left foot in the stirrup, to help counteract the frantic throes of the victim which is now lacerated by balls from his pistols. Sometimes in its phrenzy of madness the victim rushes upon his pursuers, causing a precipitate retreat, and not unfrequently both horse and rider fall victims to their own temerity.

As our team had not yet arrived, we walked on one mile to Grime's fort, a similar structure, and I believe the owner is a claimant of Sutter's claim. We walked on to the river, prepared ourselves and waded through. On the opposite side, as we ascended the bank, we found ourselves on the margin of a plain, stretching away as far as the eye could reach, with nothing but an occasional oak to relieve the monotony. On the bank, a short distance above, is a rancho, to which belongs the ferry, used only during high water. This rancho belongs to the Sutter estate. There are several thousand head of cattle and horses belonging to it, and about two hundred *head* of Indians. The soil has the appearance of being extremely fertile, but at this time vegetation was parched with drought. Sutter claims most of the country drained by the Sacramento and its branches, which is all, of any agricultural value, in the north part of the State.

Our team soon came up, and our driver informed us that it was ten miles to the next water, consequently we were obliged to encamp on the bank of the river, notwithstanding it was only 3 o'clock, P. M. We had averaged one mile per hour. I loaded my rifle and went down the river to hunt; I had promised myself a supper of wild duck, but they proved to be, on that particular day, all crows, and I compensated myself in part by picking a quantity of grapes. These were put into our camp-kettle and served up for supper. We thought them delicious, but the next morning, to our regret, we learned that we had forgotten to sweeten them. Late in the afternoon, a party of Indians started, fully equipped, to lasso horses, that were herding on the bottom lands of the Sacramento, six miles distant. They rode at the top of their speed, the horse and rider seeming moved by the same impulse. At night we spread our blankets in the open air. Some one of the party had been throwing out insinuations reflecting upon the character of the grizzly bear, that were said to abound in our immediate vicinity; not only that they were in the habit of "running around nights," but that they had a tendency to cannibalism. One of the party took a particular fancy to my rifle; whether it was the beauty of the piece, his predilection for the owner, or the fiery appearance of the cap, that stole his affections, I am not prepared to say. He folded it in his blanket and seemed to sleep the better for it. Soon after dark the California serenade commenced. The performers being two packs of wolves, the prairie (coyotas) and large gray wolf, each carrying a part, and in the latter were incorporated some of the best alto voices I ever heard. We were aroused early in the morning by a member of the above choir, who passed over the foot of our bed.

After breakfast we filled our flasks with water from the river and started. Our team travelled in a cloud of dust which hid them from our view. We moved on in advance. The day was excessively hot, and we were obliged to stop often for our team, in order to refill our flasks. After traveling five miles we overtook an ox-team loaded, and several mules packed, on the way to the mines. (See Plate). There were also several teams in the distance, moving in the same direction. We soon saw three men mounted on mules, coming toward us, who appeared to be returning from the mines. They were in high *spirits*, galloping along a little off the main track. One of them, in order, probably, to show a proper respect, pulled out his revolver and fired. His mule, taking the cue from his master, wishing to

G. V. COOPER DEL. BROWN & SEVERIN LITH. G. W. LEWIS PRINT.

BETWEEN SACRAMENTO, AND THE MINES.

make a proper demonstration in the presence of his fellow mules, gave a few peculiar gyrations with his tail, threw his head up, then threw it down, and threw his heels up, and at this particular time his master threw his heels up, and they parted company. It would be difficult to imagine a position more humble than the one assumed by the above mentioned master. He was literally with his face in the dust, and I never saw a more peculiar cast of countenance. If I had not seen the above transaction, but had met him with the same expression of countenance, I should have thought he had stolen the mule he was on, or would steal one if he had an opportunity. He didn't give us his card, but hurried on in the direction of Sacramento city.

We found the country a continuous plain entirely destitute of water, vegetation parched, and nothing showing signs of life excepting the few scattering oaks, an occasional wolf, and numerous gray squirrels. These last have much the appearance of the gray squirrels of the forests of New York; but they burrow in the ground, in families. We exhausted the supply of water we had put on board, and were suffering with thirst. The sun had gained the meridian, and his rays were almost consuming. We hurried on through clouds of dust, and at 2 P. M. reached the point at which we expected to find water. To our painful surprise, the spring was dry. It was three miles to the next, and we were almost crazy with thirst. It was no time for deliberation. There was no alternative but to push on. On arriving at the next spring, we found a puddle containing a quart of water, the surface covered with yellow wasps. We were, however, not fastidious, and drank all excepting the wasps. It again filled and was again drained, until all had replenished their flasks. We here took dinner, and moved on until about 5 P. M., when, after a most fatiguing day's journey, we reached the "half-way tent." I here saw a herd of deer, and notwithstanding the fatigues of the day, indulged in a "hunt," but without success.

Here, in the way of public accommodations, we found a tent, luxuriating in the name of the "half-way house." A rough board running the entire length served as a table, the guests sleeping in the open air outside, under the protection of their own blankets. A blacksmith had erected, under a temporary covering of canvas, his anvil-block and forge, and was busily engaged in repairing a damaged vehicle. (See Plate.)

Our cook is busily engaged in preparing supper, while Mr. Cooper and myself devote the few remaining moments of twilight, to sketching the surrounding scene. The snowy peaks of the Sierra Nevada are seen looming up in the distance, now gilded by the last rays of the setting sun, and now a dark imposing mass. Our teamster has just returned after a weary search for pasturage for our mules. I am visited by an individual whose personal appearance proclaims his own history more eloquently than it can be described. He might be termed one of the oldest inhabitants, having taken up his residence in the country before the gold excitement. He claimed to be on terms of intimacy with the *delirium tremens*, was deaf, had the rheumatism and scurvy, and said "he was not very well himself." His entire system seemed palsied by the use of rum, and so little control had he over the lineaments of his face, that he could only open his eyes by opening his mouth at the same time; hence, in closing his mouth upon his pipe (which was in constant use) he was obliged to part the lids of his left eye with his thumb and finger; so confirmed had he become in this habit, that a protuberance had raised upon his eyebrow and cheek-bone by the appliance. He was extremely loquacious and imparted much *valuable* information gratis, constantly keeping that *piercing* eye upon our brandy bottle. Mr. Cooper, who was seated upon a log near, cast an inquisitive glance upon him, and I tried to detect a family resemblance between the two. I was unable to learn, however, that they were in the least connected, nor am I prepared to say that their present acquaintance ripened into an intimacy. Two amiable donkeys are standing patiently under their loads while their masters are extracting "vegetables" from a demijohn.

We were serenaded, as usual, during the night. We had been under the impression that the music was gratis, but learned, on this occasion, that it was supported by *direct taxation*, one of the worthies having taken a ham from our camp-kettle during the night. In addition to this, I had the pleasure, in the morning, of *adding a note to his scale*, with which he seemed so much pleased, that he went off *repeating it*, until he was out of sight.

G. V. COOPER DEL. ON STONE BY J. CAMERON LITH. OF G. W. LEWIS, 111 NASSAU ST N.Y.

AUTHOR AND ARTIST

We took an early start and found the country more rolling, with an occasional pine tree. It was evident that we were ascending into a more elevated region, and from the higher points we could plainly see the Sierra Nevada, their slopes pointing out the location of the river to which we were journeying—the north branch of the American river. The country abounded in massive rocks, sometimes piled up in ledges, and sometimes forming the entire summits of the hills.

Chapter Thirteenth.

VENISON—FIRST VIEW OF THE GOLD REGIONS—SURROUNDING SCENERY—"MORMON BAR"—A POCKET—MY MACHINE IN MOTION—CERTAINTY OF SUCCESS—FIRST DINNER—"PROSPECTING"—A GOOD "LEAD"—DISAPPOINTED MINERS—A NEW COMPANION—A HIGHER POINT ON THE RIVER—VOLCANOES—SNOWY MOUNTAIN—AUBURN—LONELY ENCAMPMENT.

WE passed the night in the open air, and the next morning at eight o'clock arrived at an encampment of teamsters who were just dressing a deer and preparing breakfast. (See Plate.) The tree under which they were encamped was on fire, on one side, to its very top—the other supporting a luxuriant branch. The coffee-pot is on the fire and the cook stands by, frying-pan in hand, waiting for the steak. At the left the cattle are seen feeding; one of them, however, having resigned himself to the "coyotas." In the distance is seen a herd of deer bounding away over the hill. On the right are seen teams wending their way to the banks of the "North Fork" of the American river—freighted with provisions and utensils for mining. It will be seen that we have ascended into a more elevated region since leaving the last Plate. The ascent has been gradual—almost imperceptible—still everything indicates our elevation.

At ten we arrived at a junction in the roads, four miles from our point of destination; we remained here until after dinner; we now felt that we were about to try the realities of that for which we had left home and friends, traveled thousands of miles, and endured hardships and privations, the very thought of which makes the heart sick—we felt a degree of anxiety, as a few hours would probably decide whether we were soon to return to our friends or endure a long period of hardships in the mines. After dinner we were again under way, and soon, leaving the main road, we were running in the direction of the

G. V. COOPER DEL.

ON STONE BY J. CAMERON

TEAMSTERS BREAKFASTING.

LITH. OF G. W. LEWIS, 111 NASSAU ST. N. Y.

river. The road was good; but little timber; and the soil appearing well adapted to agriculture. It was soon evident that we were in close proximity to the river—the ravines all tending in the same direction; frequent rocks of enormous size, and from the more elevated points we could see a range of mountains rising on the other side. Having left the team behind, we pressed forward, eager to get a glimpse of the river and those employed in the golden pursuit; we soon arrived among the pines which stud the banks, but were still obliged to climb a slight ascent forming the immediate bank.

We soon gained the summit, and stood enraptured with the scene around us. The river, saluting our ears with its restless murmurs, meandered at the base of the mountain which had lifted us a mile above it. The banks were dotted with tents and teeming with the Liliputian owners. On the opposite side were mountains piled one above the other, terminating in a range covered with eternal snow, presenting a scene of grandeur and sublimity nothing can excel. The whitened peaks, reflecting the sun, resembled the domes of some vast cathedral. Looking back, the entire valley of the Sacramento was stretched out before us, bounded by the coast range of mountains, beyond which we could look upon the Pacific ocean—presenting a scene which, in extent, diversity, and grandeur is rarely if ever equalled. In the valley we could see extensive fertile plains, deserts of white sand, marshes, numerous lakes, dense forests, marking the water courses; and no doubt, with a glass of sufficient power, could have seen herds of elk, deer, antelope, and wild cattle. There is but little vapor in the atmosphere at this season of the year, and the vision is almost unbounded. Our team soon came up, and we prepared to descend the mountain, which was very precipitous, and the only place within ten miles at which the river can be reached with a team. Our teamster chained the wheel and with much difficulty descended the first step. He having been engaged in the same capacity during the Mexican war, managed the descent with much skill, and reached the base without accident.

We found ourselves at the "Mormon Bar," forty-five miles from Sacramento city. We pitched our tent and cooked dinner after which I paid the teamster seventy-five dollars for three hundred pounds freight and started off to visit the miners. I well remember that as I was going down the side of the cañon I saw a hole in a rock, which I thought such an excellent "pocket" that I resolved to pay it a secret visit, not doubting that it contained a rich deposit. I afterward learned that the "pockets" in California had not all been filled, and the one above mentioned was never picked to my knowledge. I found a great many in eager pursuit, some digging up the dirt, carrying it in buckets, or tin pans, and throwing it into the rocker, while their companions would rock the machine and pour in water, which would wash out the dirt, the gold being retained by riffles, or cleats, in the bottom. The first machine I saw in operation was being rocked by Mr. Devoe, and fed by Gen. Winchester and his brother—all of New York. The two last named were in the water knee deep, getting dirt from the bottom of a hole. I loaned them a late New York paper, and we were soon acquainted. They were about to take the gold from their machine and wished me to stay. This was just what I wished to do, and, after a five minutes' detention, they raised the screen, exhibiting the bottom of the rocker, which was covered with gold. I started for the tent, and it seemed that every rock had a yellow tinge, and even our camp kettle, that I had thought in the morning the most filthy one I had ever seen, now appeared to be gilded—and I thought with more than one coat. During the night, yellow was the prevailing color in my dreams. In the morning, hiring out two of the men temporarily at ten dollars per day, I hired a machine at two dollars per day, took the other man, went a short distance above Gen. Winchester's "lead" and soon found myself in a "lead" which I thought much better than his.

"Bent" rocked and I put in the dirt. We resolved to run through twenty buckets before raising the screen, and soon the perspiration began to flow. He had a strong arm and I exerted every nerve to keep the machine supplied. The dirt would pass through the screen almost instantly, leaving the pebbles which he would scan very minutely, but finding no large pieces of gold consoled himself with the thought, "the smaller the more of them." But now, after an hour's incessant labor, we were about to finish our first task, and had in the machine as

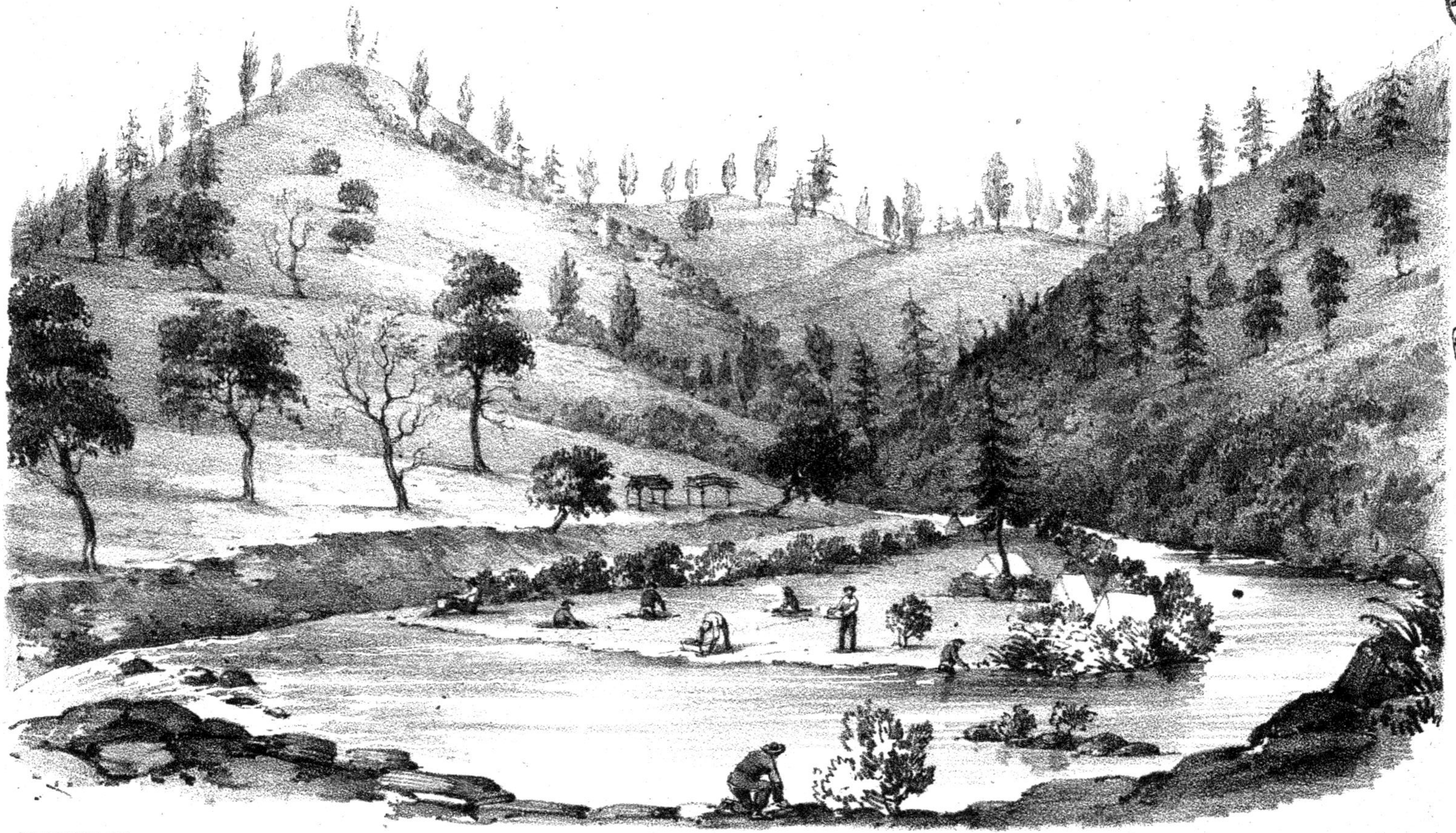

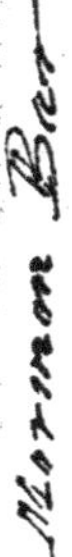

C. V. COOPER DEL. BROWN & SEVERIN LITH. G. W. LEWIS PRINT.

MORMON BAR, ON THE NORTH FORK, AMERICAN RIVER

Mormon Bar

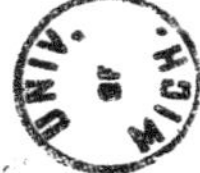

much as we thought it prudent to have at any one time; I stopped digging but my heart kept on. The heat was most intense, the perspiration gushing from every pore. Bent was in a fever of excitement. He was naturally of a sandy complexion, but now his face added a deeper tinge to his red flannel shirt collar. Our reward was in our machine, and after putting in several dippers of water we raised the screen. It did not look as we expected it would; there was any quantity of dirt and *some* gold.

We were not altogether satisfied with the result; still, we had just commenced, and, perhaps, were not sufficiently near the granite. Our "lead" was the best one on the bar—we *knew* by the looks of it—and the next twenty buckets must show a different result. Our ambition was again up, and our machine in motion, and, if possible, with increased energy. After running through several buckets of dirt, we raised the screen. There was not much gold on the top, but there was *some;* and we worked on, thinking that we had not yet reached the best part of our lead. I noticed that after raising the screen, the machine was rocked with less energy; and it seemed to add to the weight of my pick-axe. We resolved to visit the General. They had done a fine morning's work, and were in high spirits. They told us of many who had opened "leads," and worked them two or three days without success, when some one else would step in, and make a fortune the first day. This was precisely our case. We had got our "lead" almost opened, and if we should step out, some one would step in, and get the fortune. This we were not disposed to do. We had got on track, and were determined not to give way to any one. We looked up, but there was no one in our "lead." On our way back we discovered many natural advantages that our "lead" had over the General's, and an even exchange would have been to us no object.

Our machine was again in motion. The sun had now almost gained the meridian. The heat was excessive. Bent's red flannel was outside of his pantaloons, dripping with perspiration. My blue one was in the same condition. I would think of those abandoned "leads," and wish I had two buckets. He would think of them, flourish his dipper, and rock the machine, until its very sides would quake. We finally prepared to adjourn for dinner, took out the screen, put the contents of our machine in a pan, and commenced to wash out the dirt, which required some time, then walked up to dinner. On our arrival at the tent, we weighed the gold, and found it worth one dollar.

As it was our first day in the mines, we resolved to dine on pork, a favorite dish in California. We cut a quantity into slices, put it into the frying-pan, laying on it a quantity of sea-biscuit, filling the pan with water, and covering it with a tin plate. We kept it on the fire until the water evaporated—it was then ready for use. Our coffee, in the mean time, was boiled in the tin coffee-pot. Seating ourselves on rocks in front of the tent, we expressed our appreciation of the swine tribe in unmeasured terms. We take a respite of an hour, and return to our labor. We are anxious to get down to the granite, as we are sure of finding there a rich deposite. Towards evening we struck the granite, and were within reach of a fortune, deposited here by nature for our express benefit. As it was late, we resolved to wash down what we had in the machine, and prepare for a successful effort on the following day. On our arrival at the tent, we found "Harry" and "Sam," stretched out on the ground, groaning with fatigue, declaring that they had never worked so hard before, nor would they again. They had seen enough of the mines, and were determined to return to Sacramento. After telling them of the brilliant success that was about to attend our efforts, they agreed to remain another day. We had pork for supper, and spent the night in dreams of luxury. After an early breakfast we were again at our "lead." We were particular to scrape the granite, as we uncovered it, and after running through ten buckets, we raised the screen; to our surprise, we were doing no better than on the previous day. This we could not account for. The only solution was, that the gold had never been there, and why, we could not divine. It had the same appearance as the General's lead, which was paying the three from fifty to eighty dollars per day.

We worked on for some time, when "Bent" went up to cook the dinner, (we had resolved to have pork,) and I took the pick, shovel, and pan, and went "prospecting." After walking some distance, I found a place which combined, as I thought, every indication of a rich deposit, and my only surprise was, that it had not been discovered before. It was on the lower side of a large rock, which must, at high water, break the current, forming an eddy below, where the gold must settle. On discovering a "lead," one has only to leave his pick, and his title is indisputable. I left my implements, and hurried up to the tent. After dinner we carried our machine to the spot, and were soon in a profuse perspiration. "Bent" would frequently lift the screen, and it was very apparent that the prospect beneath was not brilliant. He had become a kind of thermometer to our success, and at every inspection his energy would lag, and my bucket would grow the heavier. Late in the afternoon we washed down our half-day's work, and went up. Harry and Sam were writhing with fatigue. Harry had over-heated himself; Sam, being a mulatto, could endure the heat,—but his muscles had lost their tension, and every bone was cracked. He was willing to stay, if I wished him to, but Harry was bound for Sacramento. Bent said but little, still I could plainly see a cloud in his horizon. He had an impediment in his speech; and when I asked him what he thought of the prospect, he got into close proximity to some very hard words, and, with great magnanimity, wished the mines in the possession of an individual of brimstone notoriety, whose name I will not mention. After supper, we weighed our afternoon's work, and had seventy-five cents. The man for whom Harry and Sam had been working, had taken possession of a bar, which was paying him well. As a general thing, the bars had been "prospected," and the parts that would pay taken possession of. There was, however private "leads" opened daily, from which something could be made. Harry and Sam were too sore to start down the next day, consequently they resolved to rest; and Bent was willing to work the machine another day. As for myself, I must confess that the camp-kettle had lost one coat of its gilding, and the rocks were about the same color as those in the States.

We took an early start, and devoted an hour to "prospecting." This time we were more successful, we found a "lead" from which we got twenty particles of gold in the first pan-full.

We soon had our machine on the spot. As we were placing it several miners passed on the way to their work. They all looked, *we thought*, as if they considered us the most fortunate of men, and we detected a lurking envy in their expression. As soon as they left, our machine was put in motion; we now had no doubt as to the result, and after running through ten buckets of dirt we raised the screen, but, to our astonishment, there was not a particle of gold to be seen. This was beyond our comprehension. We could not conceive of a more convenient place for gold to deposite than this particular one, and determined not to abandon it until we had reached the granite. This we reached, and toiled on until noon, when we emptied our machine, and had two dollars' worth of gold. We adjourned to dinner, and learned that a team had just arrived and was to return to Sacramento city the next day. Harry, Sam, and Bent immediately resolved to take passage. They had had their expenses paid to California, and were to work under the direction of the Company, and have a portion of the proceeds. They, no doubt, considered the dividends too small in proportion to the labor. I determined to make a more thorough trial of the mines, and not wishing to be encumbered sold the provisions, cooking utensils, &c., hired the tent carried back, and the next morning the teamster had every individual that accompanied our mule-team up, excepting a young man who had been sleeping on the ground near our tent and myself. They all, no doubt, had the same exalted opinion of the mines, and returned with purses equally well filled. Harry and Sam had earned $40 beside what Bent and myself had earned. This, together with what I received for provisions, &c., amounted to $200, which I put into the hands of Harry to give to one of the firm, who was at Sacramento city.

I was now alone. The two companions of the young man spoken of above, had left him, and circumstances seemed to throw us in each other's way, and makes us companions. His name was Tracy. He and his companions, Scillinger and Hicks, were from Sante Fé; they had crossed the mountains, eaten their proportion of mule steak, and endured every conceivable hardship. We were at once friends. We determined to gain a higher point on the river, and, if possible, find a place where our efforts would be more liberally rewarded. We consequently filled a small camp-kettle with pork and hard bread, rolled up our blankets, to which we lashed our pick and shovel, and slung them over our shoulders. Our camp-kettle, coffee-pot, rifles, and tin-pans, in hand, we set out on our expedition. We first ascended the mountain, and when at the summit stopped to view the magnificent scenes around us; the heat was intense; the thermometer stood at 100°; still we were looking upon a range of mountains shrouded in eternal winter.

Our route lay over a succession of mountains, the peaks of which bore unmistakable signs of volcanic formation, being covered with lava. Our journey was a most fatiguing one, and at noon, having gained an elevated point, we sat down to rest. I here noticed, for the first time, a phenomenon which is of frequent occurrence during the summer months. A heavy white cloud resembling a bank of snow rises from the Snowy Mountains (Sierra Nevada,) and after gaining a certain altitude passes off to the south, and is succeeded by another. After disposing of a certain quantity of hard bread and pork, and kissing our flask, we stretched ourselves out on the ground under the shade of a pine tree, and were soon in the embrace of Morpheus. In one hour we were again under way, and at 3 o'clock, P. M., arrived at the "dry diggings," (now Auburn.) This was a place of three tents, situated on the main road leading to the Oregon trail, which it intersects twenty miles above. These mines were not being worked to any extent, owing to the scarcity of water. There were a few, however, engaged in carrying dirt, a mile on their backs, and washing it at a puddle, in *town*. It was very uncertain business. The gold found here was in larger particles than in the river "diggings," but there was a much greater uncertainty in obtaining it, some toiling for weeks without making a dollar, and sometimes finding pieces worth from $50 to $500. The gold has the appearance of having been thrown up in a molten state, perhaps during a volcanic eruption, and dropped into the earth.

After an hour's detention we were again under way, and after traveling sometime over mountains, changed our course, wishing to reach the river. After an hour of the most fatiguing effort we were on a brink, with the river beneath our feet, but so distant that it had the appearance of a meandering pencil mark. We could, however, hear its subdued murmuring as it struggled through its rocky channel. After a short rest, we commenced the descent, which we found extremely precipitous, requiring the greatest caution and attended with the most painful exertions. Sometimes losing our foothold, we would slide down until we could catch by the shrubs for support, and at others, be precipitated to the bottom of the step. We at length reached the base and found ourselves on a small bar. It being after sunset, we kindled a fire, steeped some green tea, broiled a quantity of pork, by putting it on the end of a stick and holding it in the fire, and after toasting the sea-biscuit, we sat down on the rocks and paid our cook a most flattering compliment. I must confess that I never felt the gnawings of hunger more keenly than on this occasion, nor did I ever more fully appreciate the influence of green tea. We were much fatigued, and after removing some of the larger stones, spread our blankets and prepared for sleep.

We were strangers, never having spoken until a few hours previous; yet, having been thrown together by chance in a strange land, we felt a mutual interest that could scarcely have been stronger, had we been brothers. I must here say, that I was associated with Mr. Tracy for the succeeding three months, and no brother could have been more attentive or sympathetic. Soon after we were blanketed, the moon gained a sufficient altitude to look down into the cañon upon us. Our situation was novel in the extreme. The mountains rose on either side to the height of more than a mile, almost perpendicular. The moon and stars looking in upon us with unusual brilliancy. The distant and incessant howl of numerous packs of wolves, the restless gurgling and chafing of the river, as it struggled angrily through its rocky channel, our lonely and isolated situation, all conspired to generate strange thoughts, and to bring up strange, and often unpleasant associations. To look at the moon and think that our friends might be, at that moment, looking at the same orb, and thinking of us—thinking, perhaps, that we were already preparing to return home, having accomplished our most sanguine expectations; then to look at the reality, think of the dark prospect ahead, of the time that must intervene before we could think of returning, of the innumerable hardships and privations that still awaited us, a gloom imperceptibly stole over our imaginations, and hung upon our thoughts like an incubus. But sleep soon dispelled our melancholy, and wild fancy restored us to our friends.

Chapter Fourteenth.

A SEA CAPTAIN AS COOK—A HERD OF DEER—RETURN TO MORMON BAR—KEEPING HOUSE—OUR MACHINE IN MOTION—$1,500 IN ONE HOUR—AN ELOPEMENT—WASH DAY—SPORTING—PROSPECTING—DISCOVERY OF GOLD—EXCITEMENT—FATIGUE—THE CAKES "HURRIED UP"—INCENTIVES TO EXERTION—CANALLING A BAR.

WE rose in the morning with renewed vigor, and after breakfast, thoroughly prospecting our bar, (see Plate,) we moved on up the river. We found the passage in many places extremely difficult, obliging us to climb precipices to the height of two to three hundred feet. We examined closely, but found no place sufficiently rich to pay for working. At about 12 M. we arrived at a bar that was being worked by a company that had recently purchased it of another company for $2,500.

Their labor was attended with fair success, but they did not succeed in making wages after paying the above sum. There is a law established by custom in the mines, which allows a man a certain space, generally ten feet, extending across the river. It is by this law that companies take possession of bars, and their claim is never disputed, as it is a privilege of which all wish to avail themselves. We ascended the river still higher, but found nothing to encourage us. We deliberated some time and concluded to reascend the mountain. We returned to the encampment of the above-mentioned bar, where we found an old man, a sea captain, acting as cook. They had no tent, but slept in the open air. The cook had a large camp-kettle hanging on a tripod under a live oak-tree, cooking pork and beans, and preparing dinner for thirty men. It seemed a strange occupation for a sea captain; still, it had not yet lost its novelty, and he seemed to enjoy it much. I noticed, however, that he would frequently hitch up his pantaloons and look "aloft." After resting an hour

G. V. COOPER DEL. ON STONE BY J. CAMERON LITH. OF G. W. LEWIS, 111 NASSAU ST. N. Y.

J. C. TRACY AND MYSELF "PROSPECTING."

we went to a ravine, filled our flasks with spring-water and commenced ascending the mountain. On arriving near the summit we came upon a herd of deer, and wounded one, but did not succeed in capturing it. We soon found ourselves again in view of the Snowy Mountains and resolved to encamp for the night. After partaking of a sumptuous meal, (pork and hard bread) we again reclined on the couch of nature, her sweetest incense borne by the gentle breezes to our sleeping senses. (The *dust* was blowing furiously.)

We took an early start on our return to Mormon Bar, and arrived in the evening much fatigued. We resolved to make an effort here at mining, and back it up with any amount of energy. We purchased a machine and made all the preliminary arrangements in the evening, preparatory to a start at an early hour. We had no tent, consequently resolved to rent a suit of apartments from Nature, and looking about we found a large rock on the brink of a precipice, one hundred feet above the river. The place was secluded and pleasant. In front of the rock, on the mountain side, was a kitchen sufficiently large for *our* family, including the sleeping apartment. The space was shaded by a small oak tree; and, growing against the rock, were two other trees. Behind the rock was a space about twelve feet square, well shaded and was to serve as our dressing-room. A person to jump out of the back window would land in the river.

Tracy had volunteered to act as cook, and in order to have things in harmony, I called him wife, and *he* was perhaps as well calculated to get along under the circumstances as any *one* I could have got. As to kitchen furniture, he cared more for the useful than ornamental, and was calculated to manage the domestic affairs with the strictest economy. We had a small camp-kettle, a coffee-pot, and two tin plates; I had a knife and fork and tin cup. Tracy had a pocket-knife, and a water-tight Indian basket, which served him as a coffee-cup. I slung my hammock to the trees that grew against the rock; he spread his blanket on the ground, a few feet distant, and we were keeping house.

We arose in the morning full of energy, and didn't think there were any two individuals in that "section" destined to accomplish more than ourselves. We shouldered our implements and were soon on the margin of the river. As we were placing our machine, a miner came along and informed us that, on the previous day, a Mr. Eccle had got out in one hour $1,500. We had suspected all along that there were rich deposits in the vicinity, and now our *suspicions* were confirmed. Our machine was soon in operation, and as the $1,500 would flash across our imagination, I would strike my pick the deeper. Tracy would flourish his dipper, strike up some familiar air, and the cradle would rock as if propelled by the furies. If there had been *anything* in it except dirt Tracy would have had an accompaniment to his song. We washed through ten buckets, and raised the screen; it did not look very encouraging—we run through ten more—Tracy thought there *wasn't quite as much as there was before*—he began to lag, and I must confess I was obliged to recur often to the $1,500 to keep the necessary elasticity in my suspenders; we stopped a moment to rest, and speculate on the probable appearance of the spot where the above sum was obtained; we came to the conclusion that it *must* have looked very like the spot we were then at work in. Our machine was again in motion, and with renewed energy; Tracy was really outdoing himself; the $1,500 would flit through his imagination and he would almost throw the machine into spasms; I expected every moment to see his pantaloons and red flannel shirt part company; the only connecting link was a single India rubber suspender which was stretched to its utmost tension. We resolved to run through one hundred buckets before dinner, and, by straining every nerve, accomplished it. We panned down our half-days' work—it amounted to two dollars. It had been excessively hot, the thermometer rose to 106°, and when we arrived at our encampment we were as wet as if we had been wading the river. We boiled some pork and sea-biscuit together in our camp-kettle, made coffee, and having placed two large stones against the rock, sat down to dinner. Our spirits were buoyant and our anticipations high.

Soon after dinner our machine was again making its spasmodic movements, and continued them during the afternoon; we did not allow ourselves to forget the strong resemblance between our "lead" and the one in which the $,1,500 was obtained. At night we had another two dollars to put into the company purse. It is Saturday night, and we feel that we shall hail the day of rest with pleasure. After supper we retire, having our usual serenade, and during the night one of the troupe made love to and eloped with one of Tracy's boots; I imagined from a hint thrown out in the morning that he would have preferred dispensing with the music.

Mining operations cease on the Sabbath; and miners attend to mending, washing, &c. Tracy and myself went to the river to do our washing; the vocation to me was entirely new. I commenced on a pair of white merino drawers which I sometimes used instead of pantaloons; they looked very well when I commenced, but it was different after working on them half an hour; it would have troubled an experienced washerwoman to tell what color they ought to be; I first tried soap, then sand, but it was of no use; it appeared only to *set the color*. I put them in the river and put a stone on them; what effect the rainy season had on them, I have not been able to learn. I took my rifle, and trespassed on the Sabbath by shooting a rabbit and several quails; we consequently spent the afternoon in feasting, and on Monday morning were in a condition to *tire* our machine.

We resolved to run through two hundred buckets, and no two men ought, and few could do more. When night came we had $4 to add to the purse. We resolved to spend the next morning prospecting. We started at an early hour, and after testing a number of points, decided upon one, and immediately started our machine. At noon, not liking the result, we determined to spend the afternoon in a further search. We went some distance up the river, carefully examining every point, until we came to a perpendicular ledge of rocks, overhanging the river. We thought no one had ever attempted to ascend this, and by doing so ourselves might find on the other side what had not been examined. We succeeded in gaining the summit, and on going down the other side, commenced to examine the crevices of the rocks. To our astonishment, Tracy found a piece of gold worth a dollar. We were much excited. It was too much to bear in silence. He opened his mouth to halloo but his eye again fell upon the piece of gold and he did not. We found several smaller pieces, and were now satisfied that we had at last found the place for which we had been so long and anxiously looking. We followed down the side to the river, and there found a small bar, into which the gold must find its way, as it was washed from the crevices above. We examined the bar and found particles of gold, and decided to take possession at once. It was late in the afternoon, but at this particular time, we decided not to put off till to-morrow what ought to be done to-day, and immediately started for our machine, which was a mile distant. We were soon underway ladened with our implements, with perspiration gushing from every pore. We found our task a hard one; were often obliged to rest, and as often would our success flit across our imaginations, when we would again shoulder our machine, and push on. It was dark long before we reached our destination; we were obliged to climb over crags of rocks, where one misstep would have precipitated us into the river below. We toiled on, and at length reached our destination. We would gladly have remained here during the night, but our clothes were saturated with perspiration, and, although the days were hot, the nights were on the other extreme, sometimes rendering it uncomfortably cold, even under our woollen blankets. There was no alternative but to return, and we again ascended the precipice, and after a most fatiguing march reached our encampment. I had heard of people's bones aching "out loud," but this was the first exhibition of the kind I had ever witnessed. We were soon in the embrace of Morpheus, and fancy carried us home.

We arose much fatigued, but hope was preëminent, and we were soon under way, with the brightest anticipations. Our machine was again in motion; I never felt stronger, and at every bucket-full Tracy would give his dipper an extra flourish, his India-rubber suspender fairly grinning with excitement. We did not fear for the result, and kept our machine in motion until noon, when on raising the screen we found we had made about fifty cents. We had, however, not yet reached the granite, and our spirits were not dampened. We worked during the afternoon, reaching and scraping the granite, and at night would have been one dollar richer than in the morning, if some one had been boarding us gratis. We had exhausted our lead and took our implements back to the first scene of operations. We continued to labor hard during the week, and Saturday night, on making out our balance sheet, we had earned $13.50 each, which was less than the cost of our provisions. It is said that prosperity begets want, and it was precisely so in our case. On Sunday morning we went to the store, purchased flour at seventy-five cents per pound, and a frying-pan for $5, determined to spend the day in feasting.

A team had just arrived from Sacramento with eight fortunate individuals, who had heard that this was the place where men were getting $1,500 per hour, and as they had just arrived from the States, they were willing to *commence even at that rate.* The teamster informed me that Bent, Harry, and Sam "*put in*" at Sacramento, in "stress of weather," having got on a drunken spree, and spent the $200. On our arrival at the encampment Tracy took his basket, put in some water, stirred in flour, and was soon using our frying-pan. I practiced turning the cakes, and soon became so skilled that I could hit the pan every time. We held a consultation. Tracy was determined to continue mining, but I resolved to go to Sacramento and prepare to embark in something that would pay better. A few individuals were doing well in the mines, and there were comparatively but few. Ours was about the average success. The mass were merely paying expenses. There were a thousand extravagant stories constantly circulating, of men who had made fortunes in an hour, and Mr. Eccles did really in that length of time, get $1,500 in our immediate vicinity. Each one naturally considered himself destined to be one of the fortunate ones, and if he has only made a dollar to-day, he is quite confident that he will make a hundred to-morrow, or, perhaps, a thousand. The same influences operate upon the mind as in gambling, and chances of success are about equal, although mining is not attended with the same disastrous results.

The country is rich in gold, the supply is inexhaustible. The entire soil of the mountainous parts is impregnated with it. It seems an ingredient or constituent of the soil. Still, in its natural distribution, it is not sufficiently abundant to pay for collecting. It is found most plentifully on bars in the rivers, where it is deposited during freshets, or at the confluence of ravines, which sweep down the side of the mountains uniting at the base, where the gold naturally deposits during the rainy season. "Bars," in California *parlance*, are the low tongues of land at abrupt bends in the river. (See Plate.) They are generally formed in whole, or in part by freshets. During the rainy season, torrents rush down the sides of the mountains, freighted with gold, dirt and stones, which, when coming in contact with the main stream, are borne along until an abrupt bend in the river checks the current, an eddy sets back a certain distance, at which point the heavy substances are deposited. A canal is cut across the root of the tongue, at the head of which a dam is thrown across the river, which turns the water from its natural channel, enabling miners to work below water-mark.

Chapter Fifteenth.

START FOR SACRAMENTO CITY—THE "NIAGARA CO."—FREDERIC JEROME—A LOVE-CHASE—HEROINE UNDER A BLANKET—SUSPICIOUS BOOTS—PART OF A LADY'S HAT FOUND—A BALL—ARRIVAL AT SACRAMENTO CITY—POOR ACCOMMODATIONS—RETURN TO THE INTERIOR—A CHASE—A NEW YORK MERCHANT—BEALS' BAR—EMBARK IN TRADE—A MOUNTAINEER—INDIAN CHARACTERISTICS.

ON Monday morning I bade Tracy farewell, and started for Sacramento, promising to report at the earliest possible moment. After walking four miles I was taken sick and stopped at a tent until morning, when, feeling better, I left my rifle and pursued my journey. The heat was excessive, and the road a dreary one, with nothing to break the monotony. I exhausted the contents of my flask and was soon suffering with thirst; I met a gentlemen who supplied me with water, and I moved on. After traveling some twelve miles, as I was pursuing my course I was surprised at hearing a voice, and immediately heard my name called. I looked up and saw at a short distance from the road, two tents, and on approaching, found a company of gentlemen of Lockport, N. Y., who had been fellow passengers up the Pacific. They had started for the interior, and on reaching this point their wagon broke down, the team strayed, and left them no alternative but to encamp. As they were in the immediate vicinity of the river, they had commenced mining, and I am happy to add, with unexpected success. This they richly deserved, for a more gentlemanly, hospitable and energetic set of men, it was never my fortune to fall in with. They styled themselves the "Niagara Co.," and I have had the pleasure of meeting one of the gentlemen in this city since my return. At their solicitation I visited their works, and remained over night, and when I parted with them in the morning, it was like parting with brothers.

I started at day-break and after traveling an hour, fell in with

Frederick Jerome, well known for his heroic efforts, in saving the passengers of the Ocean Monarch. He and his companions were bound for the interior. I soon came out on the margin of a prairie, some four miles in diameter, the road running through its center; I had but just entered upon it, when I discovered the track of a—not a grizzly bear, dear reader, but of a female. I did really discover the track of a female in California. It may seem a trivial circumstance to you, it was not so to me. A galvanic battery would not have created a more startling sensation, and I was half-tempted to faint in honor of the occasion. It was a small foot, encased in a slipper of the finest mould; then there was such a witching air about it, so pert, the toes turned a little out, the heel set down with just enough decision, and a something coquettish in the way she raised it up; then there was a sprightliness and elasticity, quite perceptible. I soon came to where she had turned round, as if she had been expecting me, and without designing to be silly, I soon found myself on a "round trot." I hurried on, buried in thought and conjecture, sometimes imagining it some one I had seen in the States; the track seemed familiar. Sometimes I would remember having met her at a cotillon party, and then I would notice a change in the track, as if she had been thinking of the same thing, and taking some of the "old steps;" I could see that the toe had removed a greater quantity of dust, as if she had been taking the standing, instead of the "chessa" balance. But the distance between us was fearful. I could see several miles and could not see her, and she might take another road. As these thoughts were running through my mind, I would come to myself, and find myself running at the top of my speed, the perspiration oozing from every pore. I was fast gaining the opposite side, and hope was in the ascendant.

I began to think of my personal appearance, which is in such cases of the most importance. After a careful examination, I came to the conclusion that it was not very flattering. I had not shaved in six months; I had on an under-shirt and cravat, pantaloons and long boots, a Panama hat, blue flannel shirt outside, over which was a belt with a sheath-knife, and a blue sash. I had seen men as badly dressed as myself. I was in hope she had, and hurried on. I soon reached the forest, and was on the *qui vive*, scanning every rock and log, expecting to find her at rest after her fatiguing walk across the prairie. I walked on, examining every shade, without seeing her. I soon saw at some distance a thick grove of underwood, the road passing through it, and I thought I saw a smoke rising beyond it. I soon arrived near, approaching very cautiously, and keeping an eye in the direction of the smoke. I was not frightened, but my nervous system was in an unusual state of agitation. I wiped off the perspiration, and continued my cautious approach. I was soon sufficiently near to see what I at first thought to be a tent, but on a nearer examination proved to be blankets thrown over a pole, and sweeping the ground. I saw no one. I approached still nearer, and came to the conclusion that she was under the blankets taking her morning *siesta.* I still drew nearer, and stopped to take a survey of the premises. Just beyond the blankets I saw what appeared to be two pairs of heavy boots, and on changing my position they both *appeared* to have men in them. I neither fainted, nor ran, but I walked on noiselessly to a proper distance and sat down to rest. The men were sleeping on the ground, and I have no doubt the lady was doing the same under her temporary shelter. They had undoubtedly been to the mines, and perhaps became disheartened, and were returning to town.

The scarcity of ladies in California, is the theme of much conversation. There is an anecdote almost universally told in connection with the subject; it is as follows: At a certain point in the mineral regions, part of a lady's hat was discovered, which caused so much excitement and joy, that it was immediately decided to have a ball on the spot, in honor of the event. Invitations were immediately distributed throughout the country, and, on the appointed day, three hundred miners assembled, each dressed in a red flannel shirt, and accompanied by a bottle of brandy. In the *exact spot* was driven a stick, five feet high, on the top of which was placed *the* hat, and around it was wrapped a flannel blanket. It was made to represent, as nearly as possible, a female form. By the side of this was placed a miner's cradle, or machine, in which was placed a smoked ham, also wrapped in a flannel blanket. At the close of each dance the president of the meeting would rock the cradle, while the secretary would pour a bottle of brandy down the back of the lady's neck. The ball lasted two days, at the end of which time the ground was surveyed into town-lots, and called Auburn. It has been spoken of in a former chapter.

After waiting an hour without discovering any signs of life in the camp, the sun admonished me that I must move on. I pursued my lonely walk until 11 o'clock, P. M., when I reached the American river. I prepared myself and waded through, and in one hour was passing Sutter's Fort. The dogs appeared to be on duty, and hailed me with such ferocity that I have no doubt they thought I meditated an attack. I hurried on, and at midnight reached Sacramento city. I found it impossible to get lodgings, and was obliged to seek shelter under some one of the large oaks in the suburbs of the town. Even here it was difficult to find a spot unoccupied. I found a place, however, by going some distance, and spread my blanket with a fair prospect of having the bed all to myself. It had been excessively hot during the day, but now a heavy dew had fallen, the air was cold, and after laying an hour found myself stiff and lame, and chilled to the very heart. I arose, but found it difficult to walk. I succeeded in reaching an unfinished house, into which I crawled, and spent the balance of the night in a vain effort to sleep.

In the morning I took a survey of the town, purchased a horse, and prepared for another incursion into the interior. A friend wished to accompany me, and at 4 o'clock, P. M., we were under way. We crossed the river and took our course across the plain in the direction of the great bend of the American River. Late in the afternoon, as we were galloping along, we fell in with a pack of wolves (coyotas,) and as we were both well mounted we were fast overhauling them. They were crazy with fright, making two or three tremendous leaps, then turning to look at us, their alarm would increase and they would bound away. We were close upon them when my companion's girth broke, and we were obliged to give up the chase. If they have *ever* come to the conclusion to stop, I am confident it was not in that immediate vicinity, for I never saw animals so frightened. What they were doing when we came upon them, I am unable to say. It has been suggested that they may have been tuning

G.V. COOPER DEL. BROWN & SEVERIN LITH. G.W. LEWIS PRINT.

SOUTH FORK, AMERICAN RIVER.

their instruments preparatory to their evening concert. I was disposed to fall in with this suggestion, from the fact, that *that* was the only night during my stay in the country, that I did not listen to their music. If they took the trouble to stick up a notice of postponement, it read, undoubtedly, as follows: "Postponed indefinitely on account of a fright in the family."

We resumed our journey and at 10 P.M., arrived at the bend. After watering our horses we secured the ends of their lassos, and taking our supper, we rolled ourselves in our blankets. In the morning we directed our course towards Beal's Bar, a higher point on the river. As we were galloping along (California horses cannot trot) we met a gentleman whom I recognized as a New York acquaintance. He was a New York merchant, and when at home, somewhat noted for his dashing appearance. His appearance on this occasion was so extremely ludicrous, I could not withstand the temptation of taking a sketch. (See Plate.) He was returning from the mines, and at the time we came upon him, a coyota was casting inquisitive glances in that direction, as if in doubt whether it was really a man, or a fellow-member of the *California Harmonic Society*. He had on a slouched hat, which, together with his whiskers and moustache, almost hid his face; a mariner's shirt, and a pair of drawers, which were, on this occasion, serving in the place of pantaloons, being *suspended* by two strips of a woolen blanket, crossed in front. A rifle on his shoulder, pipe in his mouth, and blankets in hand, he looked the very personation of a corn-field effigy.

After a short detention we moved on, arriving at the Bar at 12 M. After dinner we went down to the scene of operations, my friend wishing to purchase an interest. The bar was divided into thirty shares, owned by as many individuals. They worked as a company and divided the proceeds at night. Shares were commanding $2,800 each. Beal's Bar was at this time paying about $20 per day to a man. They had, however, expended a large amount of money in turning the water from the channel. After remaining two hours, we started in the direction of the Mormon Bar, where we arrived at 9 P.M. Tracy was in an ecstasy. He provided supper with great alacrity, and even let my friend occupy half his bed.

I had resolved to engage in the mercantile business at this point, and having heard the present store was for sale, I called on the proprietor for his terms. They did not appear favorable, and I started the next morning for Sacramento, accompanied by my friend. We arrived that evening, and the next morning I commenced buying a stock. I was soon on my return. We were three days in reaching our destination, and such a time! We had a span of mules and a span of horses before the wagon, and a nice matched span of drivers. I paid $20 for an extra team on the route, and finally reached our destination. I deposited my goods under a tree, having canvas with which I designed to erect a store. The next morning I succeeded in buying out the other store, and before night had possession. I now felt that I had the helm of a craft I knew how to manage, and was fairly at sea. I immediately hired a Frenchman as cook at $50 per week, and Tracy became a guest. I was now pleasantly situated, with every prospect of success. I soon purchased a share in the bar—paid $1,100. At this time it was yielding abundantly, and I had every assurance of an ample remuneration. Throughout the country there is a strong propensity for gambling. People appear to engage in it for want of other amusement. The store I had purchased had been used for the purpose every night since its construction, but it became so great a nuisance, I was obliged to prohibit it excepting on particular occasions.

I here had an opportunity of seeing many of those strange adventurers who are met with only on the extreme frontiers, and who have as great an aversion to law and civilization as they have to the manacles of a prison. I had had the store but a few days, when one of these strange beings crossed my path. I must confess there was nothing, at first sight, to attract my admiration. About nine in the morning I saw, approaching the store, a strange looking being, mounted on a gray horse, a *poncho* thrown over his shoulder, over which was slung a huge rifle, skins wrapped around his legs, a pair of Mexican spurs on, and a slouched hat which partially obscured his copper complexion. As he rode up, Tracy recognized him as an old mountaineer, whom he had seen in Santa Fé. After the recognition, Tracy says "Jim! whose horse is that?" Jim—"I'll be G—d d—nd to H—ll if I know." Tracy—"where did you get him?" Jim—"*I stole him from an Indian, by G—d.*" I have no doubt his declarations were true, for he claimed the credit (and I was informed he deserved it) of being the most accomplished horse-thief in all New Mexico. He informed Tracy that he was "dead broke" and hungry, and wished him to ask me for something to eat. I requested Prince to get him some breakfast, after which he was as rich as Crœsus, and commenced giving me his life. It was a most exciting romance, interspersed with thrilling adventures and "hair-breadth 'scapes." I was convinced that his story, in the main, was true, not because he *swore* to it all, but because Tracy was acquainted with the most important facts. He was a mixture of the negro, Indian, and Anglo-Saxon blood, and born in New Mexico. His earliest training was in the art of horse and mule stealing, in which art he had become a connaisseur. He commenced by stealing one at a time, and soon became so proficient, that he could steal whole droves with perfect impunity. He declared that he furnished General Taylor's army with most of their horses and mules, and that he could raise two thousand head, with twelve hours' notice—sometimes stealing of the Indians, and at others of the Mexicans. Sometimes he would associate with the whites, and at others with the natives. He was for years, chief of the Crow Indians, and still has a wife and family with them. He led them in numerous battles against the neighboring tribes, alternately winning and losing. He was engaged in the Texan war, was at the battle of San Jacinto, and at most of the battles fought by General Taylor. He was never enrolled in the army, but always fought on his "own hook," and ready to chase the party that was defeated. He took a middle ground, and was always *just in time* to join the victorious party.

Indians in their wars have their own peculiar signs and marks by which warriors of the same tribe are informed of the locality of the enemy. These signs are made on the trees, rocks, earth, &c., &c. A detachment of a thousand warriors will start in the evening, and after arriving at a certain point, separate, to scour the country in different directions, and meet at a concerted point, when the moon is at a certain altitude. The party arriving first, drops an arrow, with the point in the direction they have taken; the latter party moving in that direction soon find their friends. But if the enemy is on the alert, the first arrow is dropped, and soon another, which is found at right angles with the first. This is a caution. They move on still farther in the direction indicated by the first arrow, and if there is danger they find two arrows, one across the other. They now stop and secrete themselves. Soon one of the first party approaches them cautiously and informs them of the position of the enemy. In cases of storm, when the sun is hidden, they resort to other indications for the point of compass. They find the moss much thicker on the north side of trees and rocks, than on the south. They also cut into the trees and find the annual growth much thicker on the south, than on the north side. Jim's legs had the appearance of being bound with cords under the skin, in consequence of the general rupture of the blood vessels. He says he was taken prisoner by the Indians, and in making his escape was chased ninety miles, without stopping for food or rest. The condition of his limbs then compelled him to stop, and secrete himself, where, in consequence of his lameness, he was obliged to remain for three weeks subsisting on roots. Jim, with his other accomplishments, was considered one of the best "*monte*" dealers in Mexico. On visiting the frontier towns, he would spend his time in gambling. Sometimes he would win several thousand dollars in one night, and the next day he would have every man drunk in town; what he could not spend in drink, he would give to the poor, or to his friends. Money was an incumbrance to which he would not submit. After remaining two or three days he mounted his horse and started up the river, designing, as I supposed, not to return.

Chapter Sixteenth.

THE MORMONS—THE ATTEMPTED MURDER OF GOV. BOGGS—CANALLING MORMON BAR—FALSE THEORIES IN REFERENCE TO GOLD DEPOSITS — INFLUENCE OF AMASA LYMAN, "THE PROPHET"—EXCITING SCENE—JIM RETURNS—A MONTE BANK "TAPPED"—JIM'S ADVENT AT SACRAMENTO CITY.

MY immediate neighbors were mostly Mormons, headed by Amasa Lyman, one of "the twelve." The person who shot Gov. Boggs, of Missouri, was also here, under an assumed name. It will be remembered that at the time of the Mormon disturbance in Missouri, it was thought by them that Gov. Boggs connived at their persecution, and several attempts were made upon his life. Scofield, alias, "Orin Porter," a reckless, daring fellow, loaded a pistol and went to his house; it was in the evening; the Governor was sitting by the light reading a paper. Porter went to the back window, and aiming at his head, discharged the pistol, the ball taking effect in the back part of his head. Porter deliberately laid the pistol on the window-sill, and left. The wound did not prove mortal, and at the time of which I am writing, Gov. B., and two sons, were in California. They had heard of Porter's rendezvous, and were supposed to be in search of him. He went armed with a brace of revolvers, and one of duelling pistols; he had a dog that was constantly with him, sleeping with him at night to give the alarm in case of danger. He declared his determination to sell his life dearly if attacked. He was much esteemed by the "*faithful*" for his heroism in the above act, consequently they kept an eye to his safety, keeping him informed of the whereabouts of the enemy.

The Mormons held no religious meetings here. They believe in the inspiration of Smith, or "Joseph," as they call him, and calculate time from the date of his death, as an era, speaking of an occurrence, as in the first, second, or third year of the death of "Joseph." They believe the Book of Mormon to be a history of the western, as the Bible is a history of the eastern continent. Those here were a *good* set of fellows, somewhat reckless, fine horsemen, fond of sprees, and an occasional fight. Many of them had belonged to the "Mormon battalion," under the late Gen. Kearney, of whom they spoke in the most enthusiastic terms. They had all been at "Salt Lake," and considered that their country, and home, many of them having left their families there. They believe all other religions heresy, and quote Scripture to prove, that the appearance of Smith, and the promulgation of his doctrine, was predicted long before the Christian era, and that that doctrine must prevail universally before the coming of the Millenium. They were all hard workers, and fond of gambling. They had spent ten weeks in canalling the bar, and the first indications were extremely favorable, but it was soon necessary to incur additional expense, in order to drain the deep holes in the bed of the river. The edges of these holes were rich with gold; in spots the granite being quite yellow, so that the gold was scraped up with spoons. It was the natural conclusion that the edges being rich, the bottoms must be more so. The company, that is to say, Amasa Lyman, (for, being one of the prophets, his word was law,) resolved to construct a hose of duck to carry off the water as it was pumped from the holes, consequently sent to town and purchased three hundred yards of duck, which, using three widths, made the hose one hundred yards in length, costing $600—the pump costing $50.

We now commenced draining the deepest and consequently the richest hole, and soon had it in working order; the richness of the margin was, as we thought, infallible evidence that the bottom must yield abundantly; we removed a quantity of dirt and stone, and commenced to wash from the bottom, but, to our surprise, it did not contain a particle of gold; this, like most of the theories in reference to operations in California, was not founded on correct principles. The influence of the stagnant water in the holes seemed to extend to the surface, holding the passing water in check. The current, as it is bearing the gold down stream, comes in contact with this dead water, and parts; receiving a sufficient check to allow the gold to deposit around the margin. Several experiments were tried without success, and it was soon apparent that the speculation was to prove disastrous. The operations were managed without system or discretion. The "*faithful*," having a majority, had it all their own way; and they managed as seemed best calculated to victimize the "Gentiles." As the sequel will show, *they* were drawn into the same vortex. I had hired a man to work my share, but the dividends did not pay his wages, and it was apparent that we must dissolve the company, and each man work or abandon his share as he saw fit. It was proposed to divide the bar into equal shares, to be drawn by numbers representing them; the "*faithful*," however, opposed this mode of distribution; they were in favor of going on, and each getting all he could; each to be allowed ten feet in width, wherever he might locate his machine. They having canalled and worked the bar, knew every foot of it, and the relative richness of the different parts. The "Gentiles" saw no alternative but to be victimized, as they must submit to the majority, and it being Lyman's motion it was sure to carry. The place of deliberation was at the tents on the side of the mountain, some distance from the bar, and as the work had been suspended for several days, many of the implements had been carried up.

There was an unusual anxiety and excitement on this particular occasion, and as the vote was about to be taken, first the implements, then the bar would be scanned, with marked solicitude; the clenched hand and determined gesture giving token of the fearful struggle that was at hand. The vote was given; each man "*broke loose*" for the bar as if his life depended upon the exertion of the moment; some with machines on their shoulders, others laden with shovels, tin pans, pickaxes, India rubber boots, and spades, all rushing down, pell-mell, some crossing the canal on the log, others, finding the log full, would rush in and wade, or swim across; the implements of some, coming in contact with others, all would tumble in to meet again at the bottom. Any one who has witnessed a charge in battle, can form a faint idea of the confusion and excitement on this occasion. The vanquished, however, instead of being drenched in blood were drenched in water, and instead of broken bones, cries of the wounded, the beating of drums, and torn uniforms, we had broken shovel-handles, curses of miners, the rattling of tin pans, and torn red flannel shirts. It so happened that the "*faithful*" all rushed for the same spot, and when their *lions* were served the *lambs* found the balance of the best in the hands of or in the possession of the "Gentiles." This occasioned considerable sparring among themselves, and resulted in the "lambs" selling out for from ten to fifteen dollars, being their entire summer's work.

I did not trust my interest at this time, to the supervision of a hired man, but joined in the foot-race, leaving Prince (the cook) in charge of the store. I knew nothing about the best points in the bar, but followed the "Prophet" and his satellites, and when they selected their "leads" I took the one next above; in this lead I had an opportunity of seeing rich deposits, although I kept it from the knowledge of the "faithful." I would go on the bar at 9 A. M. and work until 12; then from 1 P. M. to 4. On one day I got eleven and a half ounces, and on several days as high as six ounces. The bed of my lead was rotten granite, which in some places was entirely covered, being yellow with gold; in some of the crevices of the rock I would take it out with a spoon, almost entirely free from dirt. The person having the lead next above me found a piece in a crevice worth twenty-five dollars, which was thought extremely large for river gold; it was found in a cavity of its own size and form, and seemed to have dropped in in a molten state. The final result was a loss to almost all concerned in the operation; the same result attended all the canalling operations within my knowledge with one or two exceptions; such experiments require such immense expenditures that they must be extremely productive to remunerate.

Some three weeks after Jim's departure, as I was sitting in the store, in the after part of the day, I heard a peculiar whoop, and looking up the side of the mountain I saw a cloud of dust, and a something flying in the air that had the appearance of a sail that had broken loose from its lower yard during a gale; then there were four legs and two other legs, all of them seemed to be running races; whether on the ground or in the air it was difficult to tell. I soon came to the conclusion that it was a trial of speed between Old Gray and Jim; they both arrived about the same time; Jim a little ahead; as between his poncho and old Gray's *latter extremity* it was about an even race, and *they* both *settled down* quietly, as if glad the race had ended. As Jim drew up to the door, he dismounted, and throwing on the counter a large handkerchief filled with gold and silver, said, "Well, by G—d, captain, I've made a raise;" he then untied his handkerchief; there were twenty or thirty dollars in silver, the balance in gold coin; the former he insisted upon my accepting, assuring me that it was of not the least value to him. He had been up the river twenty miles, had fallen in with a Mormon who had some money, and who proposed that Jim should deal "monte" and share the profits; in a few nights they had won $13,000; the half of this was more money than he cared to have by him at any one time, and was on his way to Sacramento City to spend it. He felt in high spirits, and as there were two gamblers along in the evening, who wished to open a "monte bank," he wished me to allow them to do so, which I did; they had a capital of a few hundred dollars, and Jim was to try his luck at betting, which, by-the-way, he understood *as well* as the other branch of the game. He watched the run of the cards for some time, then wished to cut them; soon he made a small bet—it won; he made a larger bet, and won it also; after making a few successful bets, he "*tapped the bank*," and won it; at about midnight he mounted Old Gray for Sacramento City, with as much money as he could conveniently carry.

The next morning a man came to the store, who saw Jim sleeping under a tree, his money under his head, his horse tied with a lasso, having traveled about five miles on his way to town. On his arrival, he looked upon Sacramento City as his guest, and emptied his handkerchief in drinking its health. He had all the inhabitants drunk who were disposed that way, and many of them much against their will. He was quite successful in getting rid of his money, and one week after his advent, he had *invested* his last dollar. He had engaged to pilot the mail through to Santa Fé, for the government, and the time arrived while he was *entertaining* the city. Of course, he could not leave just then, and when the officer in charge ordered him to start, he declared in the *strongest* language, that he considered himself

full as good as some men, and better than others. The result was that he was put in irons. One day of such confinement would be sufficient to bring him to his senses, and make him long for his mountain air. I have no doubt that, ere this, he has seen the mail safely deposited at Santa Fé, and is, perhaps, again extensively engaged in the mule trade.

Chapter Seventeenth.

FALSE REPORTS AND THEIR INFLUENCES—DAILY AVERAGE—ABUNDANCE OF GOLD—ORIGINAL DEPOSIT—"COYOTAING"—SAILORS—THEIR SUCCESS AND NOBLE CHARACTERISTICS—THEATRICAL TENDENCIES—JACK IN THE AFTER-PIECE—MINERS ON A "SPREE"—THE WRONG TENT.

THERE was an almost universal uneasiness felt throughout the mineral regions. Not a day would pass without arrivals and departures. To-day, a report would be in circulation that at a particular point on the Juba, or Feather river, miners were getting one hundred dollars per day. A party would immediately set out, and to-morrow a party will arrive *from that particular point*, having heard that at *this* point, miners had actually got all they could carry away. They would arrive with a full supply of provisions, utensils, &c., but being disappointed, there would be no alternative but to sell out, as their provisions could not be drawn up the mountain. To-day a man arrives who has prospected throughout the southern mines without success, and fallen in with a report that has brought him to this point. Miners who are successful say nothing about it, but those who are not, are generally fond of making an *impression*. I have now in my mind's eye several individuals who were almost daily visitors at the store, who had always *just* discovered a very rich deposit. But strange as it may seem, that deposit never happened to find its way into the individual's pocket. Now, a man will come in, all excitement, having just discovered, in a mountain gorge, a deposit so rich that gold can be picked up by pounds and half-pounds. He is out of provisions, and on his way to town to lay in a stock, preparatory to availing himself of his rich discovery. He talks incessantly of his prospects, and on his arrival in town imparts the information to the press. It is published as coming from the individual himself, and, of course, worthy of credit. It is copied by papers throughout the world, and universally believed; this individual, however, in the course of a week, has engaged to drive team by the month, or if returning to the mines, goes in some other direction, as if having forgotten his rich discovery. His report, however, sends thousands to look for the spot, which, I need not say, they do not succeed in finding. The *precise spot* is rarely found; people get within twenty miles of it, but seldom nearer. As if exerting the influence of the Upas tree, they cannot approach within the prescribed limit. At the same time, many were engaged in private leads that were paying well, some averaging an ounce per day, and some even more. At the mouth of a ravine near, there were ten persons at work, who were averaging one and a half ounces per day. There were others in the vicinity doing equally well.

The country had been thoroughly prospected; there was not a bar nor ravine that did not bear the impress of the pick and shovel. There were daily discoveries of deposits, sufficiently rich to pay well; still, such discoveries, in proportion to the number in search of them, were not one to twenty. All were earning something, and the mass more than their expenses, still they were not averaging good wages. A man could place his machine almost anywhere and get two dollars per day; this, however, barely pays for the provisions consumed, and unless a lead will pay *at least* five or six dollars, it is not considered worth working. A miner finds a lead that pays six dollars, he exhausts it in six, or say ten days; his expenses are two dollars per day, leaving him, at the end of ten days, forty dollars. He now spends a week, perhaps more, before he finds another lead that will pay; his expenses have reduced the amount in hand to twenty-six dollars. If he goes any considerable distance, he must hire a mule to carry his provisions, machine, &c., which will cost him one ounce ($16) per day; two days exhausts his fund. There are in California, two hundred thousand inhabitants. Say half this number are engaged in mining—at five dollars each, it amounts to half a million daily. Now, according to statistics, this is more, by half, than is actually produced, and half this amount, or two dollars and a half, is *about the daily average*, take the mass together.

As I have already remarked, the supply of gold is inexhaustible, and late discoveries show that the rocks constituting the base of the mountains are cemented with it. When proper machinery is brought to bear, and the bowels of the earth opened, discoveries will undoubtedly be made, that will eclipse the most exaggerated calculation. The original deposits were, undoubtedly, in the depths of the earth, and all that has yet been found is that which has been thrown to the surface, by the convulsions of nature. The form and general appearance of the gold, together with the appearance of its places of deposit, are conclusive proofs of this theory. That the country has been convulsed by internal fires, no one who has visited it, can doubt. Mountains of lava are seen towering up, and caverns yawning at their base. The natural conclusion is that many of the original deposits or veins are still undisturbed; and, in the vicinity of the original deposits of those that have, gold must exist, and will be discovered to an extent almost beyond conception.

A system of mining was adopted near the commencement of the rainy season, which went to show that gold is much more plentifully distributed, as you near the original deposit. It was called in California *parlance*, *coyotaing*. It was by digging holes or pits in the ground, generally into the base of the mountains, sometimes penetrating to the depth of fifty or one hundred feet, with the opening just sufficient to admit a man. This mode was found extremely profitable. Miners now also commenced prospecting among the rocks on this side of the mountains, and with very fair success.

Among the operators in the mines, there were none, as a class, so generally successful as sailors. They were numerous, and carried with them those estimable traits for which they are so universally celebrated. They were always, both hand and purse, at the disposal of their neighbors. Nothing afforded them more pleasure than to administer to the wants of others, always acting upon the principle that what *they* had belonged to the world at large, and they were merely the agents to superintend its distribution. There was a bar in the immediate vicinity, called "Neptune's Bar," worked entirely by sailors, and of the twenty canalling operations in the vicinity, it was the only successful one. They were well remunerated, and no one envied their success. They would occasionally have a day of recreation, when all the neighbors would expect to drink; in fact, it was looked upon by all as a gala day, the amusements being of a rare and attractive character. The actors would generally drink just enough to exhibit their most prominent traits. Hogan was full of Shakspeare, and Tom of gunpowder; Charley, a true son of Neptune, would always imagine himself in a gale, and go aloft on the nearest tree; George would laugh; Bill would sing, and Geen would cry; Jack was a long, lank boy of nineteen; his eyes, *on such occasions*, had a peculiar way of closing themselves without his consent, and generally much against *his* will. The operation was somewhat like closing a lady's work-bag with a draw-string. He would tell the "yarns," and it was the only branch of the profession in which he was *au fait.* Hogan would give us a medley, made up of *gems* from "Macbeth," "Richard III.," "Much Ado about Nothing," and the "Merry Wives of Windsor." Tom would deploy into line for action, Charley would fall through the hatch, Jack would sell a magic hat to a Jew, while Prince, the cook, would be searching his pockets for yeast. On one occasion Jack was, in theatrical *parlance*, cast, in the after-piece, and he played his part with *much spirit.* He came to the store drunk, with a large sack on his shoulder, *en route* to the dry diggings. We tried to dissuade him from crossing the river that evening, but he was determined, and staggered down towards the crossing. We all followed, Dewey, being furnished with a lasso, to fish him out in case of accident. Jack was somewhat offended at the interest manifested in him, and mounted the log with an emphatic oath. He walked steadily until he had reached the middle of the stream, when, thinking no doubt that it was time to begin to climb the mountain, he raised his head, lost his balance, and fell in. The weight of the sack first took him to the bottom, but he soon rose to the surface, when Dewey threw the lasso, caught him around the neck, and drew him out. This was somewhat embarrassing to Jack, but he possessed too much courage, at this particular time, to give it up, and again mounted the log. This time he walked much farther, so that there should be no mistake about it, but he again looked up with the same result as before. The stream was very rapid, and was fast carrying him down, but Dewey's unerring lasso took effect, and he was again drawn up the bank. This way of wearing cravats Jack was not accustomed to, and it was sometime before he could raise wind sufficient to carry him from his moorings.

The third attempt was made with better success. He reached the opposite side, but in stepping off the log, stumbled, and, the bank being steep, he rolled back to the margin of the river; Dewey again threw the lasso, and Jack recrossed. This closed the scene; Jack did not come before the curtain, and, I suspect, that if there had been one near, he would have got behind it.

Occasionally the miners of that entire region of country would get on a spree, go to some drinking establishment, all get tight, and have a merry row. They would keep it up during the day, and at evening some one perhaps would propose going home. This would be favored by some, but generally met by a proposition to have another round, which would invariably carry; then some would be accused of not having treated; he would acknowledge the soft impeachment, and another round would be ordered. They would all drink to friends at home in general, then to some particular personal friend. Some one would propose going to the dry diggings the next day, prospecting. Well, all in favor of going with Price, to-morrow, to the dry diggings, will form on this side—opposed, on the other; opposed are in the minority, and must treat. Some would get mad and start for their tents, but having, at this particular time, very vague ideas of localities, instead of going down the river, they would go up the side of the mountain, and, *vice versa;* others would start, but by some mysterious movement, the earth would *fly up* and hit them in the face. The balance of the party would take the last drink and start, all wishing to go to the same place, but each, having his own peculiar ideas, as to the direction.

After wandering about for some time, each would call to the others, informing them that *he* was right, and of course when all were right none were wrong; but in the sequel not one, perhaps, out of the twenty, would reach his tent during the night. On one occasion, one of the party, after having taken the last drink, mounted his mule, designing to go one mile up the river, but, on reaching the mouth of the ravine, the worthy animal turned down stream. In the course of the night the rider, as he supposed, reached his tent, and in attempting to dismount, being somewhat *fatigued*, he fell against the side of it and rolled in at the bottom; to his surprise he found it occupied by an individual, who, disliking his abrupt *entrée*, brought his revolver into requisition; the matter was explained, and our worthy rider found himself in the tent of a stranger, five miles from his own.

G. V. COOPER DEL. ON STONE BY J. CAMERON LITH OF G. W. LEWIS 111. NASSAU ST. N.Y.

SUTTER'S MILL,

COLOMA, the spot where the Gold was first found.

Chapter Eighteenth.

ARRIVALS—PREPARATION FOR THE RAINY SEASON—NEW DISCOVERIES—COLOMA—GAMBLERS *versus* BAYONETS—"HANGTOWN"—PUBLIC EXECUTIONS—FASHIONABLE ENTERTAINMENTS—WILD CATTLE—DANGEROUS SPORTING—MURDERED INDIANS—THE WRONGS THEY SUFFER.

AFTER the result of the different canalling operations was known, being about the first of October, there was a general uneasiness felt throughout the mines, partly owing to the ill-success attending the above, and in part to a desire to make preparations for the approaching rainy season, which was expected to set in about the first of November. People were constantly arriving from San Francisco, having been informed that this was the "*precise spot.*" The overland emigration was also arriving, and there was a universal desire to change positions. Those having productive private leads, were anxious to sell, go into the "dry diggings," throw up dirt, and prepare for operating during the rainy season. Some of the canalled bars were not entirely abandoned, and much of the stock was in market; but those who purchased it, were in a similar condition to the man who purchased the bear skin, the worthy owner of which was running wild in the forest, little suspecting that so important a part of himself, had been made the subject of a mercantile contract.

There were frequent reports of rich discoveries in the mountain gorges, and many of them were found quite productive, inducing the occupants to throw up temporary habitations to protect them during winter. Those who wished to retain their claims on the river, would do so by leaving some utensil to keep possession, and spend a week in prospecting in the mountains. If successful in finding a productive spot, the pick-axe would be left in charge. A rich deposit was found in the mountains about four miles distant, to which the attention of all was directed, and many threw up temporary huts and made preparation for the approaching winter. The place immediately assumed the appearance of a town. Stores were erected and filled, and *monte-banks* established to amuse the citizens. This newly discovered dry diggings is twelve miles from Coloma, the point at which gold was first discovered; the intervening distance being a succession of mountain gorges, all containing gold, many of the vales being in the possession of herds of wild cattle, that have never, until recently, been visited by man.

Coloma is situated on the south fork of the American River, fifty-five miles from Sacramento City. The valley, though small, is one of the most beautiful in the State, being about three-fourths of a mile in width, and walled up on either side by lofty mountains. The saw-mill in the race of which gold was first discovered, is still standing and in operation. (See Plate.) The location of the town is extremely pleasant, being near a bend of the river, and commanding an extended view of the surrounding country. It was once infested by gamblers, but the miners took the matter in hand and drove them out at the point of the bayonet. A gigantic enterprise has been undertaken just below the town, by Mr. Little, of Maine. There is an abrupt bend in the river, the sweep around being three miles, and but a half-mile across; this half-mile is being tunneled to draw the water from the natural channel, which is supposed to be very rich in gold. A large frame was erected here for a flouring-mill, at the time the saw-mill was erected; but Mr. Sutter changing his plans, had it removed to the fort, and after the breaking out of the gold excitement it was taken to Sacramento City and erected, making the first hotel, in point of size and accommodations, in town, called the City Hotel. On the right of the accompanying plate will be seen a remnant of that persecuted and doomed race, the native California Indians.

Hangtown, now Placerville, is situated three miles from the south fork of the American River, twelve miles from Coloma and fifty-five from Sacramento City. It is a dry diggings, or mountain gorge, and one of the most productive in the State. The surrounding country is extremely mountainous, with innumerable gorges, from which gold has been obtained in great abundance.

C. V. COOPER DEL. | ON STONE BY J. CAMERON | LITH OF G. W. LEWIS, 111, NASSAU ST N. Y.

COLOMA.

Its first name originated in the execution of two men, a Spaniard and a Frenchman. They were guilty of murder and robbery, tried before Judge Lynch, and executed, all within twenty-four hours.

Soon after this, a man or lad, who was known as Irish Dick, had a difficulty with a person at a gaming table, in the Eldorado, after which he waylaid and murdered him. This was the second murder of which he had been guilty, and for this, his own life fell a sacrifice. The miners took him in charge, tied a rope round his neck, then giving him the other end, compelled him to climb a tree, go out on one of the limbs, fasten the end of the rope, and at the drop of a handkerchief, jump off. He complied with apparent cheerfulness, and died without a struggle.

This is now the first stopping-place for the overland emigration, from which cause, as well as that of the superior richness of the surrounding mountain gorges, it has become a place of much importance. At the time of which I am writing there were several rude houses constituting the town, all under the supervision of males—females, like the visits of their illustrious prototypes, being few and far between. I think the first one had not yet made her appearance.

No nation with less genius than the "universal Yankee," could have survived the privation, and even of these it required the genuine "wooden nutmeg" species, a couple of specimens of which are faintly portrayed in the accompanying plate. Their garments are of a cut not *generally* adopted in the Atlantic cities, yet I can assure the reader they are eminently fashionable in California. The general appearance of these individuals is a true index to the order and systematic arrangement that pervade the interior of their habitation. Nothing is done for show or ornament; everything bearing the impress of practicality and economy—one frying-pan, two tin-plates, both slightly touched with "ile," to prevent rust, their knives in their pockets and forks in their *hair*. They are just going in, having finished their day's work. They are practical miners, both having made fortunes at the business. Their house is well known by every one who has traveled through that region of the country, and many will associate with the "Yankee House" pleasant recollections, it having been a general resort and nightly scene of a sociable soirée, or something more brilliant.

There are numerous herds of wild cattle in these mountainous regions, which have never been hunted or molested by man, until since the discovery of gold, and even now their wildness and impetuosity render their capture extremely uncertain and perilous. The mountaineers, who always carry their lives in their hands and court danger in every form, are extremely loth to attack a wild bullock, even when well armed and mounted.

The grizzly bear is a universal terror, and is rarely molested by experienced hunters, yet their capture is thought less perilous than that of a wild bullock, for these when wounded become frantic, and nothing can withstand them. Mr. Lewis, a neighbor who had gained a notoriety by his success in hunting the grizzly bear, having captured two in one day, and several others at different times, all through the fleetness and superior training of his mule, resolved to make an attempt upon a herd of wild cattle that were in the mountains not far distant. He considered his mule equal to any emergency, and having a rifle that plainly spoke for itself, he started on his perilous adventure. He found the herd feeding in a ravine, and approached very near before they eyed his mule with suspicion. They seemed quite unconscious of approaching danger, until one of them, catching the scent of the foe, threw up his head, gave the peculiar signal, and all were in motion; at this instant the rifle was discharged, the ball taking effect in the neck of one of the bullocks, bringing him upon his knees; he immediately recovered, and wheeling about, bounded with headlong speed in the direction of the mule. The moment was a critical one, the mule under the sting of the spur was doing his utmost, the bullock in hot pursuit, his eyes flashing fire, his tongue hanging from his mouth, the blood streaming from his nostrils, and he foaming and bellowing with the most terrific fury, gaining upon his adversaries at every bound. At length, he was upon them, the rider seeing no other alternative, caught the limb of a tree letting the mule pass on. The next bound, however, was his last, for the bullock overtaking him, struck him in the side bringing him to the ground, and after goring him several times, bounded away in the direction taken by the herd, and soon disappeared. Upon visiting the location of the above-described occurrence a few days thereafter, in passing through a slight gorge, I came upon

G. V. COOPER DEL. ON STONE BY J. CAMERON LITH. OF G. W. LEWIS, 111 NASSAU ST. N. Y.

THE YANKEES HOUSE AT HANG TOWN

the bodies of three Indians who had been dead apparently about two weeks, each bearing the marks of the unerring rifle; they had been among the whites as their dresses indicated, two of them having on jean shirts, the other a blue flannel. Two of them were shot through the chest, the other through the head; the sight was a sad one, and gave rise to melancholy reflections, for here these poor beings are hunted and shot down like wild beasts, and these no doubt fell by the hand of the assassin, not for lucre but to satiate a feeling of revenge.

In an adjoining territory the "red man" had a quiet home; their "wigwams" were always supplied with venison, their corn-fields ripened in autumn, their rude traps furnished clothing for the winter, and in the spring they danced in praise of the "Great Spirit" for causing flowers to bloom upon the graves of their fathers; but the white stranger came and took possession of their hunting grounds and streams, and harvested their corn. They held a council and decided that the Great Spirit had sent the white stranger, and it would be wrong not to give him all he wished; they collected their traps, bows, and arrows, and prepared to fall back in search of new streams and hunting grounds; they paid the last visit to the graves of their fathers. What were their feelings? The moon threw a pale, dim light through the foliage, the air breathed a mournful sigh as they reached the lonely mound; the stout-hearted warrior drew his blanket to hide his tears as he bowed down to commune for the last time with the spirits that had so often blessed him in the chase; his heart was too full, and he fell upon his face and wept bitterly. But, a last adieu; they rise, cross the arrows over the grave, and walk mournfully away; the Great Spirit gives them a new hunting ground, and the corn ripens on the plain, but soon the white stranger comes and tells them to fall back. They are at the base of the mountain; there are no hunting grounds beyond; if they go into the mountain their corn will not ripen, and their "papooses" will starve in the wigwam; they hold a council and decide to defend their homes against the encroachments of the white stranger. The whites were strong, and drove the red man into the mountains, and for the crime of having *tried* to defend their homes and offspring, they are placed under a ban, and hunted down like wild beasts. No

matter where they are found the crime of being a red man is a forfeiture, not only of all right to property but to life itself.

Will not some philanthropist rise above sectional prejudices, and undertake the regeneration of this truly noble but downtrodden people? Had I the wealth of an Astor I would not wish a better or nobler field for immortality.

The first man I met after my arrival in the interior was an Oregonian on horseback, armed with a revolving rifle in search of Indians. He had had a horse stolen, and presumed it was taken by an Indian; he swore he "would shoot the first red-skin he met," and I had no reason to doubt his word; still the chances were ninety-nine out of the hundred, that the horse was stolen by a white man. I have no doubt the three Indians above spoken of were wantonly shot while walking peaceably along their trail.

G. V. COOPER DEL. | ON STONE BY J. CAMERON | LITH. OF G. W. LEWIS, 111 NASSAU ST., N. Y.

PLACER VILLE,
(HANG TOWN).

Chapter Nineteenth.

CANALLING OPERATIONS—UNSUCCESSFUL EXPERIMENTS—COFFEE MILLS AND GOLD WASHERS—FORMATION OF BARS—GOLD REMOVED FROM THE MOUNTAINS DURING THE RAINY SEASON—SNOW ON THE MOUNTAINS, AND ITS DISSOLUTION—RISE AND FALL OF THE RIVER—STOCK SPECULATIONS—QUICKSILVER MACHINES—SEPARATION OF GOLD AND QUICKSILVER—INDIVIDUAL ENTERPRISE—INCENTIVES TO EXERTION—EXPENSES.

To give the reader a more definite idea of the success attending mining, I will detail the result of the different operations in the vicinity of my place of business, commencing one mile above and extending four below; this is said to be as rich as the same extent on any river in the country. The Manhattan Bar was canalled and dammed by the Manhattan Co., being a party of New Yorkers, including Gen. Winchester and brother. After expending a large amount in turning the water from the bed of the river, they purchased several quicksilver machines at one thousand dollars each, and immediately put them in motion. It required but few days to convince them of the failure that must attend the enterprise; the machines did not collect enough to pay the men who worked them, and they were immediately abandoned for the common rocker, which, in their turn, were abandoned together with the entire work.

The next in order was the Vigilance Bar; here a large amount of money was expended, and almost the entire summer devoted to the construction of a dam and canal, all of which proved an entire loss to the parties concerned; they did not get enough to pay for the provisions consumed during the construction of the work. In the immediate vicinity of this was the Union Bar; a still greater amount in money and labor was expended here, but, as in the case of the Vigilance Co., it proved a total failure. In these two cases, sixty men had spent the entire summer in hard labor, and now were obliged to encounter the rainy season, many of them in debt, and but few with sufficient means to buy a month's provisions. In the latter company were several young Philadelphians, sons of the first men of that city; an adventurous spirit had induced them to leave their homes, and they were now encountering the *realities* of active life. Lacy's Bar was next in order; there were many rich private leads in the vicinity of this bar, and it contained within its bounds many rich deposits. Soon after the completion of the canal the bar was offered for sale—a *fire* or *flood* at St. Louis making the proprietors' return to the States imperative. I was unable to learn whether said fire or flood abovementioned had actually transpired or was merely in anticipation, nor am I prepared to name the *precise* amount of *net profits* made by the purchasers of the above bar. Next is the Mormon Bar; the details as well as the result of this enterprise have been heretofore given. The next is Kentucky Bar; this undertaking paid to each stockholder seven hundred dollars, which was good wages. Next was Neptune's, commonly known as "dead man's bar," the body of a miner having been found upon it; this bar was worked by sailors, and was the most productive in the country. It was said by those concerned, that they generally took out one pound ($200) per day to the man. The rainy season, however, destroyed their works before they had accumulated fortunes. The next bar was small, and without a name; operations here were unsuccessful, and soon abandoned.

The next bar I will name Woodworth's Bar; when I visited it three men were working a machine made by a Mr. Woodworth, of New York city; its construction was somewhat on the plan of, and much resembled, a large sized coffee-mill. For mining purposes the coffee-mill would have been decidedly preferable. Fortunately for miners but few of the machines made in the States ever found their way into the mineral regions; this being the only one I saw during my stay in the country. Immense numbers were shipped, and arrived in the bay of San Francisco; but, being pronounced entirely worthless, they were thrown overboard, not worth even the lighterage. This bar also proved a failure. The next below was Lehigh Bar; this was canalled, and immediately abandoned as worthless. Then came Little and Great Horse-Shoe Bars, neither of which paid for the labor bestowed upon them. Not to mention the small intervening bars, I will pass on and mention, lastly, Smith's Bar; this was one of the most gigantic works undertaken on the river. During its progress the feelings of those concerned were of the most sanguine character; in digging the canal they frequently came upon rich deposits, which would throw all into a phrensy of excitement, and some realized small fortunes by selling out during the progress of the work: after the completion of the work machines were put in operation, and all were expecting to reap golden harvests; some of the machines produced most bountifully, and others almost nothing. A few days convinced them that, as a party, they could not make wages, and the result was similar to those mentioned above.

In all the bars mentioned there were points of extreme richness. The calculations of those engaged in canalling were based upon a false, though somewhat plausible theory; the margin being rich, they very naturally came to the conclusion that the bed of the river must be much more so. It appears, however, that gold *does not* settle in the channel, but is borne along until some abrupt bend in the river checks the current, when it settles, together with the stone and earth, forming bars, which have been described in a former chapter. It is understood that these bars are formed during the rainy season. Torrents rush down the mountains, and on reaching the stream unite in bearing along the precious freight. It may seem strange that the current can convey gold to any considerable distance; it is nevertheless true, and it may seem less strange to one who has known the river to rise from twenty to thirty feet in as many hours. In such freshets the *natural* channel has no influence, the torrents claiming for their boundaries the mountains that tower up on either side. What is rain in the moderately elevated regions, is snow as you advance higher up into the mountains. This causes a long season of high water. The snow does not dissolve during the rainy season, the sun being obscured—but at its cessation torrents rush down the side of the mountains, and, not unfrequently, huge masses of snow, as if impatient of their slow dissolution, will break loose from their fastenings, and with a terrific sweep dash into the chasm below. At this season of the year the rise and fall of the rivers are as uniform as the tides.

As the sun approaches the meridian, streams become swollen, frequently rising several feet, and fall as it disappears behind the mountains. It ceases to rain about the first of March, but in consequence of the immense quantities of snow on the mountains, streams do not resume their natural channels until the first of July, at which time, deposits made during the flood are found, as a general thing, above water-mark. One cause and perhaps the main one, of the almost universal failure of canalling operations is, that the facilities attained do not counterbalance the enormous expenditures requisite. Another difficulty is that a company of thirty men cannot, in the mines, operate with the same economy of time that they can when working in pairs. As I had lost on my stock in the Mormon Bar I determined to make it up by buying in the balance, which I did at from ten to fifteen dollars per share, and eventually sold it at several hundred per cent. advance to a company designing to operate upon it with quicksilver machines. Gen. Winchester & Co. became joint owners, and soon several of the machines were in successful operation, propelled by water drawn from the canal. The success of the experiment was placed beyond a doubt. The machines used were called the "Burk rocker." They were placed on an inclined plane, and in the upper riffles, which were of iron, was placed a quantity of quicksilver. Dirt was thrown in at the upper end of the machines, and as it was washed through, the rocking motion would bring it in contact with the quicksilver, which having a strong affinity for the gold, carefully collects it without including any other substance. After the quicksilver has taken up, or freighted itself to its utmost capacity, and become a solid mass, or amalgam, it is taken out and its place supplied.

In separating the gold and quicksilver the amalgam is put into a retort, to the top of which is screwed a crooked iron tube, the end passing into a vessel of water. A heat is raised under the retort of six hundred degrees, which causes the quicksilver to evaporate and pass up into the tube, when it condenses and passes down into the water. This operation is performed at a loss of only two and a half per cent. of the quicksilver. These machines were purchased at a cost of one thousand dollars each, although in the States they are worth less than forty. Their

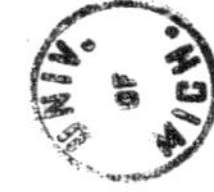

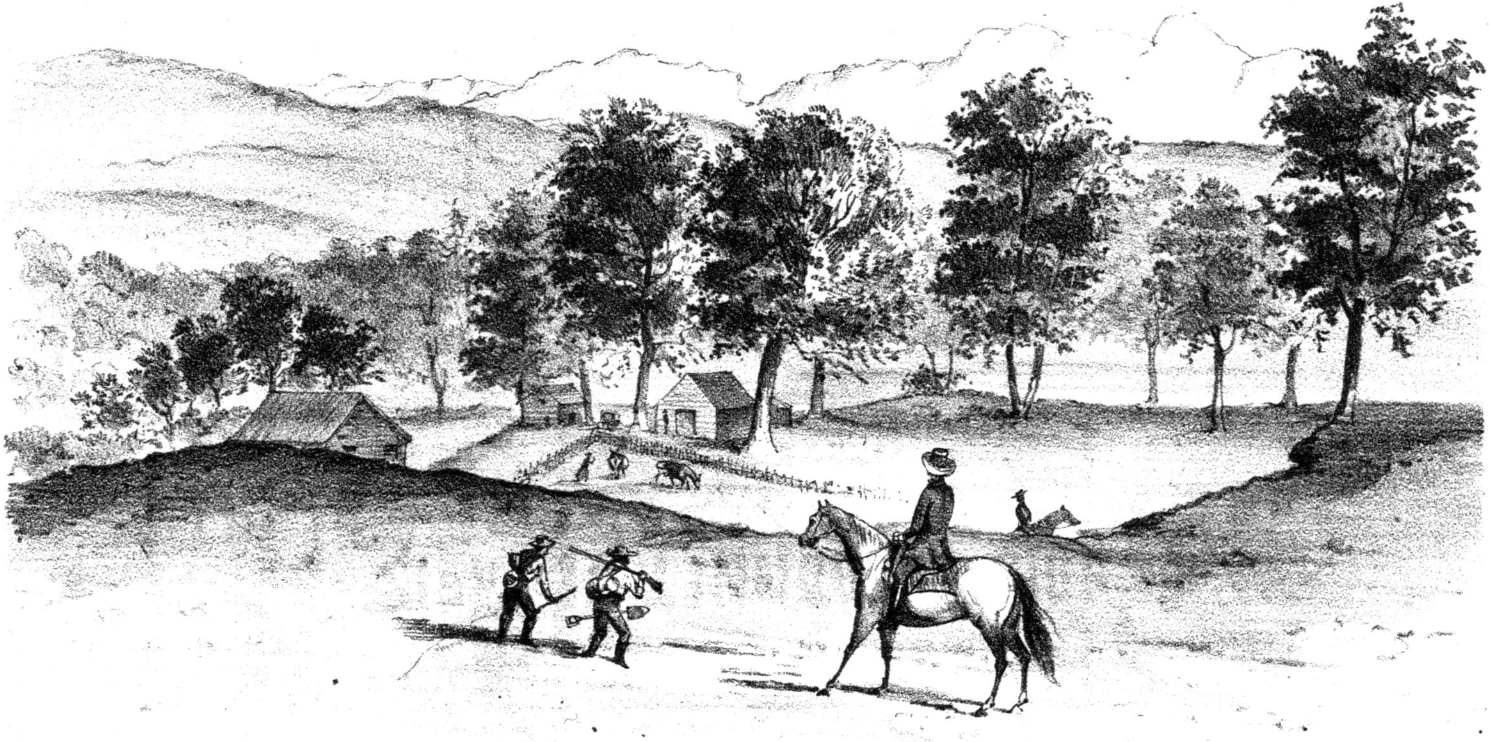

G.V. COOPER DEL. ON STONE BY J. CAMERON LITH. OF G.W. LEWIS, 111 NASSAU ST. N.Y.

WHITE OAK SPRING.

operation was very successful, and had it not been for the early deluge would have made fortunes for their owners.

The result attending individual enterprise was similar to that of canalling, with the exception that in the former case heavy debts were not contracted, and the individual, if he had not a fortune in his pocket, felt that what he earned was his own. I had a good opportunity to learn the daily proceeds of each man's labor, my scale being at their service and almost universally used. I could name one hundred individuals, take them in order as they were operating along the river, and not more than ten of the number had, at the commencement of the rainy season, sufficient means to purchase provisions for the winter. They had labored hard; to-day, opening a lead; to-morrow, getting out an ounce; and the day after prospecting. They had been all summer just on the eve of making a rich discovery and a fortune, the prospect was always bright and cheering, the prize just, almost, within the grasp—to-morrow—never more distant than to-morrow. The lead is open to-day, to-morrow the reward, that to-morrow dawned to comparatively few. It is *still* about to dawn, and sought with the same enthusiasm. Could the miners have pocketed all they took from the earth, few, perhaps, would have had reason to complain, but the attending expenses were so great that it was almost impossible to live and keep anything in the purse. They would eat up at night what they had earned during the day, consequently the proceeds of labor passed immediately into the hands of those in trade.

Chapter Twentieth.

COMMOTION IN THE POLITICAL ELEMENTS—CALIFORNIA A STATE—SLAVERY PROHIBITED—POLITICAL CAMPAIGN, AND THE RAINY SEASON—SPEECH OF A WOULD-BE-GOVERNOR—ENTHUSIASM AND BRANDY—ELECTION DISTRICTS—BALLOT-BOXES AND UMBRELLAS—MINERS IN A TRANSITION STATE—PREPARATIONS FOR THE RAINY SEASON—PRIMITIVE HABITATIONS—TRADE IMPROVING—ADVENT OF THE RAINY SEASON—ITS TERRIFIC EFFECTS—RAPID RISE OF THE RIVER—MACHINES DESTROYED—ARRIVALS—MY STORE AND BED—A BUSINESS SUIT—DISTRESSING GROANS—THE BOTTLE A CONSOLATION—SEVERAL STRANGE SPECIMENS OF HUMANITY COOKING BREAKFAST—THE SCURVY—A DEATH.

WE now, for the first time, had a commotion in the political elements, which resulted in erecting California into a State and placing her, the "bright particular star," in this glorious constellation. An election was ordered, and delegates selected to draft a Constitution for the State. They met at Monterey, and after a few days' deliberation passed upon the Constitution which is hereunto annexed, and which was eventually ratified by an almost unanimous vote of the people. The greatest unanimity prevailed at the Convention, the deliberations conducted with the utmost dignity, each seeming desirous to act for the best interests of the country. The clause prohibiting slavery, or involuntary servitude, passed by a unanimous vote, although many of the delegates were interested in slave property in the States. The nominations were made for State officers, and, although party lines were not strictly drawn, every preparation was made for a vigorous campaign.

The election was to take place on the 15th day of November, and by the time the nominees were ready to take the "stump," the rainy season was upon us. Just picture to your imagination a would-be-governor, in a slouched India rubber hat, a *poncho*, and high boots, standing near a tent on the side of the mountain holding forth to a highly patriotic audience of six, the rain pouring down in torrents. Nothing could dampen the ardor of the speaker; he had enlisted in the cause of the dear people, and nothing could induce him to swerve from the performance of his duty. The gist of his remarks was as follows:—"Fellow citizens, you *have rights to protect.* [Hurrah! Three cheers and two drinks of brandy.] *I'll spend my last breath in the vindication of those rights.* [Three more!!] The mineral lands ought to be given to the people. [Three times three!!! Three cheers and six drinks.] *Have not the sovereign people made this country what it is?* [Yes! Yes!! and great cheering.] If I am elected I will use my influence to have this immense tract of country, now claimed by Sutter, divided among the people." [Immense sensation and cheering.] After order was again restored, the speaker was invited to step out of the puddle of water that had dripped from his *poncho*, and take something to drink. The meeting was conducted with *much spirit*, and resulted in securing the votes of a majority present for the would-be-Governor.

At this time, this district of country, called the Minerva district, had become so populous that municipal officers had been elected, and now it was regularly divided into election districts, and arrangements made to open polls wherever it was deemed necessary. The qualification for an elector was to be an American citizen. The most prominent candidates for Governor were Judge Burnett, H. S. Sherwood and Rodman M. Price, of whom the former was elected. On the day of election the ballots were deposited in a hat, over which one of the inspectors held an umbrella.

The middle of October finds the miners in a transition state. There has not a drop of rain fallen during the entire summer, and the earth, six feet below, is as dry as on the surface; one cannot move without being enveloped in dust; and vegetation is as crisp as if it had just been taken from the oven. There has been no haze to shield the earth from the sun, and at night the stars have twinkled with unwonted brilliancy; but now the sun has grown dim and pale, and the stars have fled to their hiding-place. Miners are admonished that it is time to prepare for an untried winter, and on every hand is evinced a disposition not to be taken unawares. Here on the side of the mountain is a habitation, three logs high, covered with canvas, the crevices well "mudded," all the light used being admitted through the door. There is a cave, walled and roofed with rocks, the canvas closing the entrance being the only indication that it is a tenement. An army tent is also seen, which is well secured, as if in momentary expectation of the approaching blast; dirt has been thrown well over the foot, to prevent the winds from searching out the occupant. In front is a tree, under which is a camp-kettle and frying-pan, and near are a few dying embers, the smoke curling up and mingling with the foliage. It seemed hard that one accustomed to the luxury of a comfortable home, should be doomed to spend the winter in this forlorn condition. Climbing up the side of the mountain, are seen mules heavily laden with provisions and mining utensils, which are destined to some favorite spot in the mountain gorges. Trade begins to improve, miners are laying in their supplies for the winter, and merchants find their stocks exhausted, and are driven to town to replenish. The sun assumes a peculiar color, and where it is reflected in the water is a "royal" purple. Its rays had become very dim, and on the 27th of October the deluge burst upon us.

General Winchester and company had just placed their quicksilver machine, and commenced successful operations on the bar, but one night destroyed their works, carrying one of their machines, laden with twenty-five pounds of quicksilver, a distance of three miles, destroying it, and emptying its valuable contents into the river. The rise of the river was so rapid that those on the opposite side, when it commenced to rain, found it impossible to recross six hours after. The scene was most terrific; the mountain on either side of the river, rose almost perpendicularly, and the torrents rushed down, undermining huge rocks, which, after making a few leaps, would come in contact with others of equal dimensions, when both, with one terrific bound, would dash into the chasm below.

Mining operations were, for the time, suspended, and miners, many of whom were destitute of even the protection of a tent, were hovering about their fires in a most desponding mood; many were entirely destitute of means, and cooking, perhaps, their last day's supply. Teams were constantly arriving with miners fresh from the States, who would descend the mountain

G. V. COOPER DEL. ON STONE BY J. CAMERON LITH. OF G. W. LEWIS, 111 NASSAU ST. N. Y.

LOOKING DOWN THE BIG CANON.

with high hopes, having been so fortunate as to fall in with some one who had directed them to this particular spot. They were generally well supplied with provisions, and notwithstanding the drenching rain, one hour after their advent would find them busily engaged with the pan and pick-axe.

The store I occupied was made by driving stakes into the ground, and inclosing with common unbleached muslin; the roof flat, covered with the same material. It had answered a good purpose during the summer, but for the rainy season, I am not prepared to say it was exactly the thing. I do not know that the rain fell faster inside than out, but some of my neighbors insinuated that it did. I could keep tolerably dry by wearing an India rubber cap, *poncho*, and long boots, with the aid of a good umbrella, in short, this was my regular business suit. For a bed, I had a scaffold made of poles, on which I had a hammock stuffed with grass and straw, using a pair of blankets as covering. In order to keep my bed dry I had a standard at the head and foot, on which was a pole running "fore and aft," serving as a ridge-pole, over which was thrown an India rubber blanket. On going to bed I would throw up one corner of my India rubber blanket, holding my umbrella over the opening, and after taking off my boots, I would crawl in feet first, throw back the rubber to its place, then tying my umbella to the head standard I was in bed. My friends, Fairchild, Tracy, Jones, and Dean were not so fortunate. They would lay down on the ground in their blankets, and in one hour would be drenched to the skin; in this condition they were obliged to spend the balance of the night. Jones (formerly of the Cornucopia, New York) had a severe cough, his lungs being much affected, and he thought he was fast declining with the consumption. After becoming drenched and chilled his cough would set in, which, together with his distressing groans, would render night hideous, and cast a gloom over the most buoyant spirit. On rising in the morning, the bottle was our first consolation; it would elevate our spirits, and drive the chilly sensation from our limbs. A few large sticks had been thrown together and set on fire, around which would be seen a dozen strange-looking specimens of humanity, one with a red flannel shirt, part of a glazed cap, and torn unmentionables; another with a woolen-blanket, that could boast of having secured, on the previous night, what rain had fallen in its immediate vicinity; another with an India rubber *poncho* and a hat that had been used both sides out, and, as if to assume a ferocious appearance, it had adopted the color of the grizzly bear. All hovering around the fire, some with pieces of pork on the ends of sticks, others with something in a frying-pan, covered with a tin plate; one is stirring flour and water together, while his companion is trying to turn the cakes; about every other one is disposed to go into the fire.

A disease at this time manifested itself, the symptoms of which were of a peculiar nature. It was called the "land scurvy," and was caused by a want of proper vegetable diet. The blood of the system became thick and turgid, and diminished in quantity; there was but little circulation at the extremities, or near the surface of the body, the fleshy parts becoming almost lifeless; the gums became black and not unfrequently the teeth would fall out, the gums having so entirely wasted away. The malady became fearfully prevalent, and no remedy could be obtained; vegetables were not to had, there were none in the country. There had been a few, a very few, potatoes in the market, at prices varying from four shillings each to a dollar and a half per pound, but the supply was too scanty to arrest the disease, and many had become almost entirely disabled.

On the 28th of October, a man from Illinois fell a victim to this dreadful malady, and on the 29th, it was our painful duty to bear him to that lonely hill and consign him to the tomb. A board was placed at his head, on which was cut his brief epitaph. What a strange commentary upon the vicissitudes of human life. He was once an infant, fondled and caressed by an affectionate mother, a youth counseled by a doting father, and embraced and loved by sisters and brothers. He grew to manhood, pledged his hand and heart to the one he loved, combatted, perhaps, with adversity, and finally bade farewell to his own offspring, to die a stranger in a strange land.

Chapter Twenty-first.

DANGEROUS NAVIGATION—A TRIP OVER THE FALLS—A NIGHT FROM HOME—SAILOR HOSPITALITY—SCARCITY OF PROVISIONS—A HAZARDOUS ALTERNATIVE—A WAYWARD BOY—PREPARTIONS FOR LEAVING THE INTERIOR—DISTRIBUTION OF EFFECTS—OUR TRAVELING SUIT—START FOR SAN FRANCISCO—FAREWELL—THREE INDIVIDUALS UNDER A FULL HEAD OF STEAM—ARRIVAL AT THE "HALF-WAY TENT"—POOR ACCOMMODATIONS—A MORNING WALK AND POOR BREAKFAST—WADING LAGOONS—WILD GEESE—ARRIVAL AT THE AMERICAN RIVER—OUR TOILET, AND ENTRY INTO SACRAMENTO CITY.

THE river had become much swollen, and burst through among the rocks with the greatest fury. The rumbling of the rocks and stone as they were hurled from their beds, was incessant and almost deafening. Many of my friends lived on the opposite side of the river, and I had purchased a boat for their accommodation. The only place where a boat could be rowed across with safety, was above a fall occasioned, in part, by a dam. The water here was extremely rapid, but by heading well up stream, could be crossed in safety. Tracy generally volunteered to do the ferrying, but when I was disengaged I would do it myself.

On one occasion, a party of six wished to cross, and I went down with them, paddled out into the stream, and as the boat came in contact with the strongest current, it swung around, when one of the passengers becoming frightened, applied a paddle on the upper side which aimed the boat for the fall, leaving no alternative but to go over. The fall was several feet, and below it huge masses of rock; the roaring of the water was terrific, almost deafening, and it was night. We were swept along with the velocity of an arrow, and as we came to the brink I discovered the limbs of a tree, which had floated down and caught. Being in the stern of the boat, I rose up and as it was about to break over, jumped and caught to the limb, my companions going over with the boat. My situation was the most perilous imaginable. I was in the middle of the stream on the very brink of the precipice, the water up to my shoulders, and the stones tumbling from beneath my feet; my only support being the limb, to which I clung as if for life. It required almost superhuman effort to keep from being swept from my hold by the strength of the current. After feeling a little more secure, I felt below the surface and found another limb to which I clung, taking one step in the direction of the shore; after groping about, I found another and the last. I had now almost gained the upper side of a rock which rested on the brink just below the surface of the water. It was a crisis; it was extremely doubtful whether I could throw myself with sufficient force to catch the upper side of the rock. If I missed, the chances of life were against me, as I had no doubt some, if not all of my companions had already found a watery grave. It was no time for deliberation, and straining every nerve, I made one desperate struggle and gained the rock. I still had fifteen feet of the strength of the current to overcome, but by dexterous movements I succeeded in reaching the shore.

I immediately went in search of my friends; fortunately, we had two sailors with us, Billy and Charley, before spoken of. The boat ended over in passing down. Charley and Billy found their way to the shore, but Mr. Byram was dashed along among the rocks, apparently lifeless. They rushed in again and succeeded in dragging his body to the shore; we then hurried on to learn the fate of the others. On reaching the bend of the river we found the boat drifted against the rock, they clinging to its sides; they threw the hawser, and we drew the boat to the shore. Mr. Byram recovered, and we congratulated ourselves upon the auspicious termination of the adventure. They had been purchasing a quantity of provisions—flour, sugar, coffee, &c., all of which were "turned over" to tempt the appetite of the fishes.

Their encampment was a mile above, and as it was impossible to recross the river here, I went with them, in hopes of being able to ferry over in a small boat they owned, but on arriving, found it had been carried away by the freshet. The evening was chilly; I was drenched; I had left things in an unsafe condition at the store, and as my friends imagined me drowned, I determined to return and endeavor to recross in my own boat. On arriving I turned it on the side as far as possible, to relieve it of the water inside, then tying the hawser to my arm, I stepped on board. I was carried down with the greatest velocity for some distance, when I brought up against a rock. I was again in motion, and again sided against a rock with such force that the water burst over filling my boat. There was now no alternative but to try to reach the shore, which, after sundry cold baths, I succeeded in doing.

It was now late, and the night was extremely dark. One mile below were two sailor friends, and I resolved to reach their encampment. The first part of the route lay over a rocky promontory, overhanging the river. I passed over this by clinging to the shrubs and points of rocks. Occasionally one of the latter would leap from its bed, and with one terrific bound, disappear in the water below. On gaining the other side, I found the route easy, and soon gained the point of destination. I received a welcome from Tom and George (before spoken of) that sailors only know how to give. Tom cut wood, built a fire against a rock, and I was soon comfortably incased in a sailor's suit, mine hanging by the fire, George, in the meantime, boiling the tea-kettle, frying pork and toasting bread, and I was soon invited into the tent to partake of their hospitalities. Tom assisted me in the morning; I reached my tent at noon. To Tom, George, Charley, and Billy, (the latter has since died)—may fortune crown their efforts, and friendship always smile!

The mining districts soon became almost destitute of provisions, and the country impassable in consequence of the immense fall of rain. There was a reported scarcity of flour, and it rose in one day, at San Francisco, from $16 to $40 per barrel, and in the mines from 30 cents to $1.50 per pound. I had laid in a good supply at a low price, but after this was exhausted the only way in which I could keep a supply, was to buy out those who were about to return to town. There was an almost universal desire to leave the mines, and but few remained excepting those who were from necessity compelled to. Some were preparing to return to the States; the number, however, was few. We had formed strong attachments, having participated in so many vicissitudes, and the thought of separating gave rise to gloomy reflections, particularly to those who were to remain. The supply of provisions had become so entirely exhausted, that many had resolved upon the hazardous alternative of going into the mountains, and wintering on the food procured with their rifles. At the head of the list was my friend Tracy. Nothing could induce him to go to town; he had as great an aversion to civilization as his friend Jim. He had left his home when a boy, and was probably never heard of by his parents; the connection was entirely severed, and he looked upon his rifle as his only true friend and reliance.

Having sold out my stock, Mr. Fairchild, Mr. Jones, and myself had resolved to start on the 17th of November for San Francisco, Mr. F. and myself destined for home. The only preparation necessary was to distribute our surplus effects among our friends; at this particular time it afforded more pleasure to give than to receive. Nothing was movable, hardly ourselves; the earth had become so thoroughly saturated, we would either of us have been loth to accept a new suit of clothes, ragged as we were. We each reserved a pair of pantaloons, a flannel shirt, glazed cap, and stogy boots. These, in connection with our blankets, constituted our outfits. Our firearms we found it difficult to dispose of; they were entirely useless, and our friends accepted them merely as an act of courtesy. My revolver, I had carried across the Isthmus, and kept during my stay in California, and when I disposed of it, it had not had the honor of being charged.

On the morning of the 17th my successor took possession of the store, and we were preparing to start, the rain pouring down a deluge. Our friends had all collected to bid us farewell, and to give into our charge letters to their friends. It was a gloomy morning, and a feeling of sadness appeared to steal over the minds of those we were about to leave. Having contracted with a gentleman who was to leave two days after, to deliver a package for me at Sacramento City, we filled our bottles with "Monongahela," and putting a certain quantity where the effects would be more immediately felt, bade farewell to all, and started up the mountain. We were soon hailed by Tracy and Dean, who were not yet reconciled to parting with us, and who accompanied us a mile to the top of the mountain.

We here came to a halt, and took the hands of our friends for the last time. We were all most sensibly affected, and although we had become inured to hardships and privations of every description, we could not, on this occasion, restrain our tears.

It was about 2 P. M. when we resumed our journey, and we had resolved to walk to the "half-way tent," twenty-two miles distant. We were obliged to wade through mud to the tops of our boots, and on one occasion Jones sunk so deeply into the mud that we were obliged to pry him out. The first two miles found us much fatigued, and we were obliged to consult our bottles for relief; the next two found us running under a full head of steam, our walking beams in the finest working order. There was an evident disposition to try our relative speed, and the probability is that we never attained a higher rate than on this particular occasion. We did not meet any one on the road, but we met a number of trees, and although entire strangers, we made ourselves as familiar as though we had been acquainted with them for years; I hope they do not remember what we said to them. We thought Fairchild made too much lee-way; Jones had so much freight on deck that he rolled about tremendously; I found it difficult to keep on an even keel, and was so heavily laden forward, that it was almost impossible to support the "figure-head." We all, however, made good time, considering the depth of water we drew. Sunset (it did not rise that day) found half our journey performed, and three-fourths of our *fuel* consumed; we did not let the engines stop, but steamed on, the paddles frequently throwing mud into the faces of the passengers. About 9 P. M., one of the vessels was noticed to careen, but it righted, and we kept on until half-past ten, when we arrived at the half-way tent.

If I was ever glad to put into port, it was at this time, and *we* certainly put in in "stress of weather." We found the tent full, and when we called for supper were told that there was nothing to eat, except a piece of salt beef which was in the barrel. We ordered this cooked, and made a supper of brandy and beef. We now looked about for a place to sleep, but were obliged to spread our blankets on the wet ground. If I ever felt the necessity of a place on the dry dock, it was at this time; our clothes were wet with rain and perspiration, and now we were cold and stiff, and the thought of laying down for the night in the mud, was dreadful. There was no alternative, and we submitted with the best possible grace.

The "tent" was kept by Mr. Wilkin (or Wilky,) assisted by his amiable lady. They were from Scotland, having been in the United States about seven years, most of which time they had lived in their wagon or a tent; part of the time they had lived on the extreme frontier of Missouri, after which they crossed over to Salt Lake, then into Oregon, and finally down to California. They had spent the summer in the mines, and after the commencement of the rainy season had started for Sacramento City with a six-mule team. After much toil they reached this point when two of the mules were "mired," the others strayed, leaving them no alternative but to remain for the winter. They constructed temporary accommodations for travelers, and since my return to New York I met them at the Irving House, and was happy to learn that they were most bountifully rewarded for their detention. We rose the next morning, had our bottles refilled, and, as we had no particular appetite for salt beef, we resolved to walk ten miles to breakfast. Our motive powers had rusted during the night, and we found it almost impossible to move, but our bottle, like quack medicines of the present day, was a universal panacea; we applied it in this case with success. We were soon making as good time as on the previous day, but it was soon apparent that Jones must either bend on "studding-sails," or fall behind; he chose the latter alternative, and before 9 o'clock, A. M., he was "hull down." We arrived at the "blue tent" at 10, A. M., and ordered breakfast, but we had the consolation of learning from the worthy host that he had nothing to eat. This was just what we had had for supper the previous night, and informed him that we wished something a little better for breakfast. He had flour, which was full of worms, and *we had warm biscuit for breakfast.*

We were again under way, and soon came out upon an open plain which extended to the American River, fifteen miles distant. This plain, although quite elevated, was covered with "lagoons," or small lakes, all swarming with wild geese, ducks and brant. A finer opportunity for a sportsman could not well be imagined, but to us the lakes afforded but little amusement;

G. V. COOPER DEL. ON STONE BY J. CAMERON LITH. OF G. W. LEWIS, 111 NASSAU ST N.Y.

some of them we could go around, others we were compelled to wade through. The entire plain was dotted with covered wagons that had been loaded with provisions for the interior, but, in trying to cross, the teams had "mired" and the wagons been abandoned.

On arriving within sight of the ferry, we came to the margin of a lagoon that stretched away to the river, leaving us no alternative but to wade; the practicability of this could only be learned by sounding. This was not a time for deliberation, and taking my blankets, &c., on my shoulder, I waded in; after wading to my neck it grew more shallow, and my companion followed. We reached the ferry boat and were soon on the opposite bank of the river.

We were now within sight of Sacramento City, and as it was Sunday our first attention was bestowed upon our toilet. We sat down on the bank of the river, pulled off our boots, poured the water out of them, wrung out our socks, and after replacing these we took off our caps, brushed up our hair, imagined that our moustache curled, (we could not tell, for the river was too muddy to reflect our faces,) adjusted the skirt of our flannel, then throwing our chest out, with our head at an angle of about 23°, we stood in for the city, passing in at the head of J. street, which we found in fine navigable order, the water extending to the door-sills on either side.

Chapter Twenty-second.

A DRY SUIT—RESTAURANTS—WAITERS AND CHAMPAGNE—TWO INDIVIDUALS "TIGHT"—A $10 DINNER—MONTE-BANKS AND MUD—GAMBLING AND ITS RESULTS—GROWTH OF SACRAMENTO CITY—UNPARALLELED PROSPERITY—A REVULSION AND ITS CAUSE—THE FLOOD.

OUR first want was a dry suit, consequently we were on the *qui vive* for a clothing establishment; the first store we came to was unfinished, the front being hung with blue jean. This we pulled aside, and found, not only clothing, but an old acquaintance. I was soon in my dishabille, and as soon in full dress. We now feel comfortable; but near by is a restaurant, where they serve up beef and venison steak, chickens and turkeys, with coffee, tea, and champagne, &c., &c. Do not be impatient, dear reader, for only think what we had at our last supper and breakfast. We soon found ourselves seated at a table at the Empire, surrounded by three waiters, and I never saw waiters before that bore such a strong resemblance to guardian angels. I could hardly tell the difference. One hour after, *we* were in the same position. *We* were refreshed; our waiters were jaded; our champagne bottles were standing before us, with their mouths wide open; we were sitting down with ours in the same condition. My companion would look at me and give a knowing wink. I would wink knowingly at him. Then we would both laugh. We would fill our glasses and wink and laugh again. We were at this particular time rich and happy. We had money in our pockets, and felt that community were largely indebted to us. When we were informed at the bar that our bills were $10 each, we were surprised at the extreme moderation of our host.

We now sallied forth into the street, and spent the afternoon and evening in the most jovial manner, going the rounds of the

G. V. COOPER DEL. 1849

ON STONE BY J. CAMERON

LITH OF G. W. LEWIS 111 NASSAU ST N. Y.

SACRAMENTO CITY,

FROM THE FOOT OF J STREET.

gambling houses, theatres, &c. The gambling and eating-houses were thronged, and appeared to be doing all the business of the town. *Monte-banks* were even opened under tents, the patrons standing up to their knees in mud. The Round Tent contained eight tables, each letting for eight dollars per day. These, together with the profits of the bar, paid Mr. Weeks, the proprietor, at least $100 per day—a fair income for a tent, particularly one in which a man needs an umbrella and a pair of India rubber boots. The rain did not dampen the ardor of the operators, but caused them to treat more frequently, which gave them more ready access to their victims.

Here were gray-haired men commingling with boys in the game—profanity and dissipation—some of them having passed, perhaps, within the last twenty-four hours, from a competence to penury. A gloom seemed to pervade the countenance, revealing the reckless despondence that reigned within.

How truthfully were their feelings portrayed in the gloom of the surrounding elements. Here were young men, who, a few months previous, had left their friends and homes with vigorous constitutions, and characters unblemished, to seek their fortunes in this land of gold. A few short months had sufficed to accomplish the work of ruin. In an unguarded moment they were tempted from the path of rectitude; they visited the gaming-tables and halls of dissipation; and when the brief dream was over, they awoke and found ruin, like a demon, staring them in the face. They had neither means nor character, and their constitutions had been laid waste by the blighting hand of dissipation. Who can calculate the hours of anguish, or tears of blood that have been wrung from the hearts of bereaved parents and friends by that blighting curse.

Sacramento had become a large city (see Plate), and, next to San Francisco, the most important town in the State. It numbered at this time from twelve to fifteen thousand inhabitants. The town is regularly laid out, the streets running at right angles, many of which are closely built upon for the distance of a mile. The margin of the river is bold, and vessels of the largest class are moored to its banks. Some of them are used as stores, others as dwelling or boarding places. The steamer Senator runs up to the bank and puts out a gang-plank, which is all that is necessary for the accommodation of passengers The town at the time was submerged in mud, the streets almost impassable. Flour, pork, bread, &c., were piled up along the sides of the streets without protection. There were many surmises as to the probability of the city being flooded in case of freshet. It was said by the "oldest inhabitant" that the surrounding country, including the site of the town, had been flooded, so that canoes had been navigated as far as Sutter's Fort. Indications went to confirm his statement. There are gullies running through the town that have undoubtedly been caused by floods, and in the sequel, proved channels too small to relieve the city from inundation.

Many kinds of goods had become extremely scarce, and were selling at exorbitant prices. This was the case with woollen clothing, boots, and provisions. Common flannel shirts were selling at from $5 to $8 each; blankets at from $12 to $20 per pair; and ordinary boots from $20 to $32. Long boots of grained leather were held at, and selling for 6 ozs. ($96.) The interior, or mining regions, were entirely destitute, and merchants were in town from every point, trying to contract for the transportation of goods. Teamsters knew the country to be impassable, and although as high as $50, and even $100 per 100 lbs. was offered for a distance of fifty miles, no one would make the attempt. The consequence was, that miners were driven into town in many cases, to prevent starvation. Trade, during the latter part of the summer, and for the first one or two weeks of the rainy season, had been remarkably brisk in Sacramento City. The advance in prices of all the staple articles had enabled merchants to reap immense profits, and many, within a few weeks, had made fortunes.

The impetus to trade had come upon them unawares; some had leased their stores for short terms; others merely kept possession from day to day; but when this season of prosperity burst upon them, all were anxious to secure leases for the longest possible period. Thousands were eager to embark in trade, offering unparalleled rents—in many cases as high as $100 per day for a store. Long leases were granted at these exorbitant rents, and in consequence of the scarcity of tenements, lots were purchased—the prices predicated upon the above—buildings

G.V COOPER DEL.

ON STONE BY J. CAMERON.

LITH. OF G.W LEWIS 111 NASSAU ST N.Y.

ST. LUCAS.

LOWER CALIFORNIA. (Looking Northwest)

erected and immediately occupied. A season of prosperity had been experienced without a parallel. Men were not confined in their operations to their legitimate business, but would invest in anything that presented itself, and everything had been turned to advantage. But as soon as the rainy season cut off communication with the interior, a depression was felt, and soon an entire stagnation in all departments of business. This was not a time when the current of business could be safely checked; people had been borne to their present positions by one of the most buoyant seas; and should this pass from beneath them, the other extreme must as inevitably follow as the ebb follows the flood. This extreme was soon reached. Men found themselves with heavy stocks on hand that would not command one-half their cost. City lots that had cost them thousands, would not now command as many hundreds. Many found it impossible to pay their enormous rents, even with their gross amount of sales. A crash was inevitable, and it came; and all were buried beneath the ruins of their own structures. The elements seemed destined to complete the devastation, and on the 10th of December the city was inundated, the deluge running riot through the streets, carrying houses from their foundations, and causing the inhabitants to flee to the shipping for safety.

Chapter Twenty-third.

SAIL FOR SAN FRANCISCO—A FLEET—MUD—PROSPERITY—SHIPS AND STOREHOUSES—BUOYANT SEAS—SHOALS IN BUSINESS—REVULSION AND FIRE—THEIR CONSEQUENCES—SAIL FOR SANTA BARBARA—THE TOWN—DEXTEROUS FEAT BY A GRIZZLY BEAR—FASHIONS—SAIL FOR ST. LUCAS—PORPOISES AND SEA FOWLS, THEIR SPORTS—APPROACH THE TOWN—PECULIAR SKY—CAVERNS IN THE SEA—CACTUS—BEAUTIFUL SEA SHELLS—SAIL FOR ACAPULCO—MAGNIFICENT SCENERY—VOLCANOS AND CASCADES—VOLCANOS AT NIGHT—ETERNAL SNOW.

ON the 22d November we procured tickets on the steamboat "Senator," at $30 each, and at 8 A.M., were under way for San Francisco. We passed along down at North River speed, arriving at 5 P.M. As we passed through the bay, we were struck with the vast amount of shipping, numbering no less than five hundred sail—a fleet which, in tonnage and number of sail, was never before equalled. (See Plate.) The city had also made gigantic strides. The sand-hills had been leveled, and the city had, as it were, in a day, taken the whole of the surrounding country under its wings. Here, however, as in Sacramento City, the streets were most bountifully supplied with mud, requiring, in some cases, most dexterous movements to keep above ground.

Nothing had occurred, up to this time, to check the tide of prosperity, which had borne the citizens on, to the very acme of their ambition. Every one in trade had realized fortunes, and were still bountifully supplied with goods, some having large invoices piled outside for want of room within. Still all were ambitious to add to their stock, and were hiring money at ten per cent. a month to invest in provisions, boots, and winter clothing, all of which were commanding exorbitant prices. Chilian flour, in two hundred pound sacks, was purchased by the quantity at $40 per sack, in anticipation of a scarcity; other provisions at prices predicated upon the above. Rents were extrava-

G. V. COOPER DEL — ON STONE BY J. CAMERON — LITH OF G.W. LEWIS 111 NASSAU St N.Y

COAST OF LOWER CALIFORNIA,

Showing the peculiarity of the Sky.

gantly high, and real estate commanding unheard-of prices. Many magnificent buildings had been erected for banking-houses, hotels, and gambling saloons, all occupied—their tenants reaping daily fortunes; gamblers seemed to be on the very top wave of prosperity, and they were about the only class of citizens who confined themselves strictly to their *legitimate* business. Their saloons were swarming with people, who seemed to patronize them for want of other amusement.

The scarcity of facilities for storing goods, had induced parties to purchase ships, which after cutting away the spars, they would head in shore, run aground, and scuttle; then connecting them to the shore by piers, and building a story on the upper deck, they were ready for occupation, being less exposed in case of fire, and more easy of access, than buildings on shore. The Niantic and Apollo, ships well known in this latitude, were thus converted, but have since, together with the city, been converted into ashes. The water-lots belonging to the city were sold at auction, and purchased by parties, who immediately commenced extensive docks, and were soon in a condition to invite vessels along side. Improvements were commenced, and matured as if by magic and no cloud was discernible in the business horizon, to dampen the ardor or cause the business man to look out for a cross sea. No one was fearful of shoals, as none were laid down in their charts; all forgetting, that, no matter how buoyant a sea, it always finds a shoal upon which to break.

Business was transacted on a gigantic scale, and with an indomitable energy, but with a recklessness unparalleled. It must have been apparent to every one who looked upon these transactions with an eye of experience, that the least check to ruling prices must cause a revulsion that would prostrate the entire commercial interest of the country. Being entirely dependent upon the Atlantic cities for supplies, the market was liable to be overstocked at any moment; but business men did not seem to take this into consideration, but operated as if an embargo had been laid upon all shipments, and they were about to secure all the supplies that were ever to reach the shores of California. This was the foundation upon which business transactions were predicated, and, to finish the structure, money was hired at from ten to twelve per cent. a month, and invested. A revulsion was inevitable, and when it came it was accompanied by a conflagration that devastated the entire city. Business was paralyzed, and firms that had been thought to be worth millions, were not only penniless, but with heavy debts hanging upon them from which there was no prospect of relief. All found themselves overwhelmed with liabilities, and with a very few exceptions, none could even make a fractional dividend in favor of their creditors. One of the most extensive firms in the city, a firm that within two short weeks had considered themselves worth five millions, now found themselves indebted to almost that amount, without a dollar in hand, and nothing in prospect by which they could even expect to make a comfortable living. The partner who established the firm, became a citizen before the gold excitement. He was in the prime of life, universally beloved for his courteous and gentlemanly bearing, and one of those chivalrous spirits who never turn their backs upon a friend or foe. He was a terror to the "hounds," and other organizations of villainy, in San Francisco, and was the most effectual instrument in organizing the self-constituted police; this reverse of fortune, however, together with the loss of an accomplished and beloved wife, so preyed upon his spirits that he made an attempt upon his own life.

Miners were returning to town by scores, driven in by the scarcity of provisions, owing to the impassable condition of the country, and merchants of the interior were driven from their posts by the same cause. All could not get employment in town, and but few were able to remain in idleness; the consequence was that many sailed for the Sandwich and other Pacific islands in search of labor, or in hopes of finding a less expensive place to spend the winter. Others were preparing to return home. These causes, together with the arrival of large consignments of provisions, were soon most sensibly felt. Flour was offering in the market at $25 per sack; many having heavy stocks on hand for which they had paid $40, and with money for which they were then paying ten per cent. a month. Every steamer from the interior, as well as those clearing from the port, were crowded, and passage tickets selling at a premium. Every house in town was full; comfortable accommodations

G.V. COOPER DEL.

ON STONE BY J. CAMERON

LITH. OF G.W. LEWIS. 111 NASSAU ST N.Y.

SANTA BARBARA,

UPPER CALIFORNIA.

were out of the question. The lodging apartments were generally fitted up like state-rooms on a ship, with two berths, i. e. a little pen or box with two shelves, for each of which shelf, with board, the charge was $25 per week, occupant permitted to furnish his own bedding.

Dear reader, having a pressing business engagement at San Juan de Nicaragua, I will presume upon your leisure so far as to ask you to accompany me. I will give you a free passage, and return with you in thirty days, claiming your indulgence for the want of interest in the trip. You undoubtedly remember the excitement attending your advent on board the steamer, your last trip to sea—mine was similar. At 12 o'clock, M., we had the "heave ahead!" clanking of the cable, firing of cannon, and at half-past 12 passed through the "Golden Gate." Now our steamer makes her obeisance to Neptune, who steps aside to let her pass. On leaving the outer bay, we put our wheel "hard down," and stood away to the south, the coast range, as well as the Sierra Nevada, seeming in tears at our departure. We steam along, now raising a peak of the mountain, and now sinking it below the horizon, until the second day, when we stand in toward shore, and soon arrive in full view of Santa Barbara, presenting a fertile plain near the coast, with mountains in the background.

This is the point at which Col. Stevenson's regiment was disbanded. It is a small town hardly deserving the name, and has acquired its name and importance from its mission, the mission-house being a building of great capacity, containing a collection of valuable paintings. The front makes some pretensions to architectural beauty, with two towers, each containing two bells; between the towers, is a representation of the sun, the disc being the dial of a clock. (See Plate.) There is a fountain near the church, the water being brought from the mountain in a trench, and thrown from the mouths of grizzly bears. Why the grizzly bear was chosen by the worthy "Padre" to do the ornamental part, I was unable to learn, perhaps owing to feats of dexterity performed by his *bearship* on certain occasions.

At the time of the arrival of the California regiment, one of the *Bruin* family had taken up his residence on a *rancho*, not far distant. The natives, wishing to exhibit their dexterity, offered to go and lasso Bruin, for their amusement. Now, said Bruin had been a quiet neighbor, and had taken nothing excepting the appurtenances of said *rancho*, and had a most religious aversion to any additional *ties* between himself and neighbors. When said neighbors approached and attempted to present the subject, Bruin, as dignified people will do, stood up and looked them in the face. Six lassos were simultaneously thrown. He caught three of them, and, hand over hand, hauled the horses in, and with one stroke took off from one of them his entire haunch. The rider's cut their lassos, and, without bidding his bearship good-day, took the longest kind of steps toward the mission-house. Bruin is now supposed to be in his dotage, still he is said to relate this occurrence to his family circle with the greatest satisfaction.

Those interested in the prevailing fashions, are referred to the accompanying Plate. Ladies' hats are dispensed with; a scarf or parasol is used instead. Gentlemen wear white pants, over which is a pair of black velvet, open at the sides of the leg, the edges trimmed with bell-buttons. A short jacket of the same is also worn, trimmed with bell-buttons over which is thrown a *serapa* or *poncho*. A heavy *sombrero*, with a black glazed covering, is worn on the head; this is trimmed with brass ornaments, and a band with long ties serving as a streamer. In passing down from Santa Barbara the scenery is fine; a belt of fertile land stretching along the coast with mountains in the back ground.

After taking on board several passengers, a few head of cattle, and a small supply of vegetables, we again weigh anchor and stand out to sea; the weather is delightful, the sea rolls sluggishly, and our steamer speeds her way through the waters like a thing of life; now rushing through a school of porpoises, and now a school of flying-fish are driven from their element; now a whale throws a column of spray into the air; the sea-gulls collect around but soon disperse and flit along "gaily over the sea;" the albatrosses are floating about lazily; while Mother Carey's chickens display as much spirit as if the old lady had just let them from the coop.

As we approached St. Lucas we noticed that peculiarity of the sky for which the Pacific coast is celebrated. (See Plate.)

G. V. COOPER DEL. | ON STONE BY J. CAMERON | LITH. OF G. W. LEWIS, 111 NASSAU ST N. Y

MISSION HOUSE AT SANTA BARBARA.

The sun throws a ray of light through the mottled sky; the sea rolls sluggishly; porpoises are sporting about, now throwing themselves into the air, and now rushing into schools of flying-fish which are frightened from their element and pursued by the albatross. As we approach still nearer, immense rocks tower up from the margin of the ocean, some rising to the height of one hundred feet, some being columns of granite, presenting an appearance as uniform as if cut by the hand of man. (See Plate.) Here are seen huge rocks with arches worn through at the base by the action of the sea, sufficiently large to admit large row boats. The billows come dashing and thundering into these caverns, then recoil, chafing and foaming with the most terrific fury.

Here the sea rolls high, but with such uniformity that when breaking upon the shore the air is caught underneath, which bursting through throws up columns of spray. Three *coyotas*, members of the California Harmonic Society, are seen on the beach; they appear to be at rehearsal. Along the shore are huge cacti, growing to the height of thirty feet, being sufficiently large, and frequently used for building timber.

St. Lucas, like Santa Barbara, is hardly deserving the name of a town, containing but thirteen houses, which are constructed of adobes and cactus. The only peculiarity is that the natives speak the English Language. The surrounding country is extremely barren, producing but just enough to sustain the inhabitants; vessels touch here for water, which is superior, and beef, which is obtained back of the mountain. This town is situated at the outer point of the entrance to the Gulf of California. The time is probably not far distant when the river Gila will be navigated by steam, and the fertile plains bordering on its banks, and those of its tributaries, be brought into subjection to the plow, when this vast empire must disgorge its unbounded resources through the Gulf of California, and dispense its agricultural and mineral wealth to all parts of the civilized world. I say the time is probably not far distant; it is at hand; it is in the nature of things, that the Gila country within ten years will be a *State in the Union*. Then St. Lucas may become a city, and many others of great commercial importance will spring up along the shore of the Gulf of California, and at the mouth of the Gila will be one of the marts of the Pacific.

Our next point is Acapulco, distant about six hundred miles; this part of the route presents some of the finest scenery on the Pacific coast, and perhaps the most imposing in the world. It is a succession of volcanos, including Popocatapetl, the most elevated volcano in Mexico; this towers up through masses of clouds, appearing shrouded in gloom at its base, but rears its head in majestic triumph, offering its light to the stars.

Each of these volcanos presents some different features; from the craters of some the smoke issues with as much regularity as from a chimney; others are enveloped in smoke; some seem to have almost subdued the internal fires; the emission of smoke being almost imperceptible. The most striking phenomenon was exhibited by one of great elevation, rearing its head above the surrounding mountains, at some distance from the coast; it would belch forth a cloud of smoke, which for a moment would seem a huge ball suspended over the crater; this would soon commence to assume a different form, the lighter parts of the smoke ascending and expanding, while the more weighty would settle—elongating the cloud—giving it the appearance of a huge pine tree. This would float away on the atmosphere, and after an interval of half an hour, would be followed by its successor. The regularity of these manifestations was most astonishing; the volcano seemed to have entered into a contract with the atmosphere to furnish it with a cloud every half-hour.

The mountains in the background tower up, one above another, until the last loses itself in the blue of heaven. These seemed undergoing a constant change; now a cloud throws a deep cavern-like shade here, and now the sun chases it away, and shows us a vale watered by a mountain stream and teeming with the choicest plants of nature; now we see in the distant blue what appears a gigantic marble column; we look through a glass and it proves a cascade breaking from the crest of a mountain; now we see a mountain rearing its head into the very clouds, and shrouded in eternal snow, this reflecting the rays of the sun, appears the dome of some vast structure. Although volcanos are grand and impressive by day, nothing

C. V. COOPER DEL. — ON STONE BY J. CAMERON — LITH. OF G. W. LEWIS 111 NASSAU ST. N.Y.

ST. LUCAS,

LOWER CALIFORNIA (Looking East.)

will compare with their sublimity at night; their crests are surrounded by a halo of light, the smoke, illumined, crawls sluggishly out, and now are seen issuing balls and streams of liquid fire, accompanied by a most terrific shock, as if the furies were at war within; now a dark cloud floats sluggishly along, but now it is looking directly into the crater, and is burnished by the internal fires.

Chapter Twenty-fourth.

ACAPULCO—THE TREE OF LOVE—BATHING AND FEMALES—A CALIFORNIAN IN A TIGHT PLACE—EARTHQUAKES—SAIL FOR REALEJO—VOLCANO VIEJO—ITS DEVASTATING ERUPTION—REALEJO AND HARBOR—A CART AND ITS PASSENGERS—A WALL-STREET FINANCIER FLEECED—CHINANDEGA—ITS BEAUTIFUL ARBORS—BATHING—PREPARING TORTILLOS—LEON—ITS MAGNIFICENCE AND DESOLATION—DON PEDRO VACA AND FAMILY.

As we approach Acapulco, the most striking feature is the telegraph, which is erected on one of the highest peaks of the mountain, and from which, at the approach of a steamer, a blue flag is displayed, or a white one at the approach of a sailing vessel. The town is completely land-locked, there being not the slightest indication of it until passing around the bluff into the inner bay, when the castle is seen directly in our course, and passing on, bearing to the left, the town is seen stretching away up the side of the mountain. The bay has the appearance of a lake being entirely shut in by mountains. Our steamer passed on to within fifteen or twenty rods of the town when we dropped anchor and were immediately boarded by the officer of the port, also by innumerable men and boys for passengers, and females with fruit. Passengers are taken into bungoes, or canoes, which are headed in until the bow strikes the shore, when they take their stand preparatory to a jump as the sea runs back. (See Plate.) Not unfrequently they are overtaken by the next sea, which is extremely embarrassing, particularly if one has just changed his linen. We entered the town at the foot of the main street; two churches are seen, each supporting a tower, the custom-house being in the foreground at the left. The buildings are of one story, constructed of stone or *adobes*, and covered with tile. This is one of the most beautifully located towns on the Pacific coast. It is never visited by

G. V. COOPER DEL.

ON STONE BY J. CAMERON

LITH. OF G. W. LEWIS 111 NASSAU. ST. N. Y.

ACAPULCO.

blighting winds but is shut in by mountains, watered by mountain rivulets, and supplied with all the tropical fruits, which grow here spontaneously, and in the greatest abundance. It reminds one of the "happy valley" of "Rasselas." Along the margin of the bay are trees of peculiar shape called the "amata," or tree of love, the form of the top resembling an umbrella, under which hammocks are slung—and people enjoy their *siestas*. (See Plate). The castle is a work of some strength mounting several brass pieces of heavy calibre; it is however much neglected, being garrisoned only by a few barefooted soldiers. Just back of the town is a stream of the purest water from springs on the mountain side; this is the bathing place of the inhabitants, and a more inviting one could not be imagined; the stream is so limpid, and of such a congenial temperature, that one feels that he could repose in its bosom forever. In taking a bath it was difficult to rid ourself of the presence of a half dozen señoritas who would come to the bank, towel in hand, offering to prepare you for your clothes, for the moderate sum of sixpence. They were all beautiful, but I preferred seeing them under other circumstances. This want of modesty, as it will be termed, is a characteristic of Spanish America, and although it may show a want of refined delicacy according to the frigid laws of the States, they are entirely unconscious of impropriety.

The females here are celebrated for their beauty, finely developed forms, and graceful bearing, as well as for their vivacity and winning pathos in conversation. They possess many peerless traits of character, and manifest a devoted attachment to their parents and offspring. The full dress of a lady consists of a white chemise, a colored skirt flounced at the bottom, and a scarf which serves alternately as a shawl and bonnet.

The market is well supplied with every variety of fruit and cakes, and beef by the yard. The stands are mostly attended by females. The first salutation upon entering the market-place is from the little girls, who hail you with, "Say, Americano! lemonade, picayune?" holding up to you a plate containing a glass of lemonade, as will be seen by the accompanying Plate. At the left, in the foreground, is seen a Señora making love to an *hombre* who looks from underneath his huge *sombrero*, and seems to hold the tighter, his lemon basket and jug. Then there is little *Niña* with her picayune-lemonade, and *Muchacho* with his hat on his head, inverted, and filled with lemons. He was requested to stand for this drawing, and looked the very personation of a corn-field effigy. Then there is *Señora*, the second, standing demurely, supporting on her head, a basket of shells. Then comes one of the "immortal garrison;" he supports a high plume and long cigar. There is something extremely martial in his attitude, although he appears lame in one foot. Just behind this soldier, is a group of three; the man is a Californian; he was brought ashore by the boy, but does not seem anxious to pay his fare. The boy has his hand full of stones, by which he designs to convince the man that he had better pay. During the parley, a female runs out, and recognizing the man as having got his dinner of her without paying for it, she says, "Ah! you thought I wouldn't know you, but I do know you." This was coming too thick for the man, and, giving a kind of "b'hoy" bend of the knee, he runs both hands into his pockets, with a "well, I guess if I owe you anything, I can p-a-y." The range of buildings at the right are eating and drinking saloons. An officer is seen galloping across the plaza, with a sentinel at the left. Back of the town, an opening is cut through the mountain, presenting a very striking appearance, and is said to have been done by the Spaniards to give the town a circulation of air. Acapulco contains 3,000 inhabitants, many of whom are the native Indian race. It is somewhat subject to earthquakes, there being at present several ruins of buildings, including one church, that were prostrated a few years since.

In passing down from Acapulco to Realejo, there is a continuation of the same magnificent scenery, and as you near the harbor, you see towering up from the Cordilleras, Viejo, the most elevated volcano in Central America. (See Plate.) It is seen rearing its head above the clouds, and belching forth a column of smoke. This volcano, for many years, ceased to burn; but a few years since, the whole of the surrounding country became agitated; the air was filled for several days, with smoke so dense and black, that it entirely obscured the sun, rendering it dark as night. The inhabitants were appalled with terror, some fled the country, others collected their families and shut themselves up

G. V. COOPER DEL.

ON STONE BY J. CAMERON

LITH. OF G. W. LEWIS, III NASSAU. ST. N.Y

MARKET PLACE, ACAPULCO.

in their houses, or assembled *en masse* in the churches; beasts were seen near the habitations crouching with fear, and wild fowls were heard shrieking through the air. On the night of the third day, the country underwent another frightful convulsion, followed by a terrific explosion, when this volcano vomited forth a deluge of liquid fire, which swept down its sides, carrying devastation in its track. At this eruption, so great was the quantity of lava thrown out that part of the summit, near the crater, was carried away, as will be seen by the accompanying plate.

Realejo has a fine harbor, being situated on an arm of the ocean. As you pass in, passing an island at the entrance, you find yourself in a bay of sufficient capacity to accommodate the navies of the world. Our steamer passed up three miles to a dock which was being constructed by Howard and Son, and to which we made fast. This is one of the coal depots for the line, and preparations were making to construct suitable buildings. After landing our baggage, we engaged "bungoes" to convey us to Realejo, three miles distant, and as we passed along up, we found the margin of the bay low and swampy, and, in some places, as will be seen at the right, above the dock, forests of mango-trees growing up from the water. Several rivers put in at the head of the bay, their banks low and swampy, presenting a very unhealthy appearance.

Realejo is a town of 400 inhabitants. The houses are one story, built of *adobes*, and covered with tile. There are several churches in ruins, and one much dilapidated, but still used; the natives are the most squalid I saw in Central America, and everything is done on that behind-the-age principle that characterizes Spanish America.

At the left, in the accompanying Plate, will be seen a cart, drawn by two yoke of oxen, and lashed to their horns are sticks, four feet in length, which fall against their foreheads, and by which they draw. The cart-wheels are made by sawing two cuts from a log, and boring holes through at the heart; a pole is run through, with a linch-pin hole in each end. A rude frame of reed or cane is put on to keep the wheels from running together, and as this is covered with raw hides, it serves as a protection to the passengers in case of rain. When all are ready, the driver mounts the tongue, with a long pole, prepared to "stir up the animals;" he gives the inimitable whoop, and they are under way. When he wants them to bear to the left, he applies the end of the pole to the right-hand leader, shoves him out, and they come to, and *vice versa.* On the road there is always in attendance a little boy, whose duty it is to "grease the wheels." He is supplied with a quantity of green bark, and when the wheels creak he applies a piece; it winds around the axle, and seems to ease the pain. This, to a person accustomed to an easy carriage, would seem an uncomfortable mode of performing a journey; yet, dear reader, in this same cart, at this particular time, there is a gentleman and lady, well-known in New York circles, on their way to Nicaragua, *en route* to the United States. They are seated on their trunks, in a recumbent attitude, with heads uncovered, each drop of the wheel seeming to *give rise* to new phrenological developments.

There is a spacious hotel now being built here, and there is a prospect that the town will become Americanized. We were obliged to take lodgings at a private house. We lived on chickens, eggs, and *carna*, or beef dried in strings, and sold by the yard. At night we slung ourselves up in hammocks, at the mercy of the mosquitos. After a detention of two days, we succeeded in hiring passage, in carts, for Chinandega. Our driver was anxious to start at an early hour, and *hitched his oxen to the cart at* 2 P. M. We seated ourselves on trunks, inside, and were soon under way.

Nothing could have been more ludicrous than the appearance of the passengers, as each had assumed a peculiar attitude. Here sat a lank doctor of six feet three, his feet hanging out at the fore-end of the cart, his legs and body being warped up along the side of the covering, his head sticking out behind. On the other side, seated flat in the bottom, was a man very nearly as tall, but not half so amiable, who had somewhat the appearance of a clothes-rack unshipped, and seemed to think this a suitable occasion for the use of *hard words.* He was under oath all day, and swore himself to sleep at night. Soon after starting, our driver, with the greatest precision, brought up against a rock, which not only caused a great mortality

G. V. COOPER DEL.

ON STONE BY J. CAMERON

LITH. OF G. W. LEWIS 111 NASSAU ST. N. Y.

BARACO REALEJO.

among the hats inside, but broke our axle. Our driver hacked down a sapling with his matchet, and soon had a new one, and was again under way.

Our driver was a decided genius in his way, and with a suitable pair of pantaloons, and a clean shirt, would have done honor to Wall-street. He would hide his oxen every opportunity, and then throw a native boy in our way, who would offer to find them for $5. I need not add that the reward was divided between them. One transaction of this kind we thought quite sufficient; and in his subsequent financial transactions he was not so successful, as the sequel will show. His entire wardrobe was a shirt, which he carried in his hat. Our *muchacho*, who attended to the wheels, was much less encumbered. We gave him a shirt, which he very judiciously rolled up and tied around his neck; I say judiciously, for when he arrived at Chinandega he had a clean shirt to put on.

The country from Realejo to Chinandega, is a continuous mud-hole, and, together with the intense heat and our wretched conveyance, made our sufferings intolerable. The distance was but seven miles, still as night overtook us, and our team gave out, we were obliged to encamp before reaching the town. In the morning, our driver went out in search of the team, but soon returned, pronouncing them *unfindable*. This was most vexatious. We were almost in sight of Chinandega, but with the prospect of being detained for hours. Our driver was accompanied by a worthy, of about his own age and personal appearance. We sent our driver out again in search, but his companion remained. After loitering for half an hour, he proposed going out in search of the team, thought he could find them for five dollars; we, as if wishing to drive the best bargain we could, asked him if he could not find them for less; he came down to four, three, two, and one dollar, and finally to twenty-five cents. We took him, tied his hands behind him, then tied him to a tree; we then cut a half-dozen good sized *saplings*, designing to "put him through a course of sprouts." He was almost frantic, and seemed to look upon this as a crisis in his affairs. We asked him where the oxen were, he said, "just over the hill;" we asked him if our driver knew it, he said, "Si, Señor." We told him to call him, and in a moment he was at hand. He looked with apparent concern at the situation of his *companion*, and endeavored to keep beyond the orbit of our *saplings.* We ordered him to back up to a tree, he fell on his knees and said he would find the team in "*una momento*," and in a moment they were at the tongue of our cart; we now demanded his half of the five dollars already extorted, which he immediately paid over, and seemed to breathe more freely. We now released his companion, in part, in order to give him an opportunity to escape, which we saw he was anxious to do. He improved the golden moment, for as we were making certain demonstrations with our *saplings* he made one tremendous leap and disappeared in the chaparrals. We were soon at Chinandega, and did not forget to deduct the other two dollars and a half from our freight bill.

Chinandega is a beautiful town, well laid out, the streets running at right angles, and built upon compactly. In the suburbs, the streets are walled up, with the fluted cactus, with an occasional opening through which you enter into ornamented groves and arbors. Nothing can exceed the beauty and luxury of these retreats. Fruits of the most delicious flavor grow spontaneously, every vine blooms, and the air laden with incense, breathes through, whispering gently to the foliage; here are also innumerable tropical birds, lending their notes and plumage to the scene. This town is celebrated for its beautiful women, and never did I look upon such specimens of female grace and loveliness. Their eyes were dark and lustrous, and their countenances, like their native clime, always beaming with sunshine. The town numbers several churches and convents of great extent, one of the former being surmounted by a spacious dome and spire, (see Plate,) and furnished with an organ and valuable scriptural paintings. Near the town is a stream and pool, the favorite bathing-places of the inhabitants. (See Plate.) In the pool are seen both sexes, the Señoritas displaying their graceful forms, without the least reserve or sense of impropriety. Water is obtained here for the use of the town; bathers fill the earthen jars, when the Señoritas place them upon their heads and walk gracefully away. Here are seen a party of females preparing corn for "tortillos;" they boil it in water into which is thrown a handful of ashes; it is then put into a basket and the hull removed, by getting in with their feet; it is then washed, dried,

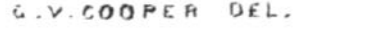

G. V. COOPER DEL. ON STONE BY J. CAMERON LITH OF G. W. LEWIS 111 NASSAU ST. N.Y.

CHURCH IN SHINANDAGUA.

and parched, placed upon a flat stone, and with another stone ground to a flour.

I engaged a cart to take myself and baggage to Grenada, but after waiting one day, with no prospect of starting, I purchased a horse, and engaged passage for my trunk in a cart that was about to start, and was soon under way. We passed through Chichigalpa, Poselagua, &c., small towns, and at night, put up at a miserable *rancho*, with the prospect of a poor supper, and poorer lodgings. We had traveled, during the day, through a level, densely timbered country, the road having been a continuous mud-hole, in many places almost impassable; I stretched myself out on a bench, half my length, and after paying court to Morpheus for an hour, fell into his arms. The next morning, at ten, we arrived at Leon, the capital of Nicaragua; we had not breakfasted, consequently this was our first care, after which we took a survey of the town.

This is a place of much importance, being the home of the aristocracy and talent of the country. It is ornamented with public buildings, churches, and convents which, for extent and magnificence, are not equalled in the country. The plaza is spacious, and surrounded by public buildings, elaborately ornamented with stucco, all indicating the work of a master-hand. My first impressions were of the most pleasing character, but upon extending my walk, a feeling of sadness insensibly stole upon me. Here, too, amidst the beauties, I might say the perfections of nature, here in this almost celestial atmosphere, is found the impress of those sanguinary revolutions, with which this doomed country has been laid waste. One half the town is in ruins. Palaces that were once the scene of regal banquests, are now roofless, and tenanted only by loathsome reptiles. Here, are figures, representing Liberty and Peace, now half-buried beneath the ruins, their faces bearing the marks of the ruthless sabre. The political, like the natural existence of this country, has always been precarious; her social elements, like her subterranean caverns, have always been in a state of agitation; the lava of human passions frequently bursting forth, devastating, and drenching the country with blood.

The inhabitants of Leon were, as a class, superior to any I had seen in the country; the men were robust, active, and intelligent, and the females beautiful. They seemed more nearly allied to the Castilian than any I had seen in any of the departments of Spanish America. Hospitality is the predominant characteristic; we frequently found ourselves under obligations, and owing debts of gratitude I fear it will never be in our power to cancel. We feel under particular and lasting obligation to Don Pedro Vaca, and family, for their unsolicited attentions. It was to them we were indebted for a bountiful repast, which was prepared and served by the accomplished daughters,

> Whose sympathetic smiles chased fatigue away,
> And changed the night of melancholy into day.

They were beautiful, and unconsciously so. I was at a loss which most to admire, the graceful forms, finely-chiseled features, lustrous eyes, and flowing hair, or that soft winning artlessness, which was so preëminently theirs. There was a daughter-in-law in the family; she was also beautiful, but her beauty was in strong contrast with that of the daughters—she having auburn hair, light eyes, and an alabaster complexion. I here fell in with Capt. B., an "old salt," who very kindly received my trunk into the cart with his own.

G. V. COOPER DEL. ON STONE BY J. CAMERON LITH. OF G. W. LEWIS 111. NASSAU ST. N. Y.

BATHEING AND WASHING CORN,

AT CHINANDAGA.

Chapter Twenty-fifth

A PROBLEM IN MATHEMATICS WORKED OUT WITH A CANE—PUEBLO NUEVA—CULTIVATING THE ACQUAINTANCE OF A HORSE—LOOKING FOR THE RIDER—AN "OLD SALT" STUCK IN THE MUD—UNCOMFORTABLE NIGHT'S REST—NAGAROTES—LAKE LEON AND THE SURROUNDING VOLCANOS—MATARES—DELIGHTFUL COUNTRY—MANAGUA—DON JOSE MARIA RIVAS—NINDAREE—RUINS OF A VOLCANO—A LONG INDIVIDUAL IN SPURS—A DILEMMA—ONE OF MY HORSE'S LEGS IN MOTION—A BOY IN A MUSICAL MOOD—ENTRY INTO MASSAYA—BLOOMERISM.

AFTER remaining three hours at Leon, we were again in motion; not, however, without the usual "*poco tiempo*." Our driver now had half a dozen "*compañeros;*" and in this country people are slow, in mathematical progression, or retrogression—what takes one half an hour to do, takes three six hours. Our captain, however, worked out this problem with his cane upon the back of one of the drivers, which produced a very different result. Our team did not get hungry, nor our drivers fatigued; the latter manifested a particular aversion to the captain's system of mathematics. The very sight of his cane would create a *stampede* among them.

Our route, during the day, lay through a densely timbered country, the road muddy, and heat excessive; our team becoming much jaded. We moved on until 11 P.M., when, finding feed, we encamped for the night; we found neither a downy pillow nor a musquito net, but were obliged to drop down in the mud at the mercy of those vile insects. Three hours of *rest* sufficed, and at 2 A.M., we were again in motion, and at nine arrived at Pueblo Nueva. Here we found nothing new, excepting that the inhabitants wore hats and pantaloons. We had breakfast and were again in motion, our route, as on the previous day, being through a densely timbered country, with extremely muddy roads. I had purchased a horse and equipage, and anticipated a pleasant day's ride. My horse and myself were strangers, but I was soon in a fair way of *cultivating* his acquaintance. The party had gone on. After arranging my saddle, I mounted, gave the word, and started, myself, but my horse did not; I applied my spur gently, but no signs of life; I applied both spurs, with the same result. I dismounted, examined the saddle, and finding all right, I again mounted; but with all my arguments I could not induce him to take the first step. Presuming there was something wrong, I again dismounted, and went into a critical examination. The saddle was properly adjusted, he had the usual number of legs, and seemed in good condition. There was nothing malicious in his eye, nor was he stuck in the mud. I cut a fair-sized cane and again mounted, but with this additional argument I could not induce him to move, although it was accompanied by the most vehement jestures. He would occasionally look me in the face, and seem to say, "I don't *exactly* understand what this means." Three natives coming along at this particular juncture, I induced them to go behind and push; their first effort caused a general relaxation of the muscular system, and the next moment my horse was on his back, his eyes rolled up, the very picture of resignation; *I* was looking around on the ground for the rider. We stood in momentary expectation of seeing him breathe his last, but he soon got up and very deliberately commenced eating; I tried to lead him, but no. As the natives were going in the same direction, we each cut a long pole and went behind, soon convincing him that he was a very fair traveler.

I soon overtook the captain, he being on foot, a short distance in the rear of the party, and informed him of the difficulty I had had with my horse. He thought it was owing to his reluctance at leaving home, and proposed to buy a half-interest, and I pay half the expenses of the cart. Two influences operated upon my mind in coming to a conclusion; one, that my trunk was already on the cart, the other that I thought one owner quite insufficient for *such* a horse. The captain mounted, and I hurried on to overtake the team. Night soon overtook us, and with it a terrific thunder storm. It was extremely dark, and we were obliged to grope about to find our way, the rain pouring down in torrents. We had distanced the captain, but he soon informed us of his locality by bawling out lustily for help. We were startled, and hurried back to his assistance, when we found him

G. V. COOPER DEL.   ON STONE BY J. CAMERON   LITH. OF G. W. LEWIS 111 NASSAU ST. N. Y.

HARBOUR OF REALAJO.

mounted, the only difficulty being that our horse imagined himself stuck in the mud. The captain had exhausted all the arguments of spurs and stogy, but could not succeed in dispelling from his mind this strange hallucination. We cut a couple of *saplings*, and after warping him "fore and aft," half a dozen times, he came to the conclusion that there must be some mistake about it, and moved on. We were destined to encounter other difficulties, for soon after overtaking our cart the axle broke, we unloaded, cut a new one, and after a detention of two hours, were again in motion.

As if to seal our fate for the night, our cart became entangled, and fastened in a mud-hole; this was a most inauspicious state of things, and to say that we were vexed is using a tame term. There is always one alternative, in our case there were two; we could either stand up in the rain, or lay down in the mud; we chose the former, and as soon as it was sufficiently light, disentangled our cart, and at nine arrived at Nagarotes.

We were in a sad plight to make our appearance among bright eyes. We were in a similar condition to the individual who had not slept any for three nights—last night, to-night, and to-morrow night, with the addition, in our case, of having been thoroughly saturated with rain. Our driver, as if to show his superior wisdom, took his hat from beneath a rawhide in the cart, and dressed in dry pants and shirt, the first clothing he had had on since our first acquaintance with him. Nagarotes is a miserable town; the inhabitants a mixture of Spanish and Indian, the latter predominating. They are all extremely robust and healthy in appearance.

After breakfast we moved on, and at 12 M. arrived at Lake Leon. The appearance of this lake as it opened to our view was peculiarly striking. It is shut in by lofty mountains, which tower up in innumerable peaks of volcanic origin, from many of which the smoke curls gracefully out, commingling with the clouds. From the center of the lake rises an island of conical form, which towers up as if to look into the surrounding craters. While our driver was feeding his team we prepared for a bath. We were, however, much disappointed in the anticipated pleasure, finding the heat of the water almost insufferable. Our first sensation was that of pain, and we were soon again in our clothes. This phenomenon added a peculiar interest; the lake seemed a huge cauldron, steaming over an invisible furnace, the surrounding craters serving as flues or chimneys.

We passed along down to Matares, a small town situated on an eminence overlooking the lake, and inhabited by descendants of the African race. We breakfasted on chickens, *frijoles*, *tortillos*, eggs, &c., and after an hour's detention started for Managua. We passed through a delightful region of country, the soil, in many places, highly cultivated, bearing the impress of thrift and industry, I had not before seen in the country. Fruits grow in abundance, cattle had an unlimited range, and were the finest I ever saw; the country was broken, the mountains towering up to the clouds, and some covered with perpetual snow; but at their base were vales watered by mountain rivulets, and shaded by groves of orange and fig, seeming a retreat fit for the angels.

Night overtook us, and we encamped on the bank of the lake; starting early in the morning we descended a hill, being the immediate bank of the lake, and at sunrise arrived at Managua, which is situated at the foot of the lake. We breakfasted with Don Jose Maria Rivas. He was a man of much intelligence, and seemed to feel a lively interest in the affairs of the United States, as well as those of his own country. He alluded to General Taylor's career, and spoke of his death as a national calamity. We could not prevail upon him to accept remuneration for our breakfast, but pressed it upon a member of the family. We hope we may some day have the honor of serving the worthy Don at our own board.

After a detention of two hours, we were again under way, passing through a most delighful country, with highly cultivated plantations, watered by rivulets running from the mountains. We passed along on the margin of the stream which connects Lake Leon with Lake Nicaragua, running in the direction of the latter. After a fatiguing day's march night overtook us, and our driver very considerately got the cart fast in another mud-hole. We encamped, and soon had the satisfaction of hearing the rumbling of distant thunder, and soon were wet to the skin. In the morning at sunrise we were at Nindaree; soon after leaving this town we came to what appeared the *ruins* of

G. V. COOPER DEL.

ON STONE BY J. CAMERON

LITH. OF W. C. LEWIS 111 NASSAU ST. N. Y.

OUR ARRIVAL AT MASAYA.

a volcano. It had consumed itself to its very base, and the surrounding country was strewn with lava, which, in color and form, much resembled blooms or pigs of iron. We moved on, and soon saw indications of the city of Massaya.

I had two companions who were mounted on donkeys. (See Plate). Our *long* friend was obliged to hold up his feet to keep them from dragging on the ground; he wore spurs, but they were, *at first*, of no use to him; when he would raise his feet to apply them, they would be so far *aft* they would not touch the animal; he, however, with Yankee ingenuity, put them on just below the knee; this had a perceptible influence, enabling him to lead the party.

We were disposed to make as favorable an impression upon our *entrée* as possible. My other companion had hoisted his umbrella, and got his donkey well waked up; I had been leading *our* horse all the morning, wishing to make my advent on a *fresh* animal. As we were about to ascend the hill I mounted; my horse at this moment was seized with a most voracious appetite. I applied my spurs, which only seemed to give him a keener relish for the grass. I pulled upon the bridle—it seemed to open his mouth the wider, but go he would not. My companions had left me, and even the cart had passed; and now a party of females, laden with corn for the market, walked leisurely by, not, however, without giving a mischievous wink at my perplexity. This was too much; I dismounted, cut a heavy stick, and again mounted. Under the influence of this, he seemed to devour small brush with the greatest avidity. I must confess I felt cornered; what to do I did not know. I hailed a native lad who was passing, and requested him to go behind and push; this the horse seemed to think derogatory to his *standing*, and raising one of his hoofs, he struck the lad about *midships;* the precise number of summersets he turned, I am not prepared to say. He soon gained his feet, and, in a most musical mood, took the longest kind of steps in the direction of a *rancho*, where, no doubt, his mother lived.

One of the horse's legs having got in motion, I applied, most vigorously, spurs and cudgel, and soon the other three started, and I was under way at a rapid pace. I soon gained the summit of the hill, when my horse raised his head, pricked up his ears, and with his nostrils distended looked a very Bucephalus. Never did I make a more auspicious entrée into a city than on this occasion; the natives stood all agog, and even the Bloomer-clad señoras, that had looked upon me sneeringly but a few moments before, now courtesied with veneration. *Apropos* of Bloomerism—this is the prevailing fashion in Central America; it has become so deeply rooted that it will be difficult to eradicate it. I would recommend this as a favorable retreat for ladies of the North who wish to dispense with the long robe.

Chapter Twenty-sixth.

MASSAYA—THE CARNIVAL—FEMALE LABORS—GOURDS—MAIDENS CONSIGNED TO A VOLCANO—A DONKEY "NON EST"—OX *versus* DONKEY—SAME MEDICINE PRESCRIBED—LAKE NICARAGUA—GRENADA—A "PRIEST" IN A CONVENT—"OUR" HORSE—A GROUP OF ISLANDS—CROSS THE LAKE—MR. DERBYSHIRE'S PLANTATION—BREAKFAST—BULLOCKS STEPPING ON BOARD—SAIL FOR SAN CARLOS—MAGNIFICENT SCENE—A HYMN OF THANKS—A MOUNTAIN CITY—GOLD MINES—ARRIVAL AT SAN CARLOS—CUSTOM-HOUSE REGULATIONS REPUDIATED.

AFTER breakfast we strolled about to see the town; the location is commanding, being on the bank of a lake of the same name. The town is large, well laid out, with an open plaza in the centre, which serves as a market-place. At this time everything wore a business-like appearance. Extensive preparations were being made for the carnival, which was to come off in a few days. Here are many fine buildings, including churches, monasteries, and convents, all elaborately ornamented, and decorated with paintings.

This is considered one of the most pleasant towns, if not the most pleasant, in the country. Yet, strange as it may seem, it is wholly dependent, for water, upon the lake, the bank of which is a perpendicular ledge of rocks, one hundred feet in height. Up this precipice females are toiling, day after day, for life, in the service of inhuman masters. The water is conveyed in gourds of immense size, which are held to the back by a strap and netting of grass, the former passing over the forehead. These gourds grow on trees, and are natives of the tropics; they grow sufficiently large to contain one and a half or two gallons, perhaps more.

The surrounding country is a mass of lava, the mountains frequently towering up, terminating in volcanic peaks, the most prominent being that of Massaya. This was once the terror of the country, but has now ceased to burn. It is said that the natives formerly, in order to appease its rage, were in the habit of consigning their most beautiful maidens to its terrific bosom. After stopping two hours we were again under way, *en route* to Grenada, distant twelve miles.

The country is rolling, and timbered with cedars, our route laying along a stream emptying into Lake Nicaragua. After traveling six miles we encamped for the night. In the morning our companion's donkey was *non est;* there were three drivers now in the party; four *reals* was the first charge for finding said donkey; the proposition being readily accepted by the owner, they thought it was worth *five*; this being accepted, six were demanded, or two *reals* each for the drivers. Now, we still had fresh in our minds a certain transaction, the subject of which was an ox instead of a donkey. After a word of consultation we came to the conclusion, that notwithstanding the disparity in the length of ears, the same remedy might prove effectual in both cases. We immediately acted upon this hypothesis, and prepared a liberal dose of *saplings*, and in order that the medicine might reach the system *unadulterated*, we ordered them to take off their shirts. The medicine proved too strong for their nerves, even before tasting it, and forgetting the *reals*, they assured us that they would have "*mula aqui una momento*," and in five minutes his donkeyship was under the saddle. It was the donkey belonging to our *long* friend, and it was shrewdly suspected that he (the above-named donkey) was in collusion with the drivers. Whether the accusation was true or false, I am not prepared to say; I noticed, however, that in the course of the morning his master administered to him a dose of the same kind of medicine.

At 9 A. M., we were on the banks of Lake Nicaragua, at Grenada. This is a beautifully located town, with paved streets, and magnificent churches. A description of one town in Central America describes them all. They are all built upon the same plan, with spacious plazas in the centre;—extensive churches and convents, all after a similar order of architecture, some of them ornamented with a degree of splendor seldom surpassed, if equalled, on this continent. The streets, when paved, are paved with cobble-stone, with the gutter in the center. This mode has its advantages when carriages are seldom used.

We here found an American, Mr. Priest, of Philadelphia, who had just entered a convent; not, however, with a view to taking the veil, but to take down the superfluous crosses and ornaments, preparatory to converting the building into a hotel. The building had attained the advanced age of two hundred and forty years; it seemed almost sacrilege to divest it of its ornaments. The natives were accustomed to seeing priests enter convents, but they looked upon the demonstrations of our Philadelphia Priest with a suspicious eye.

In Spanish America, a horse that is led through the street is always considered "up" for sale. We hired a *muchacho* to lead ours through Grenada, and soon had several applicants. One, wishing to try him, mounted, and the horse being thirsty, walked very deliberately down to the lake, and waded in until the water came up to his sides. After remaining for a certain length of time, the rider pulled on the reins, and invited the horse to step ashore; but, no—he was perfectly satisfied with his situation, and did not wish to change it. He applied the spurs—the horse appeared to have fallen into a quiet slumber; he swore in Spanish, but it was of no use. There was no alternative but to dismount, and wade or swim ashore. He reached the shore in safety, but did not buy the horse. We offered him to Mr. Priest for six dollars, including saddle, bridle, and spurs. He offered two, at which price we "closed him out."

Our first efforts were directed to hiring conveyance to San Carlos and San Juan; we applied to Mr. Derbyshire, an English merchant from Jamaica, and succeeded in hiring a *bungo* of sufficient capacity to carry our party of fifteen, including baggage. There were two other *bungoes*, hired by Americans that were to be our company down; and after a protracted and vexatious detention of two days, the time of starting arrived. We now, however, had a new and unexpected difficulty to encounter, the boatmen refused to go on board; but after a long parley, a complaint was lodged with the Alcalde, who ordered out a file of soldiers, they forming in line along the river bank to protect the agents, while they were *whipping* the boatmen on board. At length the oars were plied, and we shot out into the lake, and laid our course for a group of islands three miles distant, in order to lay in a stock of plantains for the voyage. This group number one hundred islands, each having one house and one proprietor. Nothing can excel the beauty and fertility of this group; tropical fruits grow spontaneously and in the greatest abundance, and the islands seem to nestle, with feeling security, in the bosom of this lake, which sleeps in perpetual calm. The foliage is most luxuriant, interlaced with vines bearing flowers of every conceivable hue; these flowers generally hang from the vines on tendrils, and spend their hours fondling with the air, loading its breath with perfume. The trees grow to the very margin of the lake, and seem to look admiringly into the mirror at their feet.

Remaining during the night we took an early start, laying our course in the direction of Mr. Derbyshire's plantation, which is on the opposite side of the lake, thirty miles distant. Our mission here, or that of our boatmen, was to take in cattle for the San Juan market. We arrived early in the morning of the second day from the islands. Our ambitious boatmen would work only in the evening and morning; in the middle of the day they would lay and broil in the sun.

We arrived at an early hour, and commenced preparing breakfast. We had chickens, and rice, and chocolate on board; we sent to the plantation for eggs, milk, and bananas, and soon sat down to a breakfast that would have pleased the most fastidious palate. The manner in which it was served I am not prepared to say was quite so satisfactory. (See Plate.) One was sitting on a rock, drinking his coffee from a tin basin; another standing up, doing likewise; a third holding a chicken by a leg and wing, trying to dissect it without the use of edged tools. One of our party has finished his breakfast, and is sitting on a rock, in a very aldermanic attitude, smoking a pipe, probably the only one ever introduced into Central America.

While we were taking breakfast, the natives were taking in a cargo of bullocks; the manner was truly Spanish. The bungoes were anchored a short distance from shore, the cattle were driven as near as convenient, when one of them would be *lassoed*, the other end of the lasso being fastened to the horse's neck; the horse is mounted and spurred into the lake, drawing the victim after him, which, in case of resistance, is unmercifully beaten. The horse tows him around on the seaward side of the

G. V. COOPER DEL. ON STONE BY J. CAMERON. LITH. OF G. W. LEWIS 111 NASSAU ST. N. Y.

BREAKFASTING ON SHORE,

bungo, when the lasso is slipped and the bullock beaten and *booted* until he jumps on board. Two passengers of this class will be seen cozily chewing their cuds in the midships of the two *bungoes* in the foreground, and one is just *stepping on board* that on the right. In the background is seen a party of natives, cooking and eating breakfast. They put rice and plantains together into an iron pot, and stew them into a chowder which is served out in small gourds. After spending an hour on shore, there was a simultaneous move to go on board; the inexpressibles of some were rolled up, others pulled off. Before starting we saw one native moving towards the *bungo*, and one only; he was dressed in nature's garments, with a palm-leaf hat in his hand, and a bunch of stolen bananas on his shoulder. On arriving at the side of our bungo, we found the best apartments occupied by his bullockship, to which we immediately protested, as contrary to the rules of polite society; not that we wished to limit any one of the passengers in the number of legs used, but then his head-dress was "positively shocking," and might put us to great inconvenience in a case of emergency. Our first impulse was to show him the depth of water on our larboard quarter, but then he seemed quiet, and as he was engaged to appear at the table of nobility at San Juan, we resolved to submit to the inconvenience, and let him ride. We soon slipped our cables, and were under way in the direction of San Carlos. Nothing can exceed the magnificence and beauty of the scene that now surrounds us. Mountains are climbing one above the other, until the last is lost in the clouds; the lake is studded with islands, some reposing modestly in her bosom, others rearing their heads as if trying to vie with the surrounding mountains. Now night throws her sable mantle over the scene, and all is hushed as death; the surrounding volcanos light their watch fires, and loom up in the most terrific grandeur. In the morning our boatmen rose up from their seats, and, in a wild strain, chanted a hymn of praise to God for protection to themselves and "los Americanos."

In the course of the morning we passed in sight of a town, which was situated on the side of the mountain, at a great elevation, presenting a most picturesque appearance. We also saw miners at work in the gold mines, on the side of the mountain. As we drew near San Carlos, we saw several volcanos rising, in pyramidal form, from the bosom of the lake; one, that of Omotepeque, towering up to the height of six thousand feet. (See Plate.)

On our arrival at San Carlos we were required to submit to custom-house regulations, the officer insisting upon searching our trunks. To this we demurred, having passed through the entire country without submitting to such an ordeal. The officer seeming anxious to compromise the matter, demanded $5 in stead from each; the Americans who had preceded us submitted to this extortion, but we were determined to resist. The officer became more moderate, coming down—down—down—to a *real;* upon our refusing to pay this, he made a move in the direction of the cannon which was near; we, however, were first to possess it, and things for the moment wore a warlike appearance. The officer, not wishing to bring things to a crisis, held a consultation with our "Padrone," and came to the conclusion that all was right, that as we were Americans he would treat us with due consideration. At the left, in the Plate, is seen the residence of this worthy officer, behind which is the village of San Carlos.

G.V. COOPER DEL. ON STONE BY J. CAMERON LITH. OF G. W. LEWIS, 111 NASSAU ST N.Y

SAN CARLOS NICARAGUA LAKE

Chapter Twenty-seventh.

PASSAGE DOWN THE SAN JUAN RIVER—CASTILIAN RAPIDS—THE "DIRECTOR"—ARRIVAL AT SAN JUAN—BOARDED BY A POSSE OF NEGROES—BRITISH PROTECTORATE—PHILANTHROPY OF GREAT BRITAIN—HER MAGNANIMOUS AND DISINTERESTED CONDUCT TOWARDS THE NATIONS OF THE EARTH—NICARAGUA GRACIOUSLY REMEMBERED—A HUNT FOR A SOVEREIGN—A FULL-GROWN KING DISCOVERED—HIS DIPLOMACY—INVINCIBILITY—AMUSEMENTS AND CORONATION—HIS FIRST PAIR OF PANTALOONS—HAIL "KING OF THE MUSQUITO COAST" !!!—ALL HAIL JAMACA I. !!!—"HEAR! HEAR!!!"

WE were soon on board, and passing around a point, were floating down the San Juan river at the rate of five knots. After a two hour's run our boatmen unshipped their oars, and commenced gambling; we were borne along by the current, at the rate of two miles an hour, until toward evening, when the oars were again manned. At nine in the evening, the roar of the water admonished us that we were approaching the Castilian rapids, and we came to anchor. The natives have a dread of this rapid, and in passing it feel that their lives are in imminent peril; in this case, however, a party of boatmen forgetting themselves in sleep, passed over, and in the morning found themselves entangled in the bushes, along the margin of the river. We descended the rapid, finding the steamboat "Director," in the act of ascending; she was making her first passage up, preparatory to taking her place on the lake for the transportation of passengers, in connection with Vanderbilt's Line of steamships. The passage up the rapid was very difficult, owing to the strong current, being about six knots; she however succeeded, and is now plying on the lake. We passed down, and at two the next morning came to anchor in the harbor of San Juan.

At an early hour in the morning we were boarded by a posse of negroes, whose mission it was to search our baggage for fire-arms; they succeeded in finding two rusty guns belonging to our padrone, which they carried off in triumph. It is well known that this harbor is under the protectorate of Great Britain, and our worthy visitors were subjects of Her Majesty, as well as of His Majesty of the "Mosquito Coast." They seem in fear of an army from Grenada, hence this precaution.

The town consists of about fifty thatched houses, tenanted by French, English, German, Spanish, and Negroes. Things here are, in a measure, *reverso;* a negro is agent for Great Britain—his boots are blacked by a white man. We found a British man-of-war in port, which is kept here to enforce their *wholesome regulations.*

The philanthropy of Great Britain has become proverbial. There is scarcely a port on the European continent that has not heard the music of her cannon, and been relieved of its surplus treasures. Three-fourths of a century ago, she *succeeded* in establishing, on the American continent, the government of the United States, and a few years thereafter voluntarily offered the use of a fleet and army at New Orleans, a part of which was *used*, the balance returned. Mexico has also been a recipient of her kind attentions. She has taken possession of the richest mines in Mexico, and worked them *gratuitously*, sending off millions under the protection of the "red cross of St. George." Her sappers and miners have found their way to Peru and Chili, as well as other divisions on the Pacific coast of South America, the mines of all of which have been taken possession of, and worked on the same *accommodating* terms as those of Mexico. She sent a fleet *free of charge* to the Argentine Republic, took possession of her ports, and *forced* the navigation of her rivers. Texas, after emerging from her glorious struggle for liberty, was offered the kind wing of protection; Great Britain even going so far as to offer her assistance in maintaining a separate republic, thinking annexation to the United States inexpedient. She visited China in the capacity of doctor, and most magnanimously forced her prescription down their unwilling throats. Her philanthropic eye next took a survey of Central America. Here she found governments of that *odious* form called republican, that of Nicaragua having an extent of sea coast, with accessible ports, and numerous rivers.

No one, up to this time, had interfered with the jurisdiction

G. V. COOPER DEL. ON STONE BY J. CAMERON LITH. OF G. W. LEWIS 111 NASSAU ST. N. Y.

SAN JUAN DE NICARAGUA

of Nicaragua, nor was her claim to this coast ever disputed. Great Britain, in her superior wisdom, however, decided that as Nicaragua had no particular use for seaports, they would be better in other hands, even if *she herself* should be *compelled* to assume the protectorate. The first step necessary to accomplish this magnanimous object was to find a suitable *sovereign*. She is supposed to have embarked in the search with her characteristic zeal and energy; it is presumed that the first inquiries were made at San Juan. At first the prospect of success was not flattering, but fortunately inquiries were made of a native Indian, who very innocently informed Her Britannic Majesty's agent that his chief was sojourning along the "Mosquito Coast."

What could have been more opportune? This was precisely the individual sought; here was a great man, a chief, in actual possession of the country, i. e., he had actually hunted 'possums there for a period of six months! The matter was immediately decided upon, and arrangements made to pay the monarch a visit on the following day, preparatory to his coronation. Artizans were employed in the manufacture of presents suitable for one who seemed pointed out by the finger of Providence to wear the "purple and ermine." Tin pans were immediately transformed into crowns and collars, sardine boxes into breastplates and stars, pill-boxes into ear and finger-rings, and "extinguishers" into ornaments for the nose. These, after a revision by chamois and soap-stone, were safely boxed, that they might not be tarnished by the touch of vulgar hands. A demijohn was filled with rum—as was supposed, to prevent his *Majesty* from fainting under the operation of putting on *his first pair* of pantaloons.

Early on the following morning, the ship having been ordered to drop along down the coast, the party were in motion under the pilotage of the Indian above mentioned. What momentous results sometimes attend the acts of individuals in the humble walks of life! This poor Indian, having been driven to the shore by hunger, had, while making a meal of raw fish, imparted a word, which single word was the means of bringing forth to the world a full-grown king. What were the feelings of this native, as he cut his way through the chaparrals? Had he aspirations? No doubt he had! In his wild delirium of pleasure, he, no doubt, dreamed of a canoe of his own, and a raw hide to sleep on; instead of going naked, as he had done all his life, he might have a red bandana to tie around his neck; he thought of abundance of broiled lizard, with plantain cooked in 'possum fat for dessert. With such bright visions in the future, it is not astonishing that, in wading swamps and cutting through chaparrals, he distanced those under his pilotage.

Nor was there a want of zeal on the part of Her Britannic Majesty's agent. He too had aspirations. He was on a mission which, if successful, must result in incalculable benefit to the world in general, and to Her Britannic Majesty's government *in particular*. If successful, knighthood was the least he could expect, with the prospect of a niche, eventually, in Westminster Abbey.

Never were mortals more eager for immortality, nor was it ever more clearly within their reach; for even now, at this point in the drama, the very dogs of his *Majesty* seemed to proclaim it—the *royal* encampment was in sight. The party deployed into a single file, and prepared to approach *the presence*. They took the *monarch* by surprise; he was stretched out at full length, on a "highly-scented" raw hide, under the shade of a palm-tree, as naked as he came into the world. He was amusing himself by trying to "get up" a fight between a parrot and a young monkey; his squaw was broiling a couple of lizards or *guanas*, and roasting plantains for dinner.

The interview was at first embarrassing, but after consulting the demijohn, they seemed imbued with a more fraternizing *spirit*, and commenced conversation on the subject of empire, and the prerogative of kings. Her Britannic Majesty's agent felt himself a man of importance, and at first seemed somewhat patronizing; but the *monarch* had consulted the demijohn too often to be outdone, and, as a proof of his invincibility, he exhibited a huge turtle, which had fallen a victim to his *machet;* he had climbed a tree that none of his men could climb, and caught sixteen "'possums," all hanging by the same tail from the same limb; he had taken his biggest dog by the tail, and swung him around his head three times, and declared he would do it again for their amusement. "Carlo" was immediately seized by the tail, but feeling a little sensitive, he curled up, bit

G. V COOPER DEL. ON STONE BY J. CAMERON LITH. OF G. W. LEWIS, 111 NASSAU ST. N. Y.

THE HARBOUR AT SAN JUAN,

NICARAGUA.

his master, and escaped. This led to a spirited footrace, and as "Carlo" dodged, the *monarch* slipped, his head coming in contact with the root of a tree. He seemed *discouraged*, and made no effort to regain his feet. The Englishman felt that he had committed a *faux pas* in allowing him free access to the demijohn, and resolved to defer negotiations until the following day. He immediately repaired to the shore, and hoisted a signal for the ship's boat.

On the following morning, the boat was again sent ashore, with an invitation for the *monarch* to visit Her Majesty's ship. Feeling as individuals will feel *next day*, he *graciously* accepted the invitation. A detail of what transpired on board has never been made public, *reporters* having been excluded. In the after-part of the day an unusual demonstration was made, flags were displayed, cannon fired, and as the band struck up "Hail to the Chief," an individual was seen descending the side of the ship, with a tin crown on his head, and a pair of red flannel pantaloons under his arm. On reaching the boat he took his position astride a barrel of rum, and moved toward the shore in triumph, having been crowned "King of the Mosquito Coast." All hail, Jamaca I. ! ! ! It is well known that Great Britain immediately recognized the government, and assumed the protectorate; hence the presence of the "red cross" at San Juan.

The distance from San Juan to Realejo is about three hundred miles. Passengers going the Nicaragua route now take a steamboat at San Juan, which runs up to the Castilian Rapids; then, after a portage of half a mile, another steamboat takes them up the river to San Carlos; thence across Lake Nicaragua to Virgin Bay. Then by pack-mules they are taken to San Juan del Sud, on the Pacific. The distances on the river and lake are about equal, being about seventy-five miles each, and from twelve to fifteen miles by land. There is every facility for crossing here, there being several steamboats plying on the river and lake. Steamships enter the mouth of the San Juan River, and the river boats come along side, consequently passengers incur no expense in the transfer, and are not obliged to land, as the small steamboats take them immediately up the river. This route has the advantage, in distance, over the Panama route, of about one thousand miles; still, the passage from

San Francisco to New York has, as yet, been acccomplished in the shortest time by way of Panama.

Now, dear reader, having finished my business here, I am ready to return. I will not trouble you to make the journey back to Realejo in a cart, but as I promised to accompany you, we will take one *psychological* leap, and salute our national flag in the main plaza of San Francisco.

G. V. COOPER DEL.

LITH. OF G. W. LEWIS, 111. NASSAU ST. N. Y.

CASTLE AT ACAPULCO.

Chapter Twenty-eighth.

SAIL FOR HOME—PASS THE "GOLDEN GATE,"—SAD CONDITION OF THE PASSENGERS—GRAVES AT THE BASE OF THE SNOWY MOUNTAINS—LAND RECEDES—LUXURIES ON BOARD—A DEATH AND BURIAL—ANOTHER DEATH—WHALES AND PORPOISES *versus* SERPENTS OF FIRE—THUNDER STORM—DEATH OF DOCTOR REED—THREE DEAD BODIES FOUND ON BOARD—THE SCURVY—FIVE OF THE PASSENGERS INSANE—EVILS OF THE CREDIT SYSTEM—A CULTIVATED MIND DERANGED—MEMORY LOST—ITS CAUSE—THE VICTIM UPON THE VERGE OF DEATH—HARPOONING PORPOISES—EXCITING SPORT.

I HAD designed to leave San Francisco for home in the steamer of the 1st December, and had purchased my ticket with that view; but the steamer, being a foreign bottom, was unable to clear for another port in California, and having but small capacity for coal, I feared detention, and was induced to sell my ticket, and take passage in the ship Edward Everett, which was to sail on the 28th November, and which, I felt confident, would reach Panama in advance of the steamer. We were notified to be on board at 9 A.M; and when Mr. Fairchild and myself reached the shore with our baggage, we saw the ship two miles out just preparing to swing from her moorings. We engaged two hardy "tars," and were soon pulling off for her; we threaded our way through the shipping, and were doing our utmost as we saw the anchor of the Everett already up, her foresail aback, and she "turning on her heel," preparatory to standing out to sea. We boarded her as she was under way. We passed the clipper-ship Architect, which was just weighing anchor for Valparaiso; the captains saluted each other through their trumpets, and we passed on through the Golden Gate, with a fair breeze, assisted by the unerring ebb tide. The passengers, eighty in number, were all on deck to take a last look at the receding landscape.

It had been but a few short days since they first beheld this scene—since they first entered through this "Gate," into the land of promise. They now look upon the same narrow passage, the same bold rocky coast, they had looked for with so much anxiety, and greeted with so much enthusiasm. But how different the feelings now! what a change! They were then accompanied by a brother or a friend, with high hopes and vigorous constitutions, looking forward with brilliant anticipations. But now the brother and friend are sleeping quietly at the base of yonder snow-capped mountain, and they are bearing the sad intelligence to the bereaved parents, brothers, and sisters. Instead of the vigorous constitutions, they are obliged to cling to the rigging for support, while they gaze for the last time upon the scene. With many it is the last time they are to view such a scene; their eyes are about to close upon the earth forever, to sleep beneath the bosom of the ocean. Many have not only sacrificed health, but are destitute of means, and are now reeling about the ship, endeavoring to earn their passage by their labor. Our ship seemed a hospital; three-fourths of all the passengers were invalids, some of them helpless. We drifted away before the wind, the mountains gradually disappearing from the horizon; one had lingered long, but as we descended from the crest of a mountain wave, we bid *it* also, a last farewell. We spent the afternoon in adjusting our baggage, and the night in sleep; the morning dawned brightly—we were still under a full press of canvas, with a fair wind. All on board had taken passage under the impression that the accommodations were superior, for which they had paid extra. We consequently felt that we were well provided for, and fairly embarked on our voyage home. As usual the first day at sea, but little attention was paid to the cook, the passengers remaining cozily ensconced in their berths.

The 30th was ushered in with a fine breeze, and we were standing on our course. At noon we found the table supplied with hard bread (sea-biscuit) and salt beef, dainties that our stomachs did not relish; the same table was kept standing for supper. Captain Smith was interrogated in reference to his supply of provisions, for which we had paid him extra; he replied that he was abundantly supplied with the above, which, if we chose, we could have served up every day during the voyage; when too late, we learned that the delicacies for the sick, with which he had by public notice proclaimed his ship abundantly supplied, were "*non est.*" He had not even a pound of fruit on board; the invalids felt this privation most sensibly many of whom had come on board without supplies, having been led to believe by advertisements, that the ship had been furnished with a direct view to the comforts of those returning in ill-health. From the fare with which our table was supplied, it was impossible for a weak stomach to extract sufficient nutriment to sustain life. This was soon manifest, as those who were destitute immediately commenced to decline, and were soon confined to their berths. We could plainly see that the lives of some were fast ebbing away.

On the 6th December, in lat, 22° 50', North, it was announced that G. W. Ray, of Maine, was dead. He died at 10 A.M; the gang-plank was placed, one end extending over the side of the ship, supported by the rail, the other supported by a cask, over this was thrown a piece of canvas, upon which was placed the corpse. A rope was tied around the body; thence, passing down was tied around the ancles, and to the end was attached a canvas bag, filled with sand. The body was then sewed up in the canvas, over which was thrown the ensign of California. The passengers now surround the corpse, with heads uncovered. A prayer is read by the captain, the ensign is removed, and at the word one end of the plank is raised, and the body passes gently into its grave. We are under a full press of canvas with an eight knot breeze; the last bubble rises to the surface, and the wind passes mournfully through the shrouds, as if sighing his last requiem.

At 8 P.M., of the same day, another death was announced. Deceased, Mr. Cook, was a young man from Sag Harbor, where he left a wife and child. One hour after the announcement of his death, he was consigned to the grave, that had so recently opened to receive his unfortunate companion. He was buried in Lat. 20° 50', N.

We were surrounded during the day (7th) by whales and porpoises, and during the evening, as they would pass through the "luminous animalculæ," they would present the appearance of enormous serpents of fire. On the 8th we were visited by a terrific thunder storm, accompanied by heavy winds. We run under close-reefed topsails; and when the storm clears up we find the wind dead ahead, and are obliged to run several days sharp on the wind.

On the morning of the 14th another death was announced; the deceased, Dr. Reed, of Massachusetts, had been, for some days, conscious of his approaching end, and manifested a strong desire to have his remains conveyed to his friends. This was his last and almost only request; the fear that this might not be complied with seemed to linger with him to the last, and died only with his last pulsation. He received some encouragement from the captain, but one short hour after his death, he followed his unfortunate companions to the grave. He was buried in Lat 16° 3′ N.

A report is in circulation that there are dead bodies on board. On inquiry, we learn that there are three—a man, a woman and child; they were preserved in casks of spirits, and being conveyed to the States. This created the greatest consternation in the minds of the sailors, and they unanimously resolved to leave the ship at the first port. They have a superstitious idea that vessels cannot be safely navigated with dead bodies on board. Many of the passengers were confined to their berths, some of them destined never again to leave them, until removed by death. The scurvy had appeared in its worst form, and there was nothing on board to relieve its victims. The food served out was most execrable; those in robust health were pining away, and for the invalids, there was no hope. Among the latter there were five who were deranged; they were all confined to their berths, and seemed waiting to be relieved by death. There is a physician on board, (whose father and captain Smith are sole owners of the ship), his services, however, are not at the disposition of all. The captain has flour, but pretends it does not belong to the ship, and refuses to serve it out to the passengers. He, however, offered to sell it, and two or three of us joined and bought a quantity of him, together with a quantity of sugar; all to be paid for in Panama, at Panama prices, and for all of which we *never had the most distant idea* of paying him a farthing. We hired the cook to prepare it for us, and thereafter were well served. With this supply, we were in a condition to inyite the invalids to our table, where we could furnish them something more palatable than sea-biscuit and salt beef.

My attention was attracted to one of the passengers, who, upon my inquiring for Spanish books, offered me one of Spanish comedy; there was something polished in his manners, yet something wayward, which very much excited my interest. His clothes were good, still, in his helplessness, they had become extremely filthy. He commenced conversation, but soon stopped for a moment, as if trying to recollect himself; and said he believed he had entirely lost his mind, that his ideas were so incoherent, he feared he could not make himself understood. He first inquired where the ship was bound; I informed him, and asked him how he came on board. He did not know, but said he was informed that he was to be sent home; he did not know why, nor from whom he received the information. He wished me to converse with him, and try to set him right; he gave me the keys to his trunks, and wished me to open them. I found them stored with clothing of the best quality, together with a well selected library of books, mathematical instruments, and materials for drawing: everything indicating a man of refinement and education. In his writing desk I found a patriotic poem, composed and read by him, on board the ship in which he sailed for California: on the anniversary of our national independence. I also found a daguerreotype; the sight of this seemed to awaken pleasing emotions. It contained the portraits of a lady and child; these he recognized as his wife and little daughter. By the sight of these, he was at first overcome; his wife appeared natural to him, but he had not the most distant idea of the age of his little daughter; he wondered if it was of a sufficient age, when he left home, to call him father, and whether it would remember and greet him when he returned. He now realized, most painfully, the gloom that hung like a pall over his memory. The sight of the articles as I would take them out, seemed to call up others, by association. The sight of rifle and pistol-balls reminded him that he had, somewhere, a rifle and revolver, where, he did not know. I requested him to run back in his memory, if possible, to the time when he first became deranged. He said that he was attacked with the fever at Benicia, and carried on board a ship that was then lying at anchor. There were several sick on board, and during his sickness, one was brought and placed on a table in front of his berth. He watched him day after day, until one night, as the light fell dimly on his pallid features, a slight convulsion passed over him, and his jaw fell. This closed the scene; from this moment his mind had been wandering in the dark labyrinths of forgetfulness. The fever had left him, and given place to that dreaded malady, the scurvy, with which he had now become reduced almost to helplessness. His feet and limbs were swollen to double their usual size, their purple hue denoting the fearful state to which his system was reduced. The name of this unfortunate man was E. W. Clark, Jr., of West Boylston, Mass. He gave me his name, and the address of his friends, at a time when he had but little hope of ever seeing them, with the request that I should write them the particulars of his death.

On the 16th, we were surrounded by porpoises; our first matet being an old harpooner, descended into the martingale of the ship, his harpoon being attached to a rope which passed through a tackle-block above, and was manned by about thirty passengers. At the first plunge of the ship, he "let go" the harpoon, taking effect in the back of a porpoise; "haul away," and the huge monster was swinging in the air. This was a moment of intense excitement; the harpoon had passed almost through the body, but in hauling him from the water, it had drawn out, holding only to a half-inch of the skin. One struggle and he would have been released; but the auspicious moment passed, and at the word "ease away," he was safely *shipped* on our forecastle deck. His struggles now were fearful; his throes causing the very spars to tremble. He strikes another and another, both of which are safely drawn on board. He strikes a fourth, and after hauling it several feet from the water, it falls from the harpoon and rushes through the water, staining its wake with blood. We are now well supplied with fish, but of a kind not calculated to tempt the appetite.

Chapter Twenty-ninth.

CLOUD AND CLIPPERTON ISLANDS—WHALES, SHARKS, PORPOISES, AND DOLPHINS—A SHARK CAPTURED—SHARK STEAK—"CAUDLE LECTURE"—DEATH OF SAMUEL B. LEWIS—A CALM—FOOT RACES BY THE SHIP'S FURNITURE—PASSENGER PECULIARITIES—SHORT OF PROVISIONS—"BOUT SHIP"—FIRST OF JANUARY—ITS LUXURIES AT SEA—A TAME SEA-FOWL—A PASSENGER DYING—A SHARK—A DELIGHTFUL EVENING SCENE—A DEATH—BURIAL AT SEA BY CANDLE LIGHT—A TURTLE NAVIGATING THE OCEAN—HIS SUSPICIOUS CONDUCT—A WRITTEN PROTEST AGAINST THE CAPTAIN—COCUS ISLAND—CAPTURING "BOOBIES."

ON the 17th, we passed under the lea of Cloud island—lat. 19°, long. 103°. 21st; passed Clipperton island, lat. 11°, long. 103°. The air is filled with sea-fowl; the island is a rocky pile, having the appearance of a dilapidated castle; and is surrounded by a low sandy beach. We are surrounded by whales, sharks, porpoises and dolphins; our first mate strikes a porpoise at midnight, and it is hauled on deck by the crew.

On the 22d, the mate struck a shark; it was hauled on deck, and we had shark-steak for breakfast. All out with the captain, and the lectures he receives are only equalled by those of the amiable "Mrs. Caudle." He finds himself wofully in the minority, and confines himself to his state-room. We not only charge the adverse winds to his account, but the destitution of the ship; of his guilt of the latter charge, the jury were unanimous.

24th. The death of Samuel B. Lewis is announced. He was buried at 9 A.M., lat. 6°–12′ north. He was from Elmira, N. Y., where he leaves a widowed mother to mourn his untimely death. On my return, I learned that subsequent to his starting for California, his father was accidently killed; the mother wrote for her son; he was her only solace; upon him she leaned for consolation; but on a dreary night, as the wind howled mournfully without, she dreamed her son returned, and as she was about to clasp him to her bosom, he shrunk from her sight and disappeared forever.

We have a calm for several days with intense heat; a general restlessness is felt, passengers are out of patience; our ship has not sufficient headway to cause her to mind the tiller; she rolls about like a log, now plunging, throwing her sails all aback, now rising on a sea, the rigging slackens, the spars and yards creak, the sails again fill, and everything is again drawn to its utmost tension; she again plunges, reers, and rises lengthwise of a sea; she careens and is thrown almost upon her "beam-ends." Trunks change sides, tables stand on their heads, barrels get up foot-races, much to the annoyance of the passengers, who, with shins in hand, enter most vehement protests, throwing in an occasional oath by way of emphasis. Jack "yarns" on the forecastle, Tom has out a shark-hook; the cook has been mast-headed by the captain; T——n comes down from the shrouds with a "damn my shirt-tail *tò* h—l," looks at his boots and goes up again; Wright exclaims, "certingly." Palmly looks from under his quaker hat, and swears at the captain; the Dutchman, with red whiskers, opens his mouth, which very much resembles a cavity in a brick-kiln; he looks an oath in Dutch, but don't speak. To calm our ruffled passions we were informed that we were short of provisions, and were to be put upon allowance.

On the 28th, the captain gave the order, "bout ship," and we stood in for the main land, 550 miles distant, lat. 6°, long. 96°. On the 29th, a fine breeze springs up, we again change our course and stand east, in the direction of Panama.

January 1st, 1850, lat. 6°, long. 9°; heat most oppressive; we have hard fare for breakfast, same for dinner and supper. Oh, ye knights of "Gotham!" did we not envy you? You, who are now cloyed with luxuries and greeted by the smiles of friends, but little dream that he who, twelve months ago, was your companion, has this moment dined upon sea-bread that has become the home of vermin, and beef on about the fourth anniversary of its salting, boiled in ocean-water.

A small bird flies on board in an exhausted condition; it is quite tame and eats food from our hands. Our inquiries in reference to its home and destination, were in vain; it remained on board during the day, and seemed to appreciate our kindness.

It is rumored that one of our passengers is dying; a shark is at this moment passing under the bow of the ship, as if anticipating his prey. 4th, rainy morning; it clears up at one, and we have a most delightful evening; a heavy cloud settles around the horizon, leaving us, as it were, in a lake as calm as a mirror. I never witnessed a more beautiful scene; I am, however, in no humor to enjoy it. This is our thirty-eighth day out, and the prospects most discouraging; I am over due at home, and half the journey yet to be performed.

At 7 P. M. it was announced that Wm. F. Capron, of Palmyra, N. Y., was dead; he was sewed up in a canvas shroud, and thirty minutes after his death, with lights on deck, in latitude 6° 34′ N., he was consigned to the ocean.

5th. Delightful morning, with fine breeze. We saw a large turtle floating on the surface of the water, asleep; we lowered a boat, and pulled off for him, but he awoke, and suspecting our movements, applied his propellers with great dexterity, and diving toward the bottom he was soon out of sight. He probably hailed from Cocus Island, distant one hundred and twenty miles; his object in cruising in these waters we were unable to learn. It being Monday, it was shrewdly suspected that he had been out, on the previous night, in search of bright eyes. His being asleep in the middle of the day, and his apparent *embarrassment* on being discovered, were evidence upon which almost any jury would have convicted him.

6th. Calm, heat insupportable, and we are short of provisions. I have a warm conversation with the captain, and draw up a protest, have it signed. by the passengers, designing to lay it before the consul at Panama.

PROTEST.

WE, the undersigned, passengers on board the ship Edward Everett, Capt. HENRY SMITH. do hereby most solemnly aver that we were induced to take passage on said ship by representations made by said Capt. Smith and his agents, which representations were, that he had on board an extra supply of ship-stores, and that extra provisions had been made for the comfort of passengers. For this *extra provision* an extra charge of $100 in the first, and $25 in the second cabin, had been made, above that of any vessel sailing from the same port for the same destination, during the present season.

The above-named Capt. Smith, through public advertisements and otherwise, called the attention of invalids *particularly*, to the superior arrangements made for their comfort, that a physician would be in attendance, &c.

Immediately upon getting under weigh we learned, to our sorrow, that we

12

had been grossly deceived; that the above representations were false. Our provisions, many of them, were damaged, and, we were credibly informed, were purchased as such at San Francisco. Of some of the articles that are indispensable at sea, we were short, and immediately put upon allowance.

Some of the passengers had made arrangements to work their passage, but upon first putting to sea were unable to do duty. The Captain called upon them in person, ordering them from their berths and on duty, threatening, in case of non-compliance, to put them ashore on the first island. Mr. Saml. B. Lewis, of Elmira, N. Y., who was working his passage as under-steward, was compelled to do duty when unable, and finally compelled to take to his berth, from which he never arose. Just previous to his death he manifested a wish to see the Captain, and said, "If I die my blood will be upon the Captain's head."

The invalids, being compelled to live on the coarse fare of the steerage, suffered for want of nourishing food, of which the ship was entirely destitute, there not being a particle of dried fruit, preserved meats, wines, or any one of the articles thought indispensably necessary on ship-board.

The physician, (whose father and Captain Smith were the owners of the ship,) paid no other attention to the sick than dealing out medicines, which he did *only* at the most exorbitant charges. In some instances, passengers, after having been sick for days without nourishment, were obliged to buy flour of the Captain at exorbitant prices, and cook with their own hands something to sustain life.

There have been five deaths on board, during the voyage. Wm. F. Capron, of Palmyra, N. Y., we do most solemnly believe died for want of proper nourishment; and in the case of Wm. B. Lewis, we believe he was brought to a premature death, by treatment received at the hands of the Captain, together with the want of proper nourishment after his prostration.

Aside from the above unheard-of conduct, Capt. Smith went to sea without a single life or quarter-boat, consequently entirely unprepared to save life in case of accident, showing a recklessness of human life in the highest degree reprehensible, which should not be passed over in silence.

We regret exceedingly that we are obliged to make the above charges against an American Captain, a class of men so justly celebrated for philanthropy and kindness; but the circumstances under which we are placed leave no alternative; and we hereby most respectfully request that our Consul at Panama will immediately enforce the law in this case, believing that a few public examples will put an end to the abuse.

At Sea, *January 6th*, 1850, *lat.* 6° *N.*, *lon.* 92° *W.*, having sailed from San Francisco, 28th November, 1849.

(*Signed*,)

Robt. N. Tate, First Mate of Ship Edward Everett.

J. M. Letts,	N. Y.	W. Cook,	Mo.	J. J. Starky,	Iowa.
N. N. Rapelye,	"	Wm. Tanner,	"	R. H. Caldwell,	Ohio.
J. R. Thorne,	"	J. Scorbough,	"	J. K. Turk,	"
J. H. R. Fairchild,	"	J. H. Hess,	"	D. McCully,	Iowa.

C. L. Hoag,	N. Y.	B. Swart,	Mo.	J. M. Richney,	Ill.
J. H. Mumby,	"	M. Z. Suzee,	"	J. Sharp,	Ohio.
A. Riley,	"	J. Turner,	"	L. H. McGee,	"
Geo. N. Seymour,	"	Z. Redwin,	"	S. Heath,	Me.
Jas. Reed, M. D.,	"	J. Albright,	"	C. B. Castella,	Ky.
H. Marks,	"	J. L. Simmons,	"	H. S. Shoudy,	"
S. H. Stevens,	"	S. D. Baldwin,	"	Wm. E. Judd,	Md.
J. F. Allen,	"	B. Holt,	"	Robt. Holland,	Conn.
J. Gaffney,	N. J.	J. N. York,	"	F. P. Berken,	N. O.
J. Pierson,	"	J. N. Clauson,	Mo.	H. Starkfleet,	"
P. D. Elmendorf,	"	J. D. Mott,	"	J. P. Peterson,	"
G. Sillcocke,	"	R. N. Sullivan,	Mass.	J. B. Hall,	Pa.
G. A. Barnes,	Ind.	J. H. Green,	"	J. Williamson,	"
J. C. Corwin,	Mo.	J. H. Ficket,	"	S. Griffin,	Va.
F. Minton,	"	J. R. Foster,	"		

7th. Pass within forty miles of Cocus Island.

8th. Indication of land; a cloud of "boobies" surround the ship, lighting on the spars and rigging; we divert ourselves by tying clubs to fishing lines, throwing them around their necks, and hauling them in. They appeared to enter into the sport with as much zeal as ourselves, for upon being released they would fly around, and seem to say, "do it again."

Chapter Thirtieth.

INTENSE HEAT—HUMAN NATURE AS EXHIBITED BY THE PASSENGERS—DANGER, NOT APPREHENDED—A TATTLER—A "DUTCH JUSTICE"—"LONG TOM COFFIN"—A QUAKER HAT—AN INDIVIDUAL RUNNING WILD—HIS OATHS, DEPREDATIONS, MUSICAL ACCOMPLISHMENTS, SHOWMAN PROPENSITIES, AND PUGILISTIC DEVELOPMENTS—"BLUBBER," BUCKSKIN, AND "THE LAST RUN OF SHAD"—A CAPSIZED WHALE-BOAT—THRILLING SENSATION—HARPOON USED—A SHARK—"LAND HO!"—GULF OF PANAMA—SOUTH AMERICAN COAST—"SAIL HO!"—DOLPHIN FOR DINNER—A WHALE—A TERRIFIC GALE—OUR SAILS AND SPARS CARRIED AWAY.

January 8th. CALM with intense heat. Our ship rolls about at the mercy of the sea, the spars creaking, and the sails displaying as little ambition as if they designed to enfold the yards in an eternal sleep. This example of tranquillity was but illy followed by the passengers; it appeared to foment their passions, bringing the evil ones to the surface. Each was disposed to demand an apology from his neighbor for wrongs either real or imaginary, (mostly of the latter;) the neighbor declaiming, in the most vehement manner, that he is the injured party.

What a motley group! what an exposition of the dissimilarity of human nature! Here are my friends Fairchild and Seymour, all they should be, disposed to look upon the brightest side of the picture; McG. offering $100 for the strength he once had; "he would whip that d—d Englishman," the Englishman, at the same time, swelling and blowing about, with the pomp and glory of "Old England" flitting through his imagination, quite ignorant of his impending danger. Gates, on the alert for news for the captain's ear, for which he gets an occasional cup of coffee, together with the universal detestation of the passengers; the "Dutch Justice" strutting about with all the pomp of brainless vanity; the professor, learned in love, law, and physic, which comprises, in his estimation, all that can be learned in this world; "Long Tom Coffin," the very "beau ideal" of the hero himself, stretched out on the quarter-deck, very much resembling a pair of oyster-tongs. He had Blackstone and Kent at his tongue's end, and swore that, on his arrival in Maine, he would prefer a "BRIEF" for the captain's especial edification; P——ly, sitting under a quaker hat, as forbidding in appearance as he is in fact, damning all indiscriminately who differ with him in opinion. T——n, who in attempting to relate an occurrence commences at the last word, throwing the balance on the top of it, in the most unintelligible confusion. He is about twenty-one years of age, has been well brought up, with a good education, but is now running wild. He blacks his boots and starts for mast-head; half-way up, he halts, looks at his boots, suspects that they might have received a higher polish, and with a "d—n my shirt-tail to h—l," comes down again. He discovers some one's can of preserved meat; he takes it to the cook, and soon *some one* is invited to dine with him, and if he discovers *some one's* bottle of wine, some one is *almost* sure to get *one* glass of it. He had a passion for music, but generally sung in parodies, as follows:

I'm sitting on a stile, Mary,
Not knowing where to jump;
My foot it slipped, I caught a fall,
And struck upon a stump,
Ittee bump, ittee bump, ittee bump.

almost indefinitely, closing up with "well, well, d—n my shirt-tail to h—l, d—n it *to* h—l," and again starting for mast-head; he would probably reach the first yard, when a new idea, and he would be again on deck, playing superintendent of a caravan, with "John, take that little monkey from his mother, or he will *suck* her to death, not that I wish to disturb the animals in their innocent amusements, but by G—d the public eye must be respected; music, ting-a-ling, ting-a-ling, well, well, &c." He is now interrupted by "Blubber," alias "Livingston & Wells' Express;" a short quarrel, and they square off for a fight. Blubber is backed by Buckskin, alias "the last run of shad," and they don't fight.

We have a steward that knows his place, and another that does not deserve one on this earth; a cook who has not been accused of washing himself during the voyage, and one who appears never to have been guilty of the act. A negro who knows his place and keeps it, a white man, his neighbor, assuming everybody's place but his own; one man with no appetite, another creating a famine in his immediate neighborhood; five crazy men, fifty invalids, a penurious doctor, two mates—Tate and Barry—noblemen of nature's own make, and a captain who was made afterwards. In one thing *only* were we unanimous, which was the condemnation of sailing vessels in general, and the "Everett" in particular, including her captain.

11th. We discover something near the horizon resembling a capsized whale-boat. This causes a great sensation; the first mate mans the quarter-boat and pulls off for the object. The passengers watch most intently, the little craft as it rises upon the crest of a mountain-wave, and now disappearing, again rises to our view, still nearing the object in the distance. As they approach still nearer, through the ship's glass, we see fowls rising from it, and now the mate, standing in the bow, elevates the harpoon, as if to strike. A large sea-fowl still clings to the object; as they approach still nearer, it flies. The mate throws the harpoon and soon they are returning to the ship. They pronounced the object a pine-log. They have a Dolphin and several small fish; a cry of shark, and a large one passes along the weather side, four are following astern, accompanied by their pilots. We use the harpoon, but without success.

12th. 4 A.M., cry of "land ho!" I dress and go on deck; we are in sight of Points Mala and Puerco, at the entrance to the gulf of Panama, 100 miles from the city. A steamer is just passing the point into the gulf; a strong wind is blowing off the land, and west and in, running close on the wind. We beat all night, and in the morning find ourselves in the same position.

13th. Wind still dead ahead; after standing in and nearing the South American coast, we put about on the other tack; the wind soon "hauls," and we stand directly for the point and soon enter the mouth of the gulf. At 4 P.M., mate cries out from mast-head, "sail ho!" "How does she bear?" "Two points off leeward bow, sir." Delightful sunset; a school of porpoises are tumbling about in ecstasies.

14th. Pleasant morning; we are just off the inner point. A fine breeze blows off, our ship bows to the impulse, and we stand along under the lee of the land. Cry of dolphin, captain strikes one with the harpoon, it struggles with the instrument, disengages itself, and disappears in the direction of the bottom; he strikes another, it is hauled safely on board and served up for dinner. A whale passes, but not sufficiently near to receive our salutation. 4 P.M., it blows a gale, captain cries out, "clue up the top-gallantsail," "aye, aye, sir." During the night we have a terrific gale; it carries away our jib, foretop-sail, foretop-gallantsail, maintop-staysail, and maintop-gallantsail.

15th. The gale still continues; we are driven out of sight of land, but arrive in sight of the South American coast at 3 P.M., the Andes towering up, hiding themselves in the clouds.

16. Strong winds; we are about sixty miles from Panama, running close in shore. At evening, the kind-hearted inhabitants light beacons upon the side of the mountain, to guide us during the night. At nine we put about on the other tack, and at four in the morning were within ten minutes run of being aground.

Chapter Thirty-first.

BAY OF PANAMA—ITS BEAUTIES—TROPICAL FRUITS—THE CITY IN SIGHT—EXCITEMENT ON BOARD—APPEARANCE OF THE CITY; HER RUINS—PREPARATIONS TO DROP ANCHOR —"STAND BY"—"LET GO THE ANCHOR"—FAREWELL TO THE SICK—A PERILOUS RIDE ON THE BACK OF AN INDIVIDUAL—ON SHORE—FIRST DINNER—NOTHING LEFT—AN INDIVIDUAL FEELING COMFORTABLE—PANAMA AMERICANIZED—A MOONLIGHT SCENE VIEWED FROM A BRASS "FIFTY-SIX"—A DILAPIDATED CONVENT, AS SEEN AT NIGHT —CHURCH BELLS—BURNING THE DEAD—EXPOSURE OF THE DESECRATED REMAINS—SICKENING AND DISGUSTING SIGHT—INFANTS CAST INTO PITS—THE RESCUE OF THEIR SOULS REQUIRING A GIGANTIC EFFORT ON THE PART OF THE CHURCH—A HETACOMB— "ETERNAL LIGHT"—IGNORANCE OF THE MASS—PEERLESS CHARACTERISTICS.

18th. WE are surrounded by islands; is there another bay that will compare with this? Certainly I never imagined anything so like a fairy scene. We are in the midst of twenty islands, all covered with tropical fruits of spontaneous growth; the orange, lime, fig, and cocoa-nut trees, interlaced with the grape, forming shelter for the inhabitants, and presenting them with food. We were in a condition to appreciate, most fully, the surrounding scene. Our voyage, which had now lasted fifty-one days, was commenced under adverse circumstances; five of the passengers had already died, and several were still confined to their berths with scurvy, some of them destined to breathe their last on board.

4 P.M. As we emerge from behind a small island, we are in full view of Panama, the towers of her cathedral looming up, and her dilapidated wall extending along the water line; all are now in a phrensy of excitement; the passengers are climbing into the rigging, gazing with astonishment upon the surrounding scene. The wind blows fresh from the land, and we are obliged to beat up directly in its eye; we passed near Tobago in the evening, and in the morning were near our anchorage. We run up the stars and stripes, and prepare to drop anchor; our trunks are in readiness, and we expect soon to be transferred to the shore.

COOPER DEL.

ON STONE BY J. CAMERON

LITH. OF G. W. LEWIS 111. NASSAU ST. N.Y.

PANAMA, FROM THE BATTERY,

The city, nestling cosily at the base of Cerro Lancon, looks enchantingly, her towers and domes being lighted up by the morning sun. Her dilapidated monasteries are also seen, and her extended wall, the base of which is washed by the gentle surf. That distant tower, shrouded in ivy, dripping with the morning dew, seems weeping over the tomb of a departed city. Everything conspired to awaken emotions of the most romantic character. Our captain mounts the quarter deck and cries out, "all hands on deck to work ship." "Aye aye, sir." "Clue up the mainsail" "hard a-lee," "main-topsail, haul;" "haul taut the weather main-braces;" the ship comes about on the other tack. A boat nears us, "Stand by to throw a rope;" a man comes on board; "bout ship," "stand by the anchor," "haul down the jib;" mate heaves the lead and cries out, "four fathom o' the deep ho!" "fore and main-sail, clue up." We are now standing towards the United States' man-of-war Southampton. "Let go the mizen top-sail braces," "stand by," "let go the anchor," and at 9 A.M., our ship rounded to and bowed submission to her chains. We are now at anchor five miles from shore; a fleet of *bungoes* are coming off for the passengers, propelled by natives in their "dishabille;" all who are able, are prepared to debark, but fourteen of our number are confined to their berths in a helpless, and almost hopeless condition; my friend Clark is one of the number; the scurvy has rendered his limbs entirely useless, and there is no hope entertained of his recovery. We bade them farewell, and started for the shore. We looked back at the ship, which now presents the trim appearance of a ship close-reefed.

It being ebb-tide our boat went aground half a mile from the shore; our boatmen, however, were prepared for the emergency, it being with them an almost daily occurrence; they got out, backed up, and wished us to mount. It was to me a novel way of riding. I had ridden "bare-backed," but always supported by a greater number of legs. After sundry stumbles and plunges, which kept my clean shirt in imminent peril, I was safely set down on shore, for which extra service my noble steed thought a *real* full compensation. I had my trunk carried to the Philadelphia Hotel. I drank freely of wine and went out on the balcony, which extends from the second story, to enjoy a cigar and my own thoughts. I soon felt as happy as a man could well feel under the influence of the same quantity of wine. I kept my eye on the table, dinner was in an advanced state of preparation; and, dear reader, you will form some idea of the voracity of my appetite when you reflect that I have not dined in fifty-one days. I must claim your indulgence here, for I must confess I am in doubt whether I am competent to write intelligibly; just on shore, you know; and then, you know, the best of wine will sometimes lead one astray; but dinner is ready, and who cares for public opinion when he has enough to eat and *drink*. I sat at table as long as there was anything visible, when I, very prudently, got up, lighted a cigar and went out for a promenade. The wine was flowing briskly through my veins, and I felt a healthful glow throughout my system. I felt that politeness was the main ingredient in my composition, and was disposed to raise my hat to every individual I met. I, however, restrained myself, and bestowed my bows only upon the half-clad Señoritas.

Panama had become completely Americanized. There was the American Hotel, the New York, the Philadelphia, the United States, the St. Charles, Washington, &c., &c., and half the business in town was done by Americans. After supper, we strolled to the "Battery," seated ourselves on a brass fifty-six, and viewed one of the most magnificent moon-light scenes I ever beheld. The bay was as placid as a mirror; the ships lying quietly at anchor, loomed up like phantoms; the islands being just visible in the distance. Behind us was a ruined monastery, the moon looking in at the roof and windows, disclosing the innumerable bats that nightly congregate to gambol through these halls of desolation. After spending an hour here, we passed through one of the dilapidated gateways and took a surf bath; we reëntered through the gateway, and passed along the wall to the convent of San Francisco, an immense structure covering an area of 300 feet square; it is now untenanted, and in ruins. Near one corner of this, standing in the street, is a stone pedestal surmounted by a cross, where the devout are wont to kneel and kiss the image of "Nuestro Señora." Passing up the main street, "*Calle de Merced*," we found the citizens all out enjoying the evening; and as we passed we could hear them modestly whisper, "Los Americanos tiene mucho oro;" during the night we had the usual procession of nuns and priests, and the next day was ushered in by the discordant clamor of church-bells. I say this without reproach, for half the bells were cracked, (and it was a great wonder they were not all so,) and every morning from daylight to nine, they were undergoing the ordeal of a severe drubbing.

The vaults of Panama in which the dead are deposited, are laid up in mason work, and resemble a succession of large ovens. They are under the control of the priests, and are the source of an immense revenue. Of the strange and often barbarous customs adopted by the church here, the most strange, the most inhuman and revolting, is that of burning the bodies of the dead. This diabolical practice cannot be contemplated without feelings of indignation and horror. Nations have praticed the burning of their dead in order to preserve their ashes, but this is not the object here—would that I could have learned an object so laudable—but here nothing can be said in mitigation. The word of the priest is potent, and considered by the people a mandate from Heaven. Whatever he requires is submitted to with cheerfulness, they thinking it the will of the Supreme Being. The priest requires a fee for his important intercessions for the dead, as well for the consecrated tapers that burn at the head of the corpse during the funeral services, as for a place in consecrated ground, and prayers for the soul which is supposed to linger a long and painful probation in purgatory, after the body is consigned to the tomb. The friends of the dead are obliged to pay, in proportion to the services rendered. A requiem in a whisper costs but half as much as one in an audible tone of voice, and one on high "C" is still much more expensive. A place for burial in the earth, even in consecrated ground, is procured at a moderate cost, but in the vaults, above described, the charge is much higher, often beyond the means of the poorer classes. These-vaults as well as the consecrated ground belong to the church, and the proceeds go into the hands of the priests. The vaults are not numerous, and are of sufficient capacity only to accommodate the deaths of a few months; but in order to serve all, the priests have hit upon the expedient of an annual "funeral pile." "All-Saint's day" in each year, is the one dedicated to this sacrilegious act. On that day the vaults give up their dead, which are carried a short distance and committed to the flames.

This act would be less revolting if done effectually, but like everything done in this country, it is but half done. Men are hired to do the work, but wood being scarce, and not expecting the priests to inspect, they do as little work as possible, keeping in view their reward. I can never forget my feelings, upon visiting this scene of annual desecration; my very soul sickens with disgust at the recollection of it. Here were coffins half-burned, exhibiting the ghastly visages of their lifeless tenants; others having turned over during the conflagration, had emptied the half-decayed bodies upon the ground; some partially consumed, others still shrouded in their grave-clothes. Here lay the head and part of the chest of a stalwart frame, the flesh having but just commenced to decay, the countenance still bearing the impress of its Maker. Very near, partially shrouded in a winding sheet, were the delicately moulded limbs of a female, who had for a brief period tenanted the house of death, now brought forth and committed to the flames.

It will be a consolation to those residing in the States, who have lost friends at Panama, to know that no one out of *the church* is allowed burial in consecrated ground; their remains, consesequently, are not disturbed. According to the *true* theory of religion, infants that die before baptism go directly to purgatory, notwithstanding their parents may belong to the *true* church. As a suitable receptacle for these unfortunate little innocents, deep pits are dug in the rear of the churches, into which they are unceremoniously cast; their influence upon consecrated ground would, it is thought, be contaminating. Curiosity led me to inspect one of these pits; what I beheld I will leave to the imagination of the reader. I am not prepared to say *positively*, but I believe that the true theory in reference to these infants is, that they are not irrevocably lost, but to reclaim them from purgatory requires a *gigantic* effort on the part of the church.

There are many things here to attract and awaken interest in the mind, but no matter how strong the desire for information, nothing can be learned from the lower classes of the population. The source of information which, in the States is inexhaustible, is here barren; for to say that a New Grenadian *even* knows his own wife and children, is awarding him, comparatively, a very high degree of attainment. Pass and inspect the ruins of a monastery or other edifice, and ask the first person you meet what it is, and what the cause of its destruction? the invariable reply is, "*no sabio, Señor.*" In passing along near the head of "*Calle San Juan de Dio,*" my attention was attracted by the movements of a little girl who, with a lighted taper in her hand, passed rapidly along to an elbow in the main wall of the city, and leaving her light hastily retreated. Upon inspecting the spot, I discovered that part of the wall was laid up of human skulls, and removing a stone which closed up an aperture, I saw a burning taper which is kept here as an "eternal light." I stepped into a small store near and inquired the history of this catacomb; the response was, "no sabi Señor." My solution was that they were the bones of heroes who had fallen in the defence of the city.

When speaking of the ignorance of the people, I wish to be understood as alluding to the mass, for, in Panama, there are ladies and gentlemen of the highest cultivation and attainments, those who are endowed in the highest degree with those peerless qualities which are so pre-eminently characteristic of the Castilian race. The stranger's friend, and friend's protector; life itself is not a sacrifice when lost in the protection of that of a friend. The ignorance of the mass, as in all the departments of Spanish America, arises from a want of noble incentives; the entire mind being enslaved and controlled by the church.

Chapter Thirty-second.

A NUN—FANDANGO—MARRIAGE ENGAGEMENT BROKEN—START FOR GORGONA—OUR EXTREME MODESTY—SAGACITY OF THE MULE—SLEEP ON MY TRUNK—A DREAM—AN ALLIGATOR WITH A MOUSTACHE—INFERNAL REGIONS—DEMONS—AN INDIVIDUAL WITH LONG EARS, AND A MULE IN BOOTS—FALLING OUT OF BED—FUNERAL PROCESSION—GORGONA—START FOR CHAGRES—OUR BUNGO FULL—SPONTANEOUS COMBUSTION, ALMOST—" POCO TIEMPO"—LIZARDS FOR DINNER—THE HOSTESS—GATUN—MUSIC OF THE OCEAN—ARRIVAL.

THERE were a number of Americans in town, *en route* to California, awaiting the arrival of the Steamer Oregon, which was, at this time, fully due; there were also here several females from the States, *unattended*, on their way to the "Eldorado." I sketched the convent of "San Francisco" and "La Mugher," and while doing the latter I was watched by a nun whose pallid features I could plainly see through the grating.

During the evening we visited the "lions," and brought up at a "fandango;" we did not, however, participate in the dance, but retired in good season, designing to set out the next morning for Gorgona. At an early hour the Philadelphia was besieged by dusky muleteers reiterating their "cargo Gorgona?" and before the sun had shown his disc above the horizon, we were under way. As we passed along *Calle de Merced*, I was very modestly recognized by an interesting Señorita, who, on the previous evening, had made to me a proposition of marriage; I, of course, accepted; but owing to numerous pressing engagements, I was not just then prepared to attend to it, and postponed it until the next evening. I did not tell her that I was to leave town early the next morning, nor did she suspect when I passed, that I was on my way, but looked as much as to say, "you won't forget, will you?" As we gained the out-skirts of the city, we were hailed by half a dozen half-clad natives, who demanded a *real* for each horse and mule in our cavalcade. We exhibited the strongest symptoms of non-compliance, and our worthy collectors were soon convinced that we were *not* the party they were looking for; they, however, succeeded in extorting from many, and claimed to be acting under a recent act of government.

As we arrived at the national bridge, we met a party of Señoritas wending their way towards the city; they saluted us with "buenos dias, Caballieros," and said by their looks that they would accompany us to the States, if we wished them to. Our extreme modesty prevented our making the proposition, and we parted with a mutual "adios." We soon entered the forest, where the gigantic palms, embracing each other, protected us from the scorching rays of the sun. Our cavalcade was made up of mules and horses, some of them mounted, others packed. Our mutual friend, J. R. Foster, whom we had expected for days to consign to the ocean, was one of our party; being mounted on a gentle horse, in an easy saddle, and buoyed up with the fond hope of again reaching home, he astonished all by his persevering endurance. The balance of the party were in good health, and enjoyed the trip exceedingly.

I was much struck, as I had often been, with the sagacity of the mule. One of them was packed with Mr. Fairchild's trunk, and my own; feeling some interest in my trunk, I naturally paid the most attention to that particular mule; and if he could have understood any language excepting the dead ones, I should have informed him that I thought him a very fine fellow. But just as I came to this very satisfactory conclusion, he was guilty of a freak that well-nigh destroyed my confidence in him. We had gained the summit of a hill, where the path stretched away for half a mile, almost level, when mule took it into his head to run, and, to my great amazement, he did run; I presumed he was making his escape, and cried out to the muleteer to stop him, but he replied "mula caro algun per comer," and so it proved, for after running a quarter of a mile, he stopped and commenced eating. As soon as the cavalcade came up, he again started, and kept repeating until he had satisfied his hunger, when he walked along in the most orderly manner, and good humored too, for his ears were erect, and a smile appeared to beam from his countenance. At our first watering-place, after drinking, he dropped himself down, in the most mechanical manner, to rest. When we were ready to start, the "mula" of our muleteer would bring him to his hoofs, all right, and off.

At 1 P.M., we reached the "half-way tent," and as some of the party were behind, we resolved to put up for the night. After supper we heard a cannon, announcing the arrival of the Oregon at Panama. I stretched myself out on my trunk in the open air, and was soon unconscious of my situation. My spirit was restless, and, as if not satisfied with one trip, spent the night in passing to and fro, over the route we had traveled during the day. Now my mule would change to a monkey, and I would ride him to the top of one of the highest trees; he would then become instantly transformed into an alligator, and there would be left no alternative but to precipitate ourselves into the mud below; in the passage down I was also transformed into an alligator, and immediately found myself covered with scales and swimming about in a pond, with an alligator on each side, holding on to my moustache, "showing me up" to my fellow alligators. The honors heaped upon me so excited and elated me, that I commenced rushing through the water, and soon found myself high and dry on land, looking around for my mule. I again mounted, and resolved to have no farther connexion with either monkey or alligator, but to ride directly through to Gorgona. Again my spirit lost its way, and I found myself on the bank of one of the most sluggish and dismal streams it is possible to imagine; the recollection of it now sends a chill to my heart. My mule stood appalled with terror, and cried for mercy, when I applied the spur. There was no alternative; it lay in the route, and we must cross it; I rode back a short distance that my mule might forget his terror; he again came up, reared and plunged, and we immediately sank below the surface; we continued to sink down, down, down, a damp chilly sensation crept over me, and I became stifled with horror; now my mule blows fire and smoke from his nostrils, and a demon of the most appalling aspect, covered with green and slime, and now another and another, all dancing along, laughing most hideously and biting their fingers in derision, as they contemplate their victim. We soon reached their abode, my blood is sent curdling to my heart, and with a feeling of horror and desperation I strike the spur into my mule, and with one terrific leap we pass through unscathed. The demons gave chase, but borne on the wings of fear we soon reached the other side of the earth. Here everything appears strange; my mule has but two legs, and wears boots and spurs; I have four legs, and a pair of enormous ears; I am led up to a block and mounted by his *muleship*, who, after lighting his cigar, applies his spurs; I determined to reach the other side by recrossing his "Satanic majestie's" dominions, and after passing through the same horrifying scene, regained the starting point. I remounted my mule, which now seemed to have the usual number of legs, and after crossing sloughs and climbing mountains, we came to a precipice which he refused to descend. After repeated applications of the spur, he reared and plunged, and as he reached the brink of the precipice he settled back, and I passed over his head; in passing over I caught hold of his ears, which, pulling out, I was precipitated into the abyss below. The concussion awoke me, and I found that I had fallen from my trunk, and was grasping tightly the bottoms of the legs of my pantaloons.

In the morning we had the satisfaction of learning that our mules had strayed, and were detained until 10 o'clock. We reached Gorgona at 4 P.M. As we were entering the town, we met a funeral procession headed by a fife and drum; the corpse borne on a bier with face uncovered, (coffins are not used,) the mother of deceased standing in the door of her dwelling, uttering the most heart-rending exclamations. The whole was accompanied by the uncouth sound of a piece of old iron hanging in the church door, serving as a bell, and at this particular time undergoing a severe castigation. Towards evening, another corpse was borne along with the same accompaniments. The deceased was a small child; its head was decorated with flowers, its face uncovered, looking the very personation of sleeping innocence.

We put up at the French Hotel, and learning that the Empire City was to remain but one day longer at Chagres, we resolved to embark early the next morning. We contracted with a native to take our party of eleven for $22, and at an early hour were *en route.* We glided down the river very pleasantly, propelled by three oarsmen, with our worthy captain at the helm.

After making two or three miles, we were brought to a dead stand on a sand-bar; our boatmen backed up, we mounted and were carried to the shore. They succeeded in getting the bungo over the shoal and we reëmbarked half a mile below.

It will be imagined that we had but little spare room in our craft after putting in eleven trunks, as many traveling-bags, as many pairs of blankets, and fifteen human beings. This was the case; and some of our passengers having tasted the luxury of a California life, looked upon our voyage down the river as a hardship unendurable, and censured the fellow-passenger who had made the contract. The latter worthy, feeling it an unjust imputation, gave the dissatisfied gentlemen above mentioned the privilege of taking passage in any craft that might come along. This led to personalities, and the feelings of our party were immediately in a state of ferment; brandy did not serve to allay the excitement, but seemed to add fuel, and we were on the eve of spontaneous combustion.

We arrived at a rancho, where it was proposed to dine. Here commenced a dissertation on "poco tiempo," (little time). These two words constitute almost the entire vocabulary of a native. Ask him how far it is to a rancho, "poco tiempo," how far it is to water, "poco tiempo." If they are employed by you, and you allow them to stop under any pretext, they never start, but are always on the point of so doing; it is "poco tiempo."

We had contracted to be taken through by daylight, and we had no time to spare; but after dinner the crew and "*el capitan*" must have their "*siesta*." We would urge them to start, but they were fatigued, they would start "poco tiempo." They would "*caro agua*," or "*caro cognac*," and after a detention of two hours we got into the *bungo* and were in the act of shoving off, when they consented to come on board, and we were again under way.

I omitted our bill of fare at the above rancho. Our worthy hostess was on the shady side of forty, and surrounded by half a dozen "*muchachos*," all as naked at they came into the world. Our hostess had paid a little more attention to her toilet, and seemed dressed with an express view to comfort, her entire wardrobe consisting of a pair slippers and a Panama hat. Our first dish was a stew of lizards and carna; this was served out in gourd-shells, which were held to our mouths, and the pieces of meat coaxed in with our fingers. Our second and last dish was boiled eggs. Our cook should have felt complimented, for we ate and drank everything in the house, and wanted more. She looked on with astonishment at the sudden disappearance of her stew and eggs, and said to one of our boatmen, " los Americanos tiena mucho hambre;" and so we were hungry, or we could not have relished lizards even when stewed, for I must confess my predilections were never very stongly in favor of that particular species of reptile. In passing along down, we came in contact with the carcase of a large alligator; it had been pierced by several balls, and was now borne along by the current, destined, perhaps, to take up its final rest in the bosom of the Atlantic. In the afterpart of the day we were overtaken by Mr. Miller of Gorgona, who was expressing to the steamer at Chagres the arrival of the Oregon at Panama. Night overtook us in a most discordant mood, and at a great distance from our destination.

We arrived at Gatun at 9 P.M.; some were in favor of stopping, others of continuing on, the former had the majority, and we made fast to the shore, and had another dissertation on "poco tiempo," and after an hour's detention were again under way.

At 2 A.M., we heard the sound of drums, and our boatmen cry out "fandango;" we could soon distinguish the ocean by the halo that rose from its surface, and could plainly hear the surf as it broke upon the beach. We could see the lights on the steamer that was at anchor outside, and an occasional light dodging about on shore.

At 3 A.M., we made fast to the American bank of the river, and had our baggage carried to the American Hotel. All were asleep, but we took possession of the dining-room and spread our blankets on the floor. The next morning we were all at breakfast precisely at the time *and a little before.*

Chapter Thirty-third.

CHAGRES, ITS GROWTH—GETTING ON BOARD THE EMPIRE CITY—MAGNIFICENT STEAMER—GOLD DUST ON BOARD—STEAMERS ALABAMA, FALCON, CHEROKEE, AND SEVERN—MY FRIEND CLARK ARRIVES ON BOARD—PREPARATIONS FOR STARTING—OUR STEAMER MAKES HER FIRST LEAP—"ADIOS"—CARIBBEAN SEA—HEAVY SEA ON—JAMAICA—PORT ROYAL—KINGSTON—"STEADY"—BEAUTIFUL SCENE—ORANGE GROVES—PEOPLE FLOCKING TO THE SHORE—DROP ANCHOR—THE TOWN—GENERAL SANTA ANNA'S RESIDENCE—"COALING UP"—A PARROT PEDLER IN A DILEMMA.

CHAGRES had undergone a great change; the American side which had contained but one hut on my first arrival, now presented the appearance of a thriving village of substantial framed houses, and appeared a place of considerable business. (See Plate). The facilities for transportation up the river and across to Panama, were ample. Several express agencies had been established, and arrangements made on a gigantic scale for the transportation of goods up the river; several barges of the largest class, furnished with India-rubber covering to protect goods from the weather, and lighters of the greatest strength and capacity for the transmission of treasures to and from the steamers. In connection with these, there were mules stationed at Panama and Gorgona, to serve in the land transportation.

After breakfast I went off to the steamer Empire City, "prospecting." It was blowing a severe norther, and it was with much difficulty we reached the steamer, and more that we got on board of her. Iron steps were let down on the side of the steamer, and as she would roll to us, the steps would be immersed, and as she would commence to roll back, one of the passengers would stand ready and jump on. After an elevation of twenty or thirty feet, the steps would return for another passenger.

The accommodations on board were unparalleled. I immediately engaged passage and sent off for my trunk, which came on board in the afternoon, in charge of Mr. Jas. Rolfe Foster,

G.V. COOPER DEL. BROWN & SEVERIN LITH. G.W. LEWIS PRINT.

CHAGRES, FROM THE CASTLE, LOOKING DOWN.
1851.

who shared my state-room. The Empire City is the "ne plus ultra" of steamers, and Captain Wilson worthy to command her. She is almost a world in size, furnished with the greatest magnificence, her bill of fare comprising the luxuries of all climates. The Steamers Alabama from New Orleans, and Falcon from New York, came in, in the afterpart of the day.

25th. The *dust* by the Oregon has just arrived from Panama, and as soon as it is on board we shall up anchor. There are $1,600,000, besides what is in the hands of passengers. *Bungoes* are coming off with passengers, and as it is blowing a gale, the steamer rolls tremendously, making it almost impossible for passengers to board her. The greatest dexterity is required, for, after reaching the steps, one is in imminent danger of being swept off by the next sea. Ladies were drawn up in chairs, as were also the invalids. In the afterpart of the day, I had the extreme pleasure of assisting on board my friend E. W. Clark, jr., I had left him in his berth on board the Everett, in a very feeble state; but the tropical fruits had operated upon his system like magic, and he had become able to cross the Isthmus on horseback. He eventually recovered, and was restored to his friends. Mr. Lewis came on board also. He had lost the use of one of his legs, and was borne across on a litter. One of our fellow passengers on the Everett was less fortunate; he lived two days after coming to anchor, when he expired and was taken on shore at Panama, and buried.

26th. The British Steamer, Severn, has just come to anchor, also the Cherokee from New York. At 3 P.M., the Alabama moved off in the direction of New Orleans, crowded with passengers. The smoke is beginning to loom up from our chimney, our quarter boats are hauled up; soon the windlass draws our anchor from its bed, and our steamer raises her head, and makes her first leap for home. We passed the Cherokee and received three hearty cheers, then the Falcon, then the Severn, and were soon on our course, in the direction of Kingston, Jamaica. Chagres is situated in lat. 9°, 21′, long. 8°, 4′. We were now fairly launched, homeward bound; the waves of the Caribbean sea fleeing from us, as if fearful of being drawn into the vortex of our wheel. I remained on deck until a late hour; we had a fresh breeze and heavy sea; the moon was almost full, and playing the coquette, now hiding her face, and now casting upon us one of her most bewitching smiles.

27th. (Sunday). It is one year this morning since I took leave of home and sailed for California. During my absence, I have passed through what has cost many a life, and once almost felt the last pulsation. But now I am in a fair way of being restored to my friends, in improved condition and health. I have not heard one word from home in six months; my anxiety can better be imagined than expressed. I can only hope they are alive. By observation at 12 M., we are 420 miles from Kingston, the only port we shall make on our passage home.

28th. Still a strong wind and heavy sea. We are running under fore sails and fore staysail. By observation at 12 M., we had run 174 miles in twenty-four hours.

26th. Still a heavy sea on, and a stiff breeze. We are under a full press of canvas, running eight knots. 11 A.M., in sight of land. We soon make the highlands, and are running for Port Royal. We have a pilot already on board, he having accompanied our steamer to Chagres. Port Royal is situated on a low island in the mouth of a small bay, upon the head of which Kingston is situated. We passed an armed brig, a steamer-of-war, seventy-four gun ship, revenue-cutter, all displaying the red cross of St. George. A four-oared boat comes off towards us; our wheels are turned back, and we are boarded by an officer in full uniform. After the usual inspection, our wheels again revolved, and we moved on up the bay, or river, in the direction of Kingston. After running a mile, the above-mentioned officer is astonished at learning that our steamer is *under weigh;* he came forward and wished to be put on shore—stupid fellow. We are standing inland, with high mountains on our right, capped with clouds. We now pass fortifications, and bearing to the right; our pilot sings out "steady!" we are now within full view of Kingston, and heading directly for the town; "steady!" "port!" steamer falls off, bringing the town on our larboard bow—"*hard a port!*" on we steam—"steady!" We are now passing a large fortification; we see houses nestling in orange groves on the side of the mountain. The town is so densely shaded with cocoa-nut and other tropical trees, that it is barely visible. We are drawing very near, the inhabitants are crowding to the shore. Our pilot sings out, "let go the anchor," the wheels are reversed, and we are warping around to the dock, which is crowded with natives as black as Erebus. Our plank is soon out, and our steamer belches forth her cargo of Californians, who, in profusion of beard and hideousness of aspect, would, no doubt, have compared favorably with those earlier adventurers under Columbus, who had the honor of landing here in advance of us. We found the inhabitants extremely attentive, particularly those who had goods to sell, and they were principally Jews. We were followed by these insinuating individuals, and kindly informed that by going a half mile we could buy anything we wanted. We were at a loss to know whether we were really in want, but were very kindly informed that we were in want of everything. Oh! Chatham street, how thou hast been defamed! Certainly, Kingston instead of Chatham street, is the Jewdom of the world.

I had a note of introduction from Mr. Moreau, whom I met at Gorgona, to his family at Kingston. I am not prepared to say that I was in a presentable condition. As near as memory serves me, I had on a gay colored "poncho," a slouched hat and long boots, saying nothing about the whiskers and moustache. I found an accomplished daughter, who was a good English scholar and fine pianist, and a mother who spoke nothing but French. My stay was short, but under other circumstances I should have wished a prolongation.

Many of the passengers visited General Santa Anna, whose villa was one mile from Kingston. He was living in great splendor, and was found extremely affable, speaking the English language fluently. Kingston is a town of considerable extent, the streets running at right angles, well-shaded; numerous churches and schools; the buildings generally of brick, built low to prevent disasters from hurricanes. The inhabitants are generally instructed in the rudiments of an English education, and are quite intelligent, but all complain of poverty. The island produces fruit in abundance, it hardly commands a price, excepting on the arrival of a steamer, when it is higher than in almost any market in the world. The natives have taken valuable lessons from the Jews, and appear to have acquired *their* peculiar business habits with the greatest facility. One of them had a quantity of shells, for which he demanded $25, but immediately fell $20, and I think would have taken two.

During the afternoon the Cherokee came in and commenced coaling up. This delicate duty is performed by the colored girls of the place, and the *modus operandi* is as novel as it is laborious. Some fifty girls are engaged, each with a vessel resembling a half barrel, holding sixty pounds of coal; this, when filled, is placed upon the head and carried up the gang-plank to the deck. As laborious as this duty may seem, it is performed with the greatest alacrity, accompanied by songs, dancing, and peals of laughter. (See Plate). The *belle* of the party, luxuriating in the name of "Flouncy," is seen on the deck, dressed in a pink muslin, flounced almost to the waist. She is in the act of taking one of those extraordinary steps for which the colored population are justly celebrated. The mate seems to have taken in charge a small specimen of humanity who pertinaciously insists upon coming on board to sell parrots. He is now receiving a "dose of sprouts," and will go off, no doubt, with a pair of stogys vividly impressed upon his imagination. A colored gentleman is seen laying against the wheel house counting the tubs as they are borne along by the "Bloomer"-clad girls; near him stands an individual who looks very like a returning Californian. A party of ladies and gentlemen are promenading the upper deck. Cocoa-nut trees with fruit are seen, with a range of mountains in the background. Boats with fruit, cactus, shells, parrots, &c., are being rowed about to tempt the passengers.

G. V COOPER DEL. ON STONE BY J. CAMERON LITH OF C. W. LEWIS 111 NASSAU ST. N.Y

COALEING UP

KINGSTON JAMAICA.

Chapter Thirty-fourth.

OUR WHEELS REVOLVE—THE NATIVES OF THE ISLAND EXTINCT—THE WRONGS THEY HAVR SUFFERED—THE ISLAND ONCE A PARADISE—SAN DOMINGO, HER MOUNTAINS—CUBA—A SHOWER BATH GRATIS—"SAIL HO!"—CAYCUS ISLAND AND PASSAGE—TURTLE FOR DINNER—A SERMON—GALLANT CONDUCT OF OUR STEAMER—WE SHIP A SEA—A SPANISH VESSEL IN DISTRESS—OUR TILLER CHAINS GIVE WAY—A KNIFE AND FORK IN SEARCH OF MINCE PIES—GULF STREAM—WATER-SPOUTS—"LIGHT SHIP"—SANDY HOOK—ANXIETY—SIGHT OF NEW YORK—FEELINGS AND CONDITION OF THE PASSENGERS—A SAD FATE—AGROUND—A NEW PILOT—AGAIN UNDER WEIGH—NEAR THE DOCK—A DEATH—MAN OVERBOARD—MAKE FAST—AT HOME—ONE WORD TO THOSE ABOUT TO EMBARK.

JAN. 30th. WE finish taking in provisions, coal, and water, and at 1 P.M., let go our hawser, our wheels revolve, and we are again under weigh, heading out to sea. We take a hearty dinner while yet in the bay, but there is a tremendous sea outside, and many will be obliged to pay tribute to Neptune. This is a delightful island, but it is changed from the paradise Columbus found it. Of the once happy, but now grossly abused natives, I saw but two, and am told they are almost extinct. What a sad commentary upon the law that "might makes right." What tenure could have been more perfect than that by which the native held this island. It was bequeathed to their forefathers by the Creator, and transmitted from father to son; but a stranger visited them, and they mistook him for a messenger from the Great Spirit, a visitor from the clouds. They worshipped the stranger, invited him to their groves and pleasure grounds, and gave him bread and wine. But alas! they have embraced the viper. The stranger taking advantage of the confidence they, in their simplicity, reposed, smites them with a ruthless hand, and hunts them down like wild beasts, until the last son, goaded to desperation, severs the cord of life and goes to meet the spirit of his fathers on the great "hunting ground." The nation sinks into oblivion, while that of their ruthless invader is emblazoned upon every tablet, and the leader in this act of infamy sleeps in triumph under an imposing cenotaph. Why does the sympathy of nations sleep while there still exists a remnant of this truly noble, but down-trodden people. As we reach the ocean we take a more easterly course, and are brought in full view of the lighthouse, which is on the extreme point of the island; we pass this point at 9 P.M., when we take a more northerly course, and stand directly for Cuba and the Caycus passage, designing to make, also, the western point of Hispaniola. We have a severe gale, but our steamer rides it out most gallantly.

31st. (Morning). We are in sight of Hispaniola, Hayti, or San Domingo, by all of which names it has been known at different times; her mountains looming up several thousand feet above the horizon. The sea is calm, our run pleasant; Cuba now appears off our larboard bow, about forty miles distant. It is indicated by heavy clouds, at the base of which, or just above the horizon, is seen the dark outline of her mountains. The mountains within the tropics are universally capped with clouds, which, in floating over, are caught by the peaks, and there waste away, the diminution supplied by the condensation of vapor, or the addition of other clouds. During the evening, a heavy sea broke against the side of the steamer, bursting our port fastening, and shooting a column of water eight inches in diameter, directly into the berth of my room-mate. It will readily be imagined that he awoke. We have just passed point St. Nicholas, the northwest point of St. Domingo, and point Mayxi, the most easterly point of Cuba.

Feb. 1st. A ship is seen, "hull down," off our larboard quarter; no land in sight, a heavy sea, and we are standing directly for the Caycus Islands, which we shall make about sunset.

2nd. We have made the Caycus passage, left the Caribbean Sea, and are now in the Atlantic, heading north by west, making a direct course for New York. We cross the tropic of Cancer at a quarter to 9 A.M. We have now nothing to do but promenade, sit in our state-rooms, and read, eat, sleep, and think of home. We have about 300 passengers on board. We have live sheep, poultry in abundance, and some twenty huge turtles, weighing from two to three hundred pounds each, some of each falling daily victims to our voracious appetites. One little turtle which looked as though he had been taken from his native island, much against his will, was thrust into a barrel, and there compelled to lay on his back. As I passed, I thought he eyed me with solicitation, and I requested one of the firemen to turn him over. This he did, much to the poor creature's apparent satisfaction. I relieved his pangs for the moment, and shall probably help devour him for dinner. Mr. Foster and myself had supplied ourselves liberally with oranges, pine-apples, limes, "forbidden fruit," bananas, &c., and spent much of our time in feasting. According to observation at 12 M., we were 920 miles from New York; we have made, in twenty-four hours, 214 miles, and are now under a full press of canvas.

3rd. (Sunday). We have a sermon by an English clergyman, from Kingston. By observation at 12 M., we had made 234 miles in twenty-four hours. We have a strong wind, and very heavy sea; boxes and barrels are running foot races on deck, it rains in torrents, hatches are closed down, but our ship rides gallantly. She rises manfully from the strife, shakes off the spray, and again leaps upon her antagonist.

4th. Stormy unpleasant day. We are now off the coast of the Carolinas, in the gulf-stream. The wind blows cold off the land, reminding us of winter. Three days ago we were picking oranges and limes, the themometer at 105°. Oh! anthracite coal! I most earnestly implore thy protection. While at dinner, we shipped a sea, which burst through the windows, putting out the lights, carrying every dish from the table, and saturating the entire company. The captain who, with a party of ladies, was sitting at the head of the table, claimed the most liberal instalment. At half past 2 P.M., a vessel appears, and bears down for us, running before the wind. She proves a Spanish bark; her rudder has been carried away, a spar is lashed on in its place, by which they are trying to manage her. She has up a foresail and spanker, and hoists a signal of distress. It is blowing a gale, raining in torrents, and the sea running mountain high. Our quarter boats could not live an instant, rendering it impossible to assist them. As they passed near us, we saw two men on the foretop-gallant yard. At 6 P.M., our tiller chains gave way, the steamer is thrown around into the troughs, and rolls so that it is impossible to keep footing on deck. The table, which has just been spread for supper, is swept of every dish; the cold beef chases the vegetables around the saloon, as if death could not dissipate the force of habit; the mustard and vinegar cruets, impelled by the same instinct, gave chase to the beef, and after a protracted run, brought up at my state-room door, *entirely exhausted.* The most amusing trial of speed took place between a knife and fork and a mince-pie; the latter lost its cap, or I think it would have won the race. Our chains are soon repaired, and we head on our course. It is dark, and we see nothing more of the last sail; wine circulates freely; our steamer seems intoxicated, and many of her passengers are *down* with the same complaint.

5th. Cold unpleasant morning; a heavy sea on. The wind blowing against the current of the gulf-stream, causes a spray, which rises in columns and seems to congeal in the air. We are in close proximity to several water-spouts, seeming the connecting links between the ocean and the clouds. We are under twenty-one inches of steam, but no canvas, the wind having been dead ahead for the past two days.

6th. Clear and cold; five sails in sight; ocean as smooth as a mirror. We fall in with a Delaware pilot, who reports us one hundred miles from New York. An exclamation of joy burst from the passengers, who are now all on deck. At 9 A. M., we saw the smoke of a steamer off our larboard quarter; ten sail in sight; the ocean presents a most sublime spectacle, not a breath disturbs its repose; as if jaded by prolonged agitation, it has relapsed into a quiet slumber. We are in sight of the light-ship off Delaware Bay; a pilot comes on board; Sandy Hook is in sight; the Jersey shore stretching away to the left, but just seen above the horizon. We passed Sandy Hook light-house, twenty-five miles from New York, at 7 P.M. As night draws her curtain round, we see looming up from the horizon, directly in our course, a halo of light, indicating the locality of the city. All are prepared to land, each, for the time being, absorbed in his own thoughts. What a diversity; the countenance of each portraying in vivid colors the hopes and fears within. Here, seated by one of the main pipes, is an emaciated form, clothed in rags; the head is reclining on the hand, the eye sunken, the visage ghastly, and now the whole frame writhes under a most distressing cough. A few short months have done their work. One year ago, a stalwart, robust, enterprising man, full of life and enthusiasm, left his wife and children to seek his fortune in a distant land. He reached his destination, and struggled hard, his prospects alternating between hope and fear; still he struggled on until at last he discovered that some lurking disease was undermining his constitution. The approach was gradual, but it did its work. The victim borrowed money and sailed for home. He is before me. He is destined to clasp to his bosom, once more, his wife and children, but in one short week is borne to a neighboring church yard.

This is the history and fate of more than one of our passengers; we, however, have many on board who are returning with robust constitutions and well-filled purses. Their countenances are lighted up with the fond anticipation of soon being restored to those whose greeting smile and warm embrace will heal the laceration of the past.

The excitement runs high; there is a prospect of reaching our dock by 10 o'clock. As we approach the Narrows, our steamer suddenly slackens her pace, and we hear a cry of "aground." Our pilot has run us upon the shoals of Coney Island; the wheels are reversed, but we are fast; the lead is thrown with a cry of "*three fathoms* o' the deep ho!" We can plainly see the light of the city looming up from the horizon, but the chances are against us. A new pilot comes on board, who points out the channel; our wheels are reversed, our tiller put hard down, and after several efforts, we are afloat, with the loss of part of our keel. As we pass through the Narrows, our pilot hands us the morning papers, containing a detail of the Hague street disaster. The city is now in sight, and we are steaming along with lightning speed; anxiety most intense. We near our pier, which we find much obstructed by ice; small boats attempt to come off for our hawser, but we are obliged to steam over toward Jersey City and come up again; this time we succeed, and as we are nearing the dock, the death of one of the passengers is announced. He was the *last* of a party of six that had embarked for, and I believe the only one of the party who lived to reach California. He lost his health soon after his arrival there, and died upon reaching his native shore.

As the steamer was being warped around, a passenger in attempting to jump to the pier, missed it, and fell through the mass of floating ice below. He soon gained the surface, but, uttering the most heart-rending screams, again disappeared. He was eventually rescued, and I jumped for the pier with better success, and stepping into a hack, was rapidly driven in the direction of Broadway. It is now midnight. Thirteen months have elapsed since I left, and for the last six, I have not had the least intelligence from home. My feelings can better be imagined than described, as I pulled the bell at No. 3 Warren street.

ONE word to those about to embark for California. Take the least possible amount of baggage, in a trunk of the smallest possible size. As no one can anticipate the circumstances under which they may be placed there, nor the wants of a life in California; it is recommended to buy *nothing* here, as purchases can be made *much more judiciously* in San Francisco, and other towns in California, and at about as fair rates, at the same time saving the trouble and expense of transportation. The transit charges, by the Nicaragua route, are fifteen cents per pound; this is *invariably* extra, even if one has a transit passage-ticket, which are issued at a charge of about $25. A limited amount of baggage is taken down the Atlantic and up the Pacific free, but *not* across. Passengers taking the Panama route, are now landed at Aspinwall (Navy Bay), thence by railroad to Miller's Station, saving thirty miles of river travel; thence in a row-boat to Gorgona, where mules are stationed in abundance to transport to Panama, twenty-five miles distant. Passengers are landed on the dock at Aspinwall, free of charge, the transit charges being about the same as by the Nicaragua route.

Constitution of the State of California.

PROCLAMATION TO THE PEOPLE OF CALIFORNIA.

THE delegates of the people, assembled in Convention, have formed a Constitution, which is now presented for your ratification. The time and manner of voting on this Constitution, and of holding the first general election, are clearly set forth in the schedule. The whole subject is, therefore, left for your unbiassed and deliberate consideration.

The Prefect (or person exercising the functions of that office) of each district, will designate the places for opening the polls, and give due notice of the election, in accordance with the provisions of the Constitution and schedule.

The people are now called upon to form a government for themselves, and to designate such officers as they desire, to make and execute the laws. That their choice may be wisely made, and that the government so organized may secure the permanent welfare and happiness of the people of the new State, is the sincere and earnest wish of the present Executive, who, if the Constitution be ratified, will, with pleasure, surrender his powers to whomsoever the people may designate as his successor.

Given at Monterey, California, this 12th day of October, A. D., 1849.

(Signed) B. RILEY,
Brevet Brig. General, U. S. A., and Governor of California.

(Official) H. W. HALLECK,
Brevet Captain and Secretary of State.

We, the People of California, grateful to Almighty God for our freedom, in order to secure its blessings, do establish this Constitution:

ARTICLE I.

DECLARATION OF RIGHTS.

SEC. 1. All men are by nature free and independent, and have certain inalienable rights, among which are those of enjoying and defending life and liberty, acquiring, possessing, and protecting property, and pursuing and obtaining safety and happiness.

SEC. 2. All political power is inherent in the people. Government is instituted for the protection, security, and benefit of the people; and they have the right to alter or reform the same, whenever the public good may require it.

SEC. 3. The right of trial by jury shall be secured to all, and remain inviolate forever; but a jury trial may be waived by the parties, in all civil cases, in the manner to be prescribed by law.

SEC. 4. The free exercise and enjoyment of religious profession and worship, without discrimination or preference, shall forever be allowed in this State; and no person shall be rendered incompetent to be a witness on account of his opinions on matters of religious belief; but the liberty of conscience, hereby secured, shall not be so construed as to excuse acts of licentiousness, or justify practices inconsistent with the peace or safety of this State.

SEC. 5. The privilege of the writ of *habeas corpus* shall not be suspended, unless when, in cases of rebellion or invasion, the public safety may require its suspension.

SEC. 6. Excessive bail shall not be required, nor excessive fines imposed, nor shall cruel or unusual punishments be inflicted, nor shall witnesses be unreasonably detained.

SEC. 7. All persons shall be bailable by sufficient sureties: unless for capital offences, when the proof is evident, or the presumption great.

SEC. 8. No person shall be held to answer for a capital or otherwise infamous crime (except in cases of impeachment, and in cases of militia when in actual service, and the land and naval forces in time of war, or which this State may keep with the consent of Congress in time of peace, and in cases of petit larceny under the regulation of the Legislature,) unless on presentment or indictment of a grand jury; and in any trial in any court whatever, the party accused shall be allowed to appear and defend in person and with counsel, as in civil actions. No person shall be subject to be twice put in jeopardy for the same offence; nor shall he be compelled, in any criminal case, to be a witness against himself, nor be deprived of life, liberty, or property, without due process of law; nor shall private property be taken for public use without just compensation.

SEC. 9. Every citizen may freely speak, write, and publish his sentiments on all subjects, being responsible for the abuse of that right; and no law shall be passed to restrain or abridge the liberty of speech or of the press. In all criminal prosecutions on indictments for libels, the truth may be given in evidence to the jury; and if it shall appear to the jury that the matter charged as libellous is true, and was published with good motives and for justifiable ends, the party shall be acquitted: and the jury shall have the right to determine the law and the fact.

SEC. 10. The people shall have the right freely to assemble together, to consult for the common good, to instruct their representatives, and to petition the legislature for redress of grievances.

SEC. 11. All laws of a general nature shall have a uniform operation.

SEC. 12. The military shall be subordinate to the civil power. No standing army shall be kept up by this State in time of peace; and in time of war no appropriation for a standing army shall be for a longer time than two years.

SEC. 13. No soldier shall, in time of peace, be quartered in any house, without the consent of the owner; nor in time of war, except in the manner to be prescribed by law.

SEC. 14. Representation shall be apportioned according to population.

SEC. 15. No person shall be imprisoned for debt, in any civil action on *mesne* or final process, unless in cases of fraud; and no person shall be imprisoned for a militia fine in time of peace.

SEC. 16. No bill of attainder, *ex post facto* law, or law impairing the obligation of contracts, shall ever be passed.

SEC. 17. Foreigners who are, or who may hereafter become, *bona fide* residents of this State, shall enjoy the same rights in respect to the possession, enjoyment and inheritance of property, as native born citizens.

SEC. 18. *Neither slavery, nor involuntary servitude, unless for the punishment of crimes, shall ever be tolerated in this State.*

SEC. 19. The right of the people to be secure in their persons, houses, papers, and effects, against unreasonable seizures and searches, shall not be violated; and now arrant shall issue but on probable cause, supported by oath or affirmation, particularly describing the place to be searched, and the persons and things to be seized.

SEC. 20. Treason against the State shall consist only in levying war against it, adhering to its enemies, or giving them aid and comfort. No person shall be convicted of treason, unless on the evidence of two witnesses to the same overt act, or confession in open court.

SEC. 21. This enumeration of rights shall not be construed to impair or deny others retained by the people.

ARTICLE II.

RIGHT OF SUFFRAGE.

SEC. 1. Every white male citizen of the United States, and every white male citizen of Mexico, who shall have elected to become a citizen of the United States, under the treaty of peace exchanged and ratified at Queretaro, on the 30th day of May, 1848, of the age of twenty-one years, who shall have been a resident of the State six months next preceding the election, and the county or district in which he claims his vote thirty days, shall be entitled to vote at all elections which are now or hereafter may be authorized by law: Provided, that nothing herein contained shall be construed to prevent the Legislature, by a two-thirds concurrent vote, from admitting to the right of suffrage, Indians or the descendants of Indians, in such special cases as such a proportion of the legislative body may deem just and proper.

SEC. 2. Electors shall, on all cases except treason, felony, or breach of the peace, be privileged from arrest on the days of the election, during their attendance at such election, going to and returning therefrom.

SEC. 3. No elector shall be obliged to perform militia duty on the day of election, except in time of war or public danger.

SEC. 4. For the purpose of voting, no person shall be deemed to have gained or lost a residence by reason of his presence or absence while employed in the service of the United States; nor while engaged in the navigation of the waters of this State, or of the United States, or of the high seas; nor while a student of any seminary of learning; nor while kept at any almshouse, or other asylum, at public expense; nor while confined in any public prison.

SEC. 5. No idiot or insane person, or person convicted of any infamous crime, shall be entitled to the privileges of an elector.

SEC. 6. All elections by the people shall be by ballot.

ARTICLE III.

DISTRIBUTION OF POWERS.

The powers of the government of the State of California shall be divided into three separate departments: the Legislature, the Executive, and Judicial; and no person charged with the exercise of powers properly belonging to one of these departments, shall exercise any functions appertaining to either of the others; except in the cases hereinafter expressly directed or permitted.

ARTICLE IV.

LEGISLATIVE DEPARTMENT.

SEC. 1. The legislative power of this State shall be vested in a Senate and Assembly, which shall be designated the Legislature of the State of California, and the enacting clause of every law shall be as follows: "The people of the State of California, represented in Senate and Assembly, do enact as follows."

SEC. 2. The sessions of the Legislature shall be annual, and shall commence on the first Monday of January, next ensuing the election of its members; unless the Governor of the State shall, in the interim, convene the Legislature by proclamation.

SEC. 3. The members of the Assembly shall be chosen annually, by the qualified electors of their respective districts, on the Tuesday next after the first Monday in November, unless otherwise ordered by the Legislature, and their term of office shall be one year.

SEC. 4. Senators and members of Assembly shall be duly qualified electors in the respective counties and districts which they represent.

SEC. 5. Senators shall be chosen for the term of two years, at the same time and places as members of Assembly; and no person shall be a member of the Senate or Assembly, who has not been a citizen and inhabitant of the State one year, and of the county or district for which he shall be chosen, six months next before his election.

SEC. 6. The number of Senators shall not be less than one-third, nor more than one-half of that of the members of Assembly; and at the first session of the Legislature after this Constitution takes effect, the Senators shall be divided by lot as equally as may be, into two classes; the seats of the Senators of the first class shall be vacated at the expiration of the first year, so that one-half shall be chosen annually.

SEC. 7. When the number of Senators is increased, they shall be apportioned by lot, so as to keep the two classes as nearly equal in number as possible.

SEC. 8. Each house shall choose its own officers, and judge of the qualifications, elections, and returns of its own members.

SEC. 9. A majority of each house shall constitute a quorum to do business;

but a smaller number may adjourn from day to day, and may compel the attendance of absent members, in such manner, and under such penalties as each house may provide.

SEC. 10. Each house shall determine the rules of its own proceedings, and may with the concurrence of two-thirds of all the members elected, expel a member.

SEC. 11. Each house shall keep a journal of its own proceedings, and publish the same; and the yeas and nays of the members of either house, on any question, shall, at the desire of any three members present, be entered on the journal.

SEC. 12. Members of the Legislature shall, in all cases except treason, felony, and breach of the peace, be privileged from arrest, and they shall not be subject to any civil process during the session of the Legislature, nor for fifteen days next before the commencement and after the termination of each session.

SEC. 13. When vacancies occur in either house, the Governor, or the person exercising the functions of the Governor, shall issue writs of election to fill such vacancies.

SEC. 14. The doors of each house shall be open, except on such occasions as in the opinion of the house may require secrecy.

SEC. 15. Neither house shall, without the consent of the other, adjourn for more than three days, nor to any other place than that in which they may be sitting.

SEC. 16. Any bill may originate in either house of the Legislature, and all bills passed by one house may be amended in the other.

SEC. 17. Every bill which may have passed the Legislature, shall, before it becomes a law, be presented to the Governor. If he approve it, he shall sign it; but if not, he shall return it, with his objections, to the house in which it originated, which shall enter the same upon the journal, and proceed to reconsider it. If, after such reconsideration, it again pass both houses, by yeas and nays, by a majority of two-thirds of the members of each house present, it shall become a law, notwithstanding the Governor's objections. If any bill shall not be returned within ten days after it shall have been presented to him, (Sunday excepted,) the same shall be a law, in like manner as if he had signed it, unless the Legislature, by adjournment, prevent such return.

SEC. 18. The Assembly shall have the sole power of impeachment; and all impeachments shall be tried by the Senate. When sitting for that purpose, the Senators shall be upon oath or affirmation; and no person shall be convicted without the concurrence of two-thirds of the members present.

SEC. 19. The Governor, Lieutenant Governor, Secretary of State, Comptroller, Treasurer, Attorney General, Surveyor General, Justices of the Supreme Court and Judges of the District Courts, shall be liable to impeachment for any misdemeanor in office; but judgment in such cases shall extend only to removal from office, and disqualification to hold any office of honor, trust, or profit, under the State; but the party convicted, or acquitted, shall nevertheless be liable to indictment, trial and punishment, according to law. All other civil officers shall be tried for misdemeanors in office, in such manner as the Legislature may provide.

SEC. 20. No Senator or member of Assembly shall, during the term for which he shall have been elected, be appointed to any civil office of profit, under this State, which shall have been created, or the emoluments of which shall have been increased, during such term, except such office as may be filled by elections by the people.

SEC. 21. No person holding any lucrative office under the United States, or any other power, shall be eligible to any civil office of profit, under this State; provided, that officers in the militia, to which there is attached no annual salary, or local officers and postmasters whose compensation does not exceed five hundred dollars per annum, shall not be deemed lucrative.

SEC. 22. No person who shall be convicted of the embezzlement or defalcation of the public funds of this State, shall ever be eligible to any office of honor, trust, or profit, under the State; and the Legislature shall, as soon as practicable, pass a law providing for the punishment of such embezzlement, or defalcation, as a felony.

SEC. 23. No money shall be drawn from the Treasury but in consequence of appropriations made by law. An accurate statement of the receipts and expenditures of the public moneys shall be attached to, and published with, the laws, at every regular session of the Legislature.

SEC. 24. The members of the Legislature shall receive for their services, a compensation to be fixed by law, and paid out of the public treasury; but no increase of the compensation shall take effect during the term for which the members of either house shall have been elected.

SEC. 25. Every law enacted by the Legislature, shall embrace but one object, and that shall be expressed in the title: and no law shall be revised, or amended, by reference to its title; but in such case, the act revised, or section amended, shall be re-enacted and published at length.

SEC. 26. No divorce shall be granted by the Legislature.

SEC. 27. No lottery shall be authorized by this State, nor shall the sale of lottery tickets be allowed.

SEC. 28. The enumeration of the inhabitants of this State shall be taken, under the direction of the Legislature, in the year one thousand eight hundred and fifty-two, and one thousand eight hundred and fifty-five, and at the end of every ten years thereafter; and these enumerations, together with the census that may be taken, under the direction of the Congress of the United States, in the year one thousand eight hundred and fifty, and every subsequent ten years, shall serve as the basis of representation in both houses of the Legislature.

SEC. 29. The number of Senators and members of Assembly, shall, at the first session of the Legislature, holden after the enumerations herein provided for are made, be fixed by the Legislature, and apportioned among the several counties and districts to be established by law, according to the number of white inhabitants. The number of members of Assembly shall not be less than twenty-four, nor more than thirty-six, until the number of inhabitants within this State shall amount to one hundred thousand; and after that period, at such ratio that the whole number of members of Assembly shall never be less than thirty, nor more than eighty.

SEC. 30. When a congressional, senatorial, or assembly district, shall be composed of two or more counties, it shall not be separated by any county belonging to another district; and no county shall be divided, in forming a congressional, senatorial, or assembly district.

SEC. 31. Corporations may be formed under general laws, but shall not be created by special act, except for municipal purposes. All general laws and special acts passed pursuant to this section may be altered from time to time, or repealed.

SEC. 32. Dues from corporations shall be secured by such individual liability of the corporators, and other means, as may be prescribed by law.

SEC. 33. The term corporations, as used in this article, shall be construed to include all associations and joint-stock companies, having any of the powers or privileges of corporations not possessed by individuals or partnerships. And all corporations shall have the right to sue, and shall be subject to be sued, in all courts, in like cases as natural persons.

SEC. 34. The Legislature shall have no power to pass any act granting any charter for banking purposes; but associations may be formed under general laws, for the deposit of gold and silver; but no such association shall make, issue, or put in circulation, any bill, check, tickets, certificate, promissory note, or other paper, or the paper of any bank, to circulate as money.

SEC. 35. The Legislature of this State shall prohibit, by law, any person or persons, association, company, or corporation, from exercising the privileges of banking, or creating paper to circulate as money.

SEC. 36. Each stockholder of a corporation, or joint-stock association, shall be individually and personally liable for his proportion of all its debts and liabilities.

SEC. 37. It shall be the duty of the Legislature to provide for the organization of cities and incorporated villages, and to restrict their power of taxation, assessment, borrowing money, contracting debts, and loaning their credit, so as to prevent abuses in assessments, and in contracting debts by such municipal corporations.

SEC. 38. In all elections by the Legislature, the members thereof shall vote *viva voce*, and the votes shall be entered on the journal.

ARTICLE V.

EXECUTIVE DEPARTMENT.

SEC. 1. The supreme executive power of this State shall be vested in a chief magistrate, who shall be styled the Governor of the State of California.

SEC. 2. The Governor shall be elected by the qualified electors, at the time and places of voting for members of Assembly, and shall hold his office two years from the time of his installation, and until his successor shall be qualified.

SEC. 3. No person shall be eligible to the office of Governor, (except at the first election,) who has not been a citizen of the United States and a resident of this State two years next preceding the election, and attained the age of twenty-five years at the time of said election.

SEC. 4. The returns of every election for Governor shall be sealed up and transmitted to the seat of government, directed to the Speaker of the Assembly, who shall, during the first week of the session, open and publish them in presence of both houses of the legislature. The person having the highest number of votes shall be Governor; but in case any two or more have an equal and the highest number of votes, the Legislature shall, by joint-vote of both houses, choose one of said persons, so having an equal and the highest number of votes, for Governor.

SEC. 5. The Governor shall be commander-in-chief of the militia, the army, and navy, of this State.

SEC. 6. He shall transact all executive business with the officers of government, civil and military, and may require information in writing from the officers of the executive department, upon any subject relating to the duties of the respective offices.

SEC. 7. He shall see that the laws are faithfully executed.

SEC. 8. When any office shall, from any cause become vacant, and no mode is provided by the constitution and laws for filling such vacancy, the Governor shall have power to fill such vacancy by granting a commission, which shall expire at the end of the next session of the Legislature, or at the next election by the people.

SEC. 9. He may, on extraordinary occasions, convene the Legislature by proclamation, and shall state to both houses, when assembled, the purpose for which they shall have been convened.

SEC. 10. He shall communicate by message to the Legislature, at every session, the condition of the State, and recommend such matters as he shall deem expedient.

SEC. 11. In case of a disagreement between the two houses, with respect to the time of adjournment, the Governor shall have power to adjourn the Legislature to such time as he may think proper; Provided it be not beyond the time fixed for the meeting of the next Legislature.

SEC. 12. No person shall, while holding any office under the United States, or this State, exercise the office of Governor, except as hereinafter expressly provided.

SEC. 13. The Governor shall have the power to grant reprieves and pardons, after conviction, for all offences except treason, and cases of impeachment, upon such conditions, and with such restrictions and limitations, as he may think proper, subject to such regulations as may be provided by law relative to the manner of applying for pardons. Upon conviction for treason he shall have the power to suspend the execution of the sentence until the case shall be reported to the Legislature at its next meeting, when the Legislature shall either pardon, direct the execution of the sentence, or grant a further reprieve. He shall communicate to the Legislature, at the beginning of every session, every case of reprieve, or pardon granted, stating the name of the convict, the crime of which he was convicted, the sentence and its date, and the date of the pardon or reprieve.

SEC. 14. There shall be a seal of this State, which shall be kept by the Governor, and used by him officially, and it shall be called "The great seal of the State of California."

SEC. 15. All grants and commissions shall be in the name and by the authority of the people of the State of California, sealed with the great seal of the State, signed by the Governor, and countersigned by the Secretary of State.

SEC. 16. A Lieutenant Governor shall be elected at the same time and place, and in the same manner as the Governor; and his term of office, and his qualifications of eligibility, shall also be the same. He shall be President of the Senate, but shall only have a casting vote therein. If, during a vacancy of the office of Governor, the Lieutenant Governor shall be impeached, displaced, resign, die, or become incapable of performing the duties of his office, or be absent from the State, the President of the Senate shall act as Governor, until the vacancy be filled, or the disability shall cease.

SEC. 17. In case of the impeachment of the Governor, or his removal from office, death, inability to discharge the powers and duties of the said office, resignation or absence from the State, the powers and duties of the office shall devolve upon the Lieutenant Governor for the residue of the term, or until the disability shall cease. But when the Governor shall, with the consent of the Legislature, be out of the State in time of war, at the head of any military force thereof, he shall continue commander-in-chief of all the military force of the State.

SEC. 18. A Secretary of State, a Comptroller, a Treasurer, an Attorney General and Surveyor General, shall be chosen in the manner provided in this Constitution; and the term of office, and eligibility of each, shall be the same as are prescribed for the Governor and Lieutenant Governor.

SEC. 19. The Secretary of State shall be appointed by the Governor, by and with the advice and consent of the Senate. He shall keep a fair record of the official acts of the Legislative and Executive Departments of the government; and shall, when required, lay the same, and all matters relative thereto, before either branch of the Legislature: and shall perform such other duties as shall be assigned him by law.

SEC. 20. The Comptroller, Treasurer, Attorney General and Surveyor General, shall be chosen by joint vote of the two houses of the Legislature, at their first session under this Constitution, and thereafter shall be elected at the same time and places, and in the same manner, as the Governor and Lieutenant Governor.

SEC. 21. The Governor, Lieutenant Governor, Secretary of State, Comptroller, Treasurer, Attorney General, and Surveyor General, shall each at stated times during their continuance in office, receive for their services a compensation, which shall not be increased or diminished during the term for which they shall have been elected; but neither of these officers shall receive for his own use any fees for the performance of his official duties.

ARTICLE VI.

JUDICIAL DEPARTMENT.

SEC. 1. The judicial power of this State shall be vested in a Supreme Court, in District Courts, in County Courts, and in Justices of the Peace. The Legislature may also establish such municipal and other inferior courts as may be deemed necessary.

SEC. 2. The Supreme Court shall consist of a Chief Justice, and two Associate Justices, any two of whom shall constitute a quorum.

SEC. 3. The Justices of the Supreme Court shall be elected at the general election, by the qualified electors of the State, and shall hold their office for the term of six years from the first day of January next after their election; provided that the Legislature shall, at its first meeting, elect a Chief Justice and two Associate Justices of the Supreme Court, by joint vote of both houses, and so classify them that one shall go out of office every two years. After the first election, the senior Justice in commission shall be the Chief Justice.

SEC. 4. The Supreme Court shall have appellate jurisdiction in all cases when the matter in dispute exceeds two hundred dollars, when the legality of any tax, toll, or impost or municipal fine is in question: and in all criminal cases amounting to felony, or questions of law alone. And the said court, and each of the Justices thereof, as well as all district and county judges, shall have power to issue writs of habeas corpus, at the instance of any person held in actual custody. They shall also have power to issue all other writs and process necessary to the exercise of the appellate jurisdiction, and shall be conservators of the peace throughout the State.

SEC. 5. The State shall be divided by the first Legislature into a convenient number of districts, subject to such alteration from time to time as the public good may require; for each of which a district judge shall be appointed by the joint vote of the legislature, at its first meeting, who shall hold his office for two years from the first day of January next after his election; after which, said judges shall be elected by the qualified electors of their respective districts, at the general election, and shall hold their office for the term of six years.

SEC. 6. The District Courts shall have original jurisdiction, in law and equity, in all civil cases where the amount in dispute exceeds two hundred dollars, exclusive of interest. In all criminal cases not otherwise provided for, and in all issues of fact joined in the probate courts, their jurisdiction shall be unlimited.

SEC. 7. The legislature shall provide for the election, by the people, of a Clerk of the Supreme Court, and County Clerks, District Attorneys, Sheriffs, Coroners, and other necessary officers; and shall fix by law their duties and compensation. County Clerks shall be, *ex-officio*, Clerks of the District Courts in and for their respective counties.

SEC. 8. There shall be elected in each of the organized counties of this State, one County Judge who shall hold his office for four years. He shall hold the County Court, and perform the duties of Surrogate, or Probate Judge. The

County Judge, with two Justices of the Peace, to be designated according to law, shall hold courts of sessions, with such criminal jurisdiction as the Legislature shall prescribe, and he shall perform such other duties as shall be required by law.

SEC. 9. The County Courts shall have such jurisdiction, in cases arising in Justices Courts, and in special cases, as the Legislature may prescribe, but shall have no original civil jurisdiction, except in such special cases.

SEC. 10. The times and places of holding the terms of the Supreme Court, and the general and special terms of the District Courts within the several districts, shall be provided for by law.

SEC. 11. No judicial officer, except a Justice of the Peace, shall receive, to his own use, any fees, or perquisites of office.

SEC. 12. The Legislature shall provide for the speedy publication of all statute laws, and of such judicial decisions as it may deem expedient; and all laws and judicial decisions shall be free for publication by any person.

SEC. 13. Tribunals for conciliation may be established, with such powers and duties as may be prescribed by law; but such tribunals shall have no power to render judgment to be obligatory on the parties, except they voluntarily submit their matters in difference, and agree to abide the judgment, or assent thereto in the presence of such tribunal, in such cases as shall be prescribed by law.

SEC. 14. The Legislature shall determine the number of Justices of the Peace, to be elected in each county, city, town, and incorporated village of the State, and fix by law their powers, duties, and responsibilities. It shall also determine in what cases appeals may be made from Justices' Courts to the County Court.

SEC. 15. The Justices of the Supreme Court, and Judges of the District Court, shall severally, at stated times during their continuance in office, receive for their services a compensation, to be paid out of the treasury, which shall not be increased or diminished during the term for which they shall have been elected. The county Judges shall also severally, at stated times, receive for their services a compensation to be paid out of the county treasury of their respective counties, which shall not be increased or diminished during the term for which they shall have been elected.

SEC. 16. The Justices of the Supreme Court and District Judges shall be ineligible to any other office, during the term for which they shall have been elected.

SEC. 17. Judges shall not charge juries with respect to matters of fact, but may state the testimony and declare the law.

SEC. 18. The style of all process shall be "The People of the State of California;" all the prosecutions shall be conducted in the name and by the authority of the same.

ARTICLE VII.

MILITIA.

SEC. 1. The legislature shall provide by law, for organizing and disciplining the militia, in such manner as they shall deem expedient, not incompatible with the constitution and laws of the United States.

Sec. 2. Officers of the militia shall be elected or appointed, in such manner as the legislature shall from time to time direct; and shall be commissioned by the governor.

Sec. 3. The governor shall have power to call forth the militia, to execute the laws of the State, to suppress insurrections and repel invasions.

ARTICLE VIII.

STATE DEBTS.

The Legislature shall not in any manner create any debt or debts, liability or liabilities, which shall singly, or in the aggregate, with any previous debts or liabilities, exceed the sum of three hundred thousands dollars, except in case of war, to repel invasion, or suppress insurrection, unless the same shall be authorized by some law for some single object or work, to be distinctly specified therein, which law shall provide ways and means, exclusive of loans, for the payment of the interest of such debt or liability, as it falls due, and also pay and discharge the principal of such debt or liability within twenty years from the time of the contracting thereof, and shall be irrepealable until the principal and interest thereon shall be paid and discharged; but no such law shall take effect until, at a general election, it shall have been submitted to the people, and have received a majority of all the votes cast for and against it at such election; and all money raised by authority of such law shall be applied only to the specific object therein stated, or to the payment of the debt thereby created; and such law shall be published in at least one newspaper in each judicial district, if one be published therein, throughout the State, for three months next preceding the election at which it is submitted to the people.

ARTICLE IX.

EDUCATION.

Sec. 1. The Legislature shall provide for the election, by the people, of a Superintendent of Public Instruction, who shall hold his office for three years, and whose duties shall be prescribed by law, and who shall receive such compensation as the Legislature may direct.

Sec. 2. The Legislature shall encourage, by all suitable means, the promotion of intellectual, scientific, moral and agricultural improvement. The proceeds of all lands that may be granted by the United States to this State for the support of schools, which may be sold or disposed of, and the five hundred thousand acres of land granted to the new States, under an act of Congress distributing the proceeds of the public lands among the several States of the Union, approved A. D. 1841; and all estates of deceased persons who may have died without leaving a will, or heir, and also such per cent. as may be granted by Congress on the sale of lands in this State, shall be and remain a perpetual fund, the interest of which, together with all the rents of the unsold lands, and such other means as the Legislature may provide, shall be inviolably appropriated to the support of Common Schools throughout the State.

SEC 3. The Legislature shall provide for a system of Common Schools, by which a school shall be kept up and supported in each district at least three months in every year: and any school district neglecting to keep up and support such a school, may be deprived of its proportion of the interest of the public fund during such neglect.

SEC. 4. The Legislature shall take measures for the protection, improvement, or other disposition of such lands as have been, or may hereafter be, reserved or granted by the United States, or any person or persons to this State for the use of a University; and the funds accruing from the rents or sale of such lands, or from any other source, for the purpose aforesaid, shall be and remain a permanent fund, the interest of which shall be applied to the support of said university, with such branches as the public convenience may demand for the promotion of literature, the arts and sciences, as may be authorized by the terms of such grant. And it shall be the duty of the Legislature, as soon as may be, to provide effectual means for the improvement and permanent security of the funds of said University.

ARTICLE X.

MODE OF AMENDING AND REVISING THE CONSTITUTION.

SEC. 1. Any amendment or amendments to this constitution may be proposed in the Senate or Assembly; and if the same shall be agreed to by a majority of the members elected to each of the two houses, such proposed amendment or amendments shall be entered on their journals, with the yeas and nays taken thereon, and referred to the Legislature then next to be chosen, and shall be published for three months next preceding the time of making such choice. And if, in the Legislature next chosen, as aforesaid, such proposed amendment or amendments shall be agreed to by a majority of all the members elected to each house, then it shall be the duty of the Legislature to submit such proposed amendment or amendments to the people, in such manner, and at such time, as the Legislature shall prescribe; and if the people shall approve and ratify such amendment or amendments, by a majority of the electors qualified to vote for members of the Legislature voting thereon, such amendment or amendments shall become part of the Constitution.

SEC. 2. And if, at any time, two-thirds of the Senate and Assembly shall think it necessary to revise and change this entire Constitution, they shall recommend to the electors, at the next election for members of the Legislature, to vote for or against the convention; and if it shall appear that a majority of the electors voting at such election have voted in favor of calling a convention, the Legislature shall, at its next session, provide by law for calling a convention, to be holden within six months after the passage of such law; and such convention shall consist of a number of members not less than that of both branches of the Legislature.

ARTICLE XI.

MISCELLANEOUS PROVISIONS.

SEC. 1. The first session of the Legislature shall be held at the Pueblo de

San Jose, which place shall be the permanent seat of goverment, until removed by law; provided, however, that two-thirds of all the members elected to each house of the Legislature shall concur in the passage of such law.

Sec. 2. Any citizen of this State who shall, after the adoption of this constitution, fight a duel with deadly weapons, or send or accept a challenge to fight a duel with deadly weapons, either within the State or out of it; or who shall act as second, or knowingly aid or assist in any manner those thus offending, shall not be allowed to hold any office of profit, or to enjoy the right of suffrage under this Constitution.

Sec. 3. Members of the Legislature, and all officers, executive and judicial, except such inferior officers as may be by law exempted, shall, before they enter on the duties of their respective offices, take and subscribe the following oath or affirmation.

"I do solemnly swear (or affirm, as the case may be,) that I will support the Constitution of the United States, and the constitution of the State of California; and that I will faithfully discharge the duties of the office of ———, according to the best of my ability." And no other oath, declaration, or test, shall be required as a qualification for any office or public trust.

Sec. 4. The Legislature shall establish a system of county and town governments, which shall be as nearly uniform as practicable, throughout the State.

Sec. 5. The Legislature shall have power to provide for the election of a board of supervisors in each county; and these supervisors shall, jointly and individually, perform such duties as may be prescribed by law.

Sec. 6. All officers whose election or appointment is not provided for by this constitution, and all officers whose offices may hereafter be created by law, shall be elected by the people, or appointed as the Legislature may direct.

Sec. 7. When the duration of any office is not provided for by this constitution, it may be declared by law; and if not so declared, such office shall be held during the pleasure of the authority making the appointment; nor shall the duration of any office, not fixed by this constitution, ever exceed four years.

Sec. 8. The fiscal year shall commence on the first day of July.

Sec. 9. Each county, town, city and incorporated village, shall make provision for the support of its own officers, subject to such restrictions and regulations as the Legislature may prescribe.

Sec. 10. The credit of the State shall not in any manner be given or loaned to, or in aid of, any individual, association or corporation; nor shall the State, directly or indirectly, become a stockholder in any association or corporation.

Sec. 11. Suits may be brought against the State, in such manner, and in such courts, as shall be directed by law.

Sec. 12. No contract of marriage, if otherwise duly made, shall be invalidated, for want of conformity to the requirements of any religious sect.

Sec. 13. Taxation shall be equal and uniform throughout the State. All property, in this State, shall be taxed in proportion to its value, to be ascertained as directed by law; but assessors and collectors of town, county and

State taxes, shall be elected by the qualified electors of the district, county or town, in which the property taxed for State, county or town purposes is situated.

SEC. 14. All property, both real and personal, of the wife, owned or claimed by her before marriage, and that acquired afterwards by gift, devise or descent, shall be her separate property; and laws shall be passed more clearly defining the rights of the wife, in relation as well to her separate property, as to that held in common with her husband. Laws shall also be passed providing for the registration of the wife's separate property.

SEC. 15. The Legislature shall protect by law, from forced sale, a certain portion of the homestead and other property of all heads of families.

SEC. 16. No perpetuities shall be allowed, except for eleemosynary purposes.

SEC. 17. Every person shall be disqualified from holding any office of profit in this State, who shall have been convicted of having given or offered a bribe, to procure his election or appointment.

SEC. 18. Laws shall be made to exclude from office, serving on juries, and from the right of suffrage, those who shall hereafter be convicted of bribery, perjury, forgery, or other high crimes. The privilege of free suffrage shall be supported by laws regulating elections, and prohibiting, under adequate penalties, all undue influence thereon, from power, bribery, tumult, or other improper practice.

SEC. 19. Absence from this State on business of the State, or of the United States, shall not affect the question of residence of any person.

SEC. 20. A plurality of the votes given at any election shall constitute a choice, where not otherwise directed in this constitution.

SEC. 21. All laws, decrees, regulations, and provisions, which from their nature require publication, shall be published in English and Spanish.

ARTICLE XII.

BOUNDARY.

The boundary of the State of California shall be as follows :—

Commencing at the point of intersection of the 42d degree of north latitude with the 120th degree of longitude west from Greenwich, and running south on the line of said 120th degree of west longitude until it intersects the 39th degree of north latitude; thence running in a straight line in a southeasterly direction to the river Colorado, at a point where it intersects the 35th degree of north latitude; thence down the middle of the channel of said river, to the boundary line between the United States and Mexico, as established by the treaty of May 30th, 1848; thence running west and along said boundary line to the Pacific Ocean, and extending therein three English miles; thence running in a northwesterly direction, and following the direction of the Pacific coast to the 42d degree of north latitude; thence on the line of said 42d degree of north latitude to the place of beginning. Also all the islands, harbors and bays, along and adjacent to the Pacific coast.

SCHEDULE.

SEC. 1. All rights, prosecutions, claims and contracts, as well of individuals as of bodies corporate, and all laws in force at the time of the adoption of this constitution, and not inconsistent therewith, until altered or repealed by the Legislature, shall continue as if the same had not been adopted.

SEC. 2. The Legislature shall provide for the removal of all causes which may be pending when this constitution goes into effect, to courts created by the same.

SEC. 3. In order that no inconvenience may result to the public service, from the taking effect of this constitution, no office shall be superseded thereby, nor the laws relative to the duties of the several offices be changed, until the entering into office of the new officers to be appointed under this constitution.

SEC. 4. The provisions of this constitution concerning the term of residence necessary to enable persons to hold certain offices therein mentioned, shall not be held to apply to officers chosen by the people at the first election, or by the Legislature at its first session.

SEC. 5. Every citizen of California, declared a legal voter by this constitution, and every citizen of the United States, a resident of this State on the day of election, shall be entitled to vote at the first general election under this constitution, and on the question of the adoption thereof.

SEC. 6. This constitution shall be submitted to the people, for their ratification or rejection, at the general election to be held on Tuesday, the thirteenth day of November next. The executive of the existing government of California is hereby requested to issue a proclamation to the people, directing the Prefects of the several districts, or in case of vacancy, the Sub-Prefects, or senior Judge of First Instance, to cause such election to be held, on the day aforesaid, in their respective districts. The election shall be conducted in the manner which was prescribed for the election of delegates to this convention, except that the Prefect, Sub-Prefect, or senior Judge of First Instance ordering such election in each district, shall have power to designate any additional number of places for opening the polls, and that, in every place of holding the election, a regular poll-list shall be kept by the judges and inspectors of election. It shall also be the duty of these judges and inspectors of election, on the day aforesaid, to receive the votes of the electors qualified to vote at such election. Each voter shall express his opinion, by depositing in the ballot-box a ticket, whereon shall be written, or printed, "For the Constitution," or "Against the Constitution," or some such words as will distinctly convey the intention of the voter. These Judges and Inspectors shall also receive the votes for the several officers to be voted for at the said election, as herein provided. At the close of the election, the judges and inspectors shall carefully count each ballot, and forthwith make duplicate returns thereof to the Prefect, Sub-Prefect, or senior Judge of First Instance, as the case may be, of their respective districts; and said Prefect, Sub-Prefect, or senior Judge of First Instance, shall transmit one of the same, by the most safe and rapid conveyance, to the Secretary of State. Upon the receipt of said returns, or on the tenth day of December next, if the returns be not sooner received, it shall be the duty of a board of canvassers, to consist of the Secretary of State, one of the Judges of the Superior Court, the Prefect, Judge of First Instance, and an Alcalde of the District of Monterey, or any three of the aforementioned officers, in the presence of all who shall choose to attend, to compare the votes given at said election, and to immediately publish an abstract of the same in one or more of the newspapers of California. And the Executive will also, immediately after ascertaining that the constitution has been ratified by the people, make proclamation of the fact; and thenceforth this constitution shall be ordained and established as the constitution of California.

SEC. 7. If this constitution shall be ratified by the people of California, the Executive of the existing government is hereby requested, immediately after the same shall be ascertained, in the manner herein directed, to cause a fair copy thereof to be forwarded to the President of the United States, in order that he may lay it before the Congress of the United States.

SEC. 8. At the general election aforesaid, viz.: the thirteenth day of November next, there shall be elected a Governor, Lieutenant Governor, members of the Legislature, and also two members of Congress.

SEC. 9. If this constitution shall be ratified by the people of California, the legislature shall assemble at the seat of government, on the fifteenth day of December next, and in order to complete the organization of that body, the Senate shall elect a President *pro tempore*, until the Lieutenant Governor shall be installed into office.

SEC. 10. On the organization of the legislature, it shall be the duty of the Secretary of State, to lay before each house a copy of the abstract made by the board of canvassers, and, if called for, the original returns of election, in order that each house may judge of the correctness of the report of said board of canvassers.

SEC. 11. The legislature, at its first session, shall elect such officers as may be ordered by this constitution, to be elected by that body, and within four days after its organization, proceed to elect two Senators to the Congress of the United States. But no law passed by this legislature shall take effect until signed by the Governor, after his installation into office.

SEC. 12. The Senators and Representatives to the Congress of the United States, elected by the legislature and people of California, as herein directed, shall be furnished with certified copies of this constitution, when ratified, which they shall lay before the Congress of the United States, requesting, in the name of the people of California, the admission of the State of California into the American Union.

SEC. 13. All officers of this State, other than members of the legislature, shall be installed into office on the fifteenth day of December next, or as soon thereafter as practicable.

SEC. 14. Until the legislature shall divide the State into counties, and senatorial and assembly districts, as directed by this constitution, the following shall be the apportionment of the two houses of the legislature, viz.: the districts of San Diego and Los Angelos shall jointly elect two senators; the districts of Santa Barbara and San Luis Obispo shall jointly elect one senator; the district of Monterey, one senator; the district of San Jose, one senator;

the district of San Francisco, two senators; the district of Sonoma, one senator; the district of Sacramento, four senators; and the district of San Joaquin, four senators:—And the district of San Diego shall elect one member of assembly; the district of Los Angelos, two members of assembly; the district of Santa Barbara, two members of assembly; the district of San Luis Obispo, one member of assembly; the district of Monterey, two members of assembly; the district of San Jose, three members of assembly; the district of San Francisco, five members of assembly; the district of Sonoma, two members of assembly; the district of Sacramento, nine members of assembly; and the district of San Joaquin, nine members of assembly.

Sec. 15. Until the legislature shall otherwise direct, in accordance with the provisions of this constitution, the salary of the Governor shall be ten thousand dollars per annum; and the salary of the Lieutenant Governor shall double the pay of a state senator; and the pay of members of the legislature shall be sixteen dollars per diem, while in attendance, and sixteen dollars for every twenty miles travel by the usual route from their residences, to the place of holding the session of the legislature, and in returning therefrom. And the legislature shall fix the the salaries of all officers, other than those elected by the people, at the first election.

Sec. 16. The limitation of the powers of the legislature, contained in article 8th of this constitution, shall not extend to the first legislature elected under the same, which is hereby authorized to negotiate for such amount as may be necessary to pay the expenses of the State Government.

R. SEMPLE,
President of the Convention,
and Delegate from Benicia.

Wm. G. Marcy, Secretary.

J. Aram,
C. T. Botts,
E. Brown,
J. A. Carillo,
J. M. Covarrubias,
E. O. Crosby,
P. D. La Guerra,
L. Dent,
M. Dominguez,
K. H. Dimmick,
A. J. Ellis,
S. C. Foster,
E. Gilbert,
W. M. Gwinn,
H. W. Halleck,
Julian Hanks,
L. W. Hastings,
Henry Hill,
J. Hobson,
J. McH. Hollingsworth,
J. D. Hoppe,
J. M. Jones,
T. O. Larkin,
Francis L. Lippitt,
B. S. Lippincott,
M. M. McCarver,
John McDougal,
B. F. Moore,
Myron Norton,
P. Ord,
Miguel Pedrorena,
A. M. Pico,
R. M. Price,
Hugo Reid,
Jacinto Rodriguez,
Pedro Sansevaine,
W. E. Shannon,
W. S. Sherwood,
J. R. Snyder,
A. Stearns,
W. M. Steuart,
J. A. Sutter,
Henry A. Tefft.
S. L. Vermule,
M. G. Vallejo,
J. Walker,
O. M. Wozencraft.

www.ingramcontent.com/pod-product-compliance
Lightning Source LLC
LaVergne TN
LVHW020224110826
845151LV00003B/815

* 9 7 8 1 4 2 5 5 3 1 2 9 4 *